How to Use Storytelling in Your Academic Writing

To my wife Sarah.

I also dedicate this book to the loved ones I've lost in recent years: my brother Bill, my parents Russ and Mickey, and my dog Marlon. I love and miss you all.

How to Use Storytelling in Your Academic Writing

Techniques for Engaging Readers and Successfully Navigating the Writing and Publishing Processes

Timothy G. Pollock

Haslam Chair in Business and Distinguished Professor of Entrepreneurship, Department of Management and Entrepreneurship, Haslam College of Business, University of Tennessee-Knoxville, USA

Edward Elgar
PUBLISHING

Cheltenham, UK • Northampton, MA, USA

© Timothy G. Pollock 2021

All rights reserved. No part of this publication may be reproduced, stored in a retrieval system or transmitted in any form or by any means, electronic, mechanical or photocopying, recording, or otherwise without the prior permission of the publisher.

Published by
Edward Elgar Publishing Limited
The Lypiatts
15 Lansdown Road
Cheltenham
Glos GL50 2JA
UK

Edward Elgar Publishing, Inc.
William Pratt House
9 Dewey Court
Northampton
Massachusetts 01060
USA

Paperback edition 2021

A catalogue record for this book
is available from the British Library

Library of Congress Control Number: 2020952018

This book is available electronically in the **Elgar**online
Business subject collection
http://dx.doi.org/10.4337/9781839102820

ISBN 978 1 83910 281 3 (cased)
ISBN 978 1 83910 282 0 (eBook)
ISBN 978 1 80220 169 7 (paperback)

Printed and bound by CPI Group (UK) Ltd, Croydon, CR0 4YY

Contents

List of figures		vi
About the author		vii
Acknowledgments		viii
1	Introduction: think like a storyteller	1
2	Structuring a story	7
3	Storytelling tools	20
4	The building blocks of storytelling: words, sentences and paragraphs	31
5	Introductions, titles and abstracts	50
6	Theory and Hypotheses	64
7	Methods and Results	76
8	Discussion section	90
9	What's different about qualitative articles, theory articles and book chapters	98
10	The writing process	114
11	The co-authoring process	132
12	Navigating the review process	144
13	Other kinds of writing	158
14	Conclusion	170
References		175
Index		181

Figures

2.1	Freytag's Pyramid	8
2.2	Freytag's Pyramid overlaid on the quantitative article structure	9
2.3	Freytag's Pyramid overlaid on the qualitative article structure	10
2.4	Freytag's Pyramid overlaid on the theory article structure	10
7.1	The three-horned dilemma	78
9.1	Proportional Freytag's Pyramid for qualitative articles	100
9.2	Proportional Freytag's Pyramid for theory articles	109
10.1	Preparing the ground	116
10.2	Blocking in the scene	118
10.3	Adding detail, refining and focusing	121
10.4	Finishing and framing	123
10.5	Where I write	129

About the author

Tim Pollock is the Haslam Chair in Business and Distinguished Professor of Entrepreneurship in the Haslam College of Business, University of Tennessee-Knoxville. He is a former Associate Editor of the *Academy of Management Journal*, has won multiple outstanding reviewer awards, and has published widely in all the top-tier journals in management. He lives in Knoxville with his wife, the artist Sarah Pollock, and his dog Maple. You can find out more about Tim at www.timothypollock.com.

Acknowledgments

This book is the culmination of twenty-seven years of experience. There are a lot of people who have helped, supported and guided me along the way. My parents, of course, who were unfailingly supportive of my leaving a good paying job to become an impoverished doctoral student and pursue an academic career. My advisors Joe Porac and Jim Wade, who taught me how to be a scholar and gave me the tools and opportunities to be successful. My many colleagues and co-authors over the years, from whom I've learned so much, and who have given me so many great writing experiences. In particular I'd like to thank Violina Rindova, who has been my friend and longest-running and best co-author. I'd also like to thank my friend and colleague of more than twenty years (and co-author) Ted Baker. It has been a joy to go through this academic journey with you. Ted also read every chapter (he was my Eulah-Beulah) and provided great suggestions. I even took some of them. I would also like to thank the rest of my friendly reviewer team, Jeff Lovelace, Yeonji Seo, and the members of my writing doctoral seminar: Ace Beorchia, Jaewoo Jung, Emily Landry, Trey Lewis, Ashley Roccapriore and Justin Yan. These folks all read and provided great feedback on the chapters as I developed them, and the students were fantastic guinea pigs as I worked out my ideas in class. That was truly one of the most fun teaching experiences of my life, even if the last five weeks were online due to Covid-19. I also owe a debt to the individuals who copy-edited my journal articles as they were prepared for publication, especially Persephone Doliner, Linda Johanson and Joan Friedman. What I've learned from these three women has made me a better writer. I must also thank my editor, Alan Sturmer for giving me the opportunity to write this book and his guidance through the process, and all the other folks at Edward Elgar who helped make it a reality. Most of all, I want to thank my wife Sarah. She's been my biggest cheerleader throughout this process, read every chapter and provided many great comments. She's also been my biggest supporter throughout my career, even though I dragged her out of Wisconsin and around the country on my academic vagabond's journey. Finally, I'd like to thank my dog Maple, who has kept me company while I write, snorted impatiently when I was late taking her on walks, and has been a sweet, loving companion.

1. Introduction: think like a storyteller

Academics are a privileged lot. Our job is to (1) think of questions other people haven't thought of and identify questions that haven't been answered, (2) figure out how to answer them, (3) do it, and then (4) tell the story. However, if your doctoral training was anything like mine, or like most of the doctoral programs I've been involved in or exposed to in the twenty-plus years since receiving my degree, the bulk of your training focused on parts two and three (i.e., research design and analytical techniques), with a reasonable amount of attention given to part 1 in your theory and content seminars, and almost no attention given to part 4—storytelling. Indeed, I'm guessing the term "storytelling" rarely, if ever, came up, and formal discussions of writing were likely relegated to one session in a research design seminar, if covered at all. Even in the professional development seminars and workshops offered at major academic association conferences, the bulk of attention is given to research methods and other topics related to figuring out how to answer the interesting questions we come up with, and the doing of it.

However, storytelling is what we do in every article, book chapter and book we write; in every presentation we give; and in every class we teach. Data does not speak for itself; the author must set the context for interpretation, ensure readers understand and accept the question's importance, and finally frame and interpret the implications of the results in ways that give the data meaning.

For example, the science historian Matthew Stanley (2019) provided a fascinating account of how British astronomer Arthur Eddington managed to build interest in and provide definitive proof for Albert Einstein's general theory of relativity during and immediately following World War I. Eddington had to decipher Einstein's complex mathematics and counter-intuitive arguments, which challenged the centuries-long received wisdom of Newtonian physics. Because of the war, only a few individuals outside of Germany were even aware of Einstein's theory, and Eddington had to work through it without the help or input of Einstein himself, who was effectively sealed off in Berlin. Eddington then translated these ideas into more accessible prose—both for other scientists and the public at large—using *Gulliver's Travels*, *Alice in Wonderland* and other relatable examples familiar to many people. He and Frank Dyson, the Astronomer Royal and one of the most influential scientists in the UK, then set about drumming up both scientific and popular interest in the theory, and the expedition Eddington was mounting (and Dyson was funding) to view a solar eclipse that would allow them to empirically test it. Eddington framed his expedition—which could provide evidence that gravity bends light, a central prediction of relativity theory—as a contest between Newton's and Einstein's theories, making it a battle between two scientific geniuses, thereby creating tension and worldwide interest in the outcome. After finding support for general relativity, he carefully orchestrated the presentation of his findings, marshaling facts and having arguments at the ready to address the objections and challenges Newtonian adherents were sure to raise. After presenting his findings, he continued spreading his interpretation of and support for the theory through both scientific lectures and public speeches before any group that invited him.

While Eddington's efforts spread well beyond the bounds of a single academic study, all the storytelling aspects that any good article or book chapter provides are reflected in his tale. He identified an interesting and important question and attracted attention to it by creating tension or conflict that his study would resolve. He clearly and carefully prepared the terrain so that the audience understood the basic context and arguments, and he laid out the central question tested. After conducting his study and carefully verifying his results, he clearly explained what he did and allowed others to examine his findings so that they were satisfied with their veracity. He then presented his findings and interpreted their meaning, setting them back into the larger framework he had previously established, and explained how they advanced our scientific understanding of gravity, space and time. British astronomer J.J. Thomson noted that "By his eloquence, clearness and literary power [Eddington] persuaded multitudes of people in this country and the Americas that they understand what relativity means" (Stanley, 2019: 317). That is, he did not simply recount the mathematical density of the theory of relativity in dry, esoteric terms; he captured his audience's attention and imagination, and brought the theory to life, through storytelling.

Good writing skills and storytelling tools are critical for successfully exposing your ideas and insights to the world. Scholars have argued (Ashford, 2013; Daft, 1985; Podsakoff, Podsakoff, Mishra & Escue, 2018) and found (Judge, Cable, Colbert & Rynes, 2007) that clearly written articles are cited more frequently and are more likely to become high-impact "home runs." As a former Associate Editor for the *Academy of Management Journal* and reviewer of hundreds of manuscripts for *AMJ* and other journals, I have seen how bad writing inhibits otherwise promising ideas from reaching the public because the papers fail to make it through the review process. Even published articles can have limited influence if their core ideas are inaccessible and they make readers think about taking a nap five minutes after they begin reading. My goal with this book is to help you improve your writing and increase the chances your insights are read and understood.

One of the most enduring and pernicious falsehoods perpetuated in academia is that being boring equals being rigorous. In this book I explain and show how scholars use the structure and tools of storytelling to make academic writing more accessible, influential and easier to read without "dumbing down" or reducing the rigor of their argumentation and work. Based on my experience and that of other authors, I also provide insights on how to approach the writing and publishing processes. I draw not only from my own experiences and work by others on academic writing, but also from noted authors of fiction and nonfiction who face many of the same struggles, and who provide insights on how to better convey your ideas to others.

In order to creatively express your ideas you have to understand the constraints and demands of the form you are writing in. I have heard complaints about the journal article format and how it inhibits writers' abilities to develop and express their ideas. My response to such whining is, "Does that mean you can't be creative writing a haiku, then, or a sonnet, because they have restrictive forms?"

Every writing form, from limericks to novels to academic journal articles, has specific structures and norms. Forms provide structure that help readers know what to expect and how to find meaning. While some forms are more flexible than others, the creativity comes from successfully conveying what you want within the bounds of the form, not from devising a new and unfamiliar form. Successful academic writers, rather than complaining about the strictures of the journal article form, figure out how to work successfully within it. In this book I discuss the general form of a journal article and what each section needs to contain, as well as the commonalities and differences across theory only, empirical quantitative and empirical qualitative articles. I also show how the structure of a drama can be laid over the general article structure, and how to employ the tools of storytelling within each section to make academic articles engaging and readable.

WRITING VERSUS TYPING

People are also often stressed by and struggle with the writing process because they conflate writing with typing. Typing occurs when you sit in front of your keyboard, as I am now, and transcribe your thoughts onto the screen (or, for a few of my older colleagues, put pen to paper, letting others do the typing). Although writing occurs during typing, it also occurs when you are far away from your computer. I have spent many dog walks thinking about how to open this chapter, for example, as well as about other aspects of this book. I've also engaged in writing—laying out the structure, logic and examples I will use in this book or in my academic work—while mowing the lawn, cooking and hiking in the woods. Does this make me an obsessive workaholic? Maybe.

But it also illustrates that writing takes place when you are thinking about your story and what you want to say, not just when you are typing it up. I will discuss the pitfalls and challenges of the writing process, but also the many ways to do it in a healthy and productive way, so that you actually put together something you are proud of and get it out the door.

ADDITIONAL PROCESS ISSUES

Odds are that most research you produce is co-authored with someone else. Fewer and fewer articles these days are sole-authored, and as productivity demands for annual reviews and promotion and tenure increase it is difficult if not impossible to generate the required amount of research all by yourself. Sole-authoring is less efficient, and a lot less fun. However, identifying and figuring out how to work with co-authors can be challenging, and most scholars with any experience have some co-author horror stories they can share. At the same time, I view writing as an inherently social activity—even though much of it occurs while you are alone—and good collaborators not only make the process more enjoyable, they help produce research that is better than any one of you could have come up with on your own. Thus, this book also covers issues of co-authorship, including selecting, working with and, if necessary, firing co-authors; determining authorship order; and putting co-authored papers together so they speak with one voice.

This takes us to what happens once your article is written. If it is a scholarly journal article, then the next step is to send it out for peer review. There is probably no other aspect of publishing research steeped in more dread, myth and urban legend than the review process. Much of the received wisdom about the review process, editors' motivations, etc., simply isn't true. Yes, it can be dispiriting and ego-damaging even when you are successful, and there are plenty of bad reviewers and editors out there. However, I can say that without exception every paper I've published has improved for having gone through the review process; whether because of ideas and insights offered by the many good editors and reviewers I've encountered, or because overcoming lazy reviewers or poorly done reviews has forced me to think through issues and sharpen my writing so that even a lazy reader can't miss the point. I've also seen many papers fail because the authors didn't manage the review process well; for example, by misinterpreting or making strategic errors in responding to comments, failing to engage with the reviewers' comments entirely, or being overly accommodating and forgetting who the authors of the paper actually are. Thus, I also address the review process and how to manage it successfully.

While publishing research comprises a significant amount of our writing time, we also engage in other types of writing in doing our jobs. Everyone drafts cover letters when they go on the job market, and research statements for use in hiring, annual reviews and the promotion and tenure process. You'll likely need money to fund your research, so you will also at some point write research grant proposals. I will spend time talking about these other kinds of writing as well, and what good writing of each type looks like.

THE BOOK'S STRUCTURE

This book is intended for any academic, at any stage of career, who is interested in improving their writing. It can also serve as a primary text for graduate student writing courses, and selected chapters could be used as readings in introductory research design courses and other courses that are either primarily focused on writing or teach writing as a core component of the course. I am a management scholar, which influences some of the particulars I discuss, especially with respect to article structure and aspects of the review process. Many of my examples will also come from the management literature because it's what I know best. However, much of this book is applicable to scholars publishing in any business discipline, or in related social sciences such as psychology, sociology and economics.

Chapters 2–4 focus on the toolkit you'll need to employ storytelling in your academic writing. Chapter 2 applies the five-act structure of drama to academic storytelling, and discusses other structural aspects such as characters, theme and storylines. Chapter 3 introduces storytelling tools, such as putting a human face on your work, motion and pacing, and showing and telling. Chapter 4 covers the building blocks of storytelling—words, sentences and paragraphs. It focuses on how to produce clear, active prose and on paying attention to the sound and cadence of your writing.

The next section of the book focuses on the article's structure, and what goes into each part. Chapter 5 addresses the Introduction (or opening), Chapter 6 covers Theory Development and Hypotheses, Chapter 7 focuses on presenting the Methods and Results, and Chapter 8 talks about how to write an effective Discussion section. In each of these chapters I cover what a good section contains and why, as well the role the section plays in the overall structure of the story. Chapter 9 brings it all together by considering the similarities and differences in writing theory and empirical qualitative articles, and the differences between writing articles and book chapters.

The book's final section largely addresses process issues. Applying the structure and tools of storytelling and developing each section of the paper can seem easy when considered as abstract concepts, but can be devilishly hard to actually do; and once the paper is ready for review, understanding how to navigate the review process is critical. Thus, Chapter 10 focuses on the writing process, Chapter 11 on the co-authoring process, and Chapter 12 on the review process. I also provide some guidance on the other types of writing (grant proposals, research statements and cover letters) that academics do in Chapter 13. Chapter 14 finishes the book with my thoughts on the pleasures of writing, and of writing well.

Although I wrote these chapters with a particular order in mind, I also tried to write them so that they do not have to be read in sequence to be helpful. If there are particular topics you are interested in, you can head right to that chapter without, for the most part, getting lost. This is a nuts-and-bolts book on how to generate good, readable academic articles. I do not engage in debates on the philosophy of science and the nature of knowledge. I hope you find it helpful and thought-provoking. Now, on to storytelling.

2. Structuring a story

How do you conceive of yourself as an academic? As a theorist? An empiricist? A creator of knowledge? A reporter of facts? How you conceive of yourself affects the way you approach the research process, including how you view the written presentation of your research. If you simply think of yourself as a reporter of facts, and the written products you generate as "research reports," then the battle for writing clear, interesting and accessible articles may already be lost. However, if you think of yourself as a *storyteller* then you can achieve these goals because you will also be open to applying the tenets of good storytelling to your academic writing.

Like any effective piece of communication, a story needs a structure. Beyond the macro-structure of an academic article (i.e., introduction, theory development and hypotheses, methods, results and discussion) it is also helpful to think about the internal structure of your story. In this chapter I focus on applying a storytelling structure that goes back thousands of years to think about how you structure your research story. I also discuss how characters, theme and storylines contribute to the storytelling structure of your academic writing.

THE DRAMATIC STRUCTURE OF A STORY

Aristotle argued that a story reflects a "whole action," which has a beginning, a middle and an end. At its core is a knot, or central challenge, that the protagonist or main character must deal with, and the drama involves first tying the knot (that is, introducing complications that increase the tension and drama) and then unraveling it (resolving the conflict and presenting the solution or outcome). Long-time *Administrative Science Quarterly* managing editor Linda Johanson (1994) argued that academic journal articles also have a clear beginning, middle and end that establish your question and why it's important; ground it in theory and present your hypotheses; describe how the question was addressed and whether or not the hypotheses are supported; and help the reader make sense of it all.

The image of tying and unraveling a knot is a powerful one to keep in mind when structuring your study's story. If there is no tension, drama or conflict to be resolved in your study (i.e., no knot to unravel), why is its story interesting? Conversely, if you cannot unravel the knot, or the unraveling does not provide any clear solution or insight into the problem at the heart of your study, what have we learned? Everything you write should either contribute to tying or unraveling the knot at the heart of your story. If it doesn't, then you need to think about whether it really needs to be included, and how it advances your story.

Freytag's Pyramid. A common dramatic structure that has been around for thousands of years is the five-act play. Gustav Freytag (1865 [1900]) reconceived the five-act structure in perhaps one of the most recognizable graphics in drama—Freytag's Pyramid. The five elements[1] of Freytag's Pyramid are exposition, rising action, climax, falling action and dénouement. Freytag organized these five elements into a pyramid, as shown in Figure 2.1.

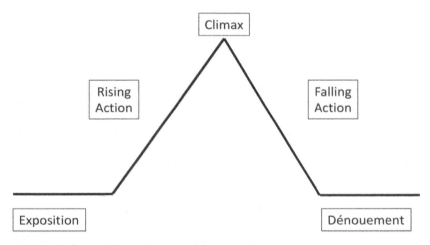

Figure 2.1   Freytag's Pyramid

The ***Exposition*** is where the background is laid. The characters are introduced, the setting is described, events that occurred before the story takes place are recounted and the characters' back stories are articulated. Although these expositional elements are also often included elsewhere in the story for dramatic effect, or to move the story along, this section is primarily dedicated to exposition. In the ***Rising Action***, a series of events and experiences occur that build the dramatic tension. This is where setbacks, challenges and complications occur, but also where evidence of the protagonist's possible ability

---

[1]   Freytag's original labels were introduction, rise, climax, fall and catastrophe, but over time the labels used here have become more standard.

to resolve the problem or overcome the challenge are introduced, or at least foreshadowed. These actions are the main guts of the story. The rising action builds to the ***Climax***, which is the point of highest tension or drama; it is the turning point that determines the protagonist's fate and where the solution starts to appear. The ***Falling Action*** is where the conflict unravels and the protagonist succeeds or fails. There may still be moments of suspense before the final outcome is known, but we eventually find out what happens. The ***Dénouement*** is the moment of catharsis for the reader, where tensions are relieved and a sense of normality and resolution is established. The drama's complexities are all unraveled and explained.

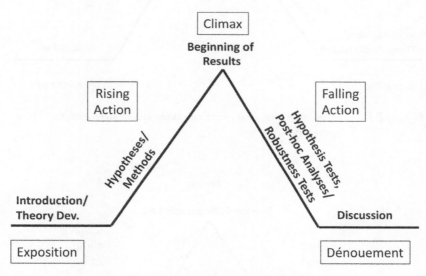

Figure 2.2   *Freytag's Pyramid overlaid on the quantitative article structure*

Freytag's Pyramid is a useful structure because it breaks the aspects of the drama into clearly defined pieces. It can also be overlaid on the basic structure of an academic article and provide structure to the story within the article format. Figures 2.2, 2.3 and 2.4 provide illustrations for quantitative, qualitative and theory-only journal articles, respectively. In all three articles the introduction is where much of the exposition occurs, as the background is laid, the reason for the study is explained, and the main characters (i.e., the primary theoretical constructs) are introduced. The beginning of the theory development section in quantitative articles, and the theoretical background sections of qualitative and theory articles, also often provide additional exposition,

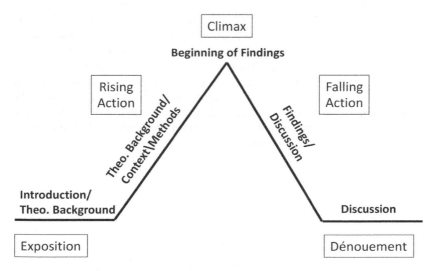

Figure 2.3   Freytag's Pyramid overlaid on the qualitative article structure

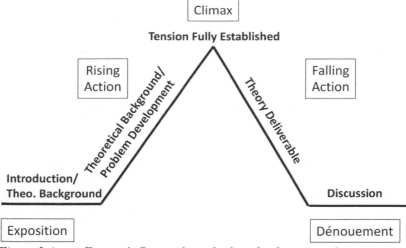

Figure 2.4   Freytag's Pyramid overlaid on the theory article structure

particularly the sections on the literature review, and for qualitative articles the research context (depending on where you choose to describe your research context).

The rising action also begins in these sections, because it is where you tie the knot. Complications are introduced and elaborated on, and the way forward—particularly in quantitative articles—is laid out as you develop and present your hypotheses. The theoretical tension and interest should build during this part of the article as expectations grow, but what will actually happen is still unclear. The methods are also part of the rising action in quantitative and qualitative studies. It describes the context, sample and data sources (i.e., the arena in which the climax will take place), defines the variables and measures (if quantitative), and explains the analysis method. At this point the knot is fully tied, setting the stage for the climax. In theory articles there are no "results"; so, for theory papers the theoretical background or literature review sections are where you develop the problem and tie the knot.

Unlike the other parts of Freytag's Pyramid, the climax is a point, rather than a segment; it's the moment of highest tension before the outcome is known. In empirical studies it's the beginning of the results or findings section. Because it's a point the climax is short, often involving ritual discussions of collinearity and descriptive statistics in quantitative studies, or the structure of the findings section in qualitative studies.

The falling action is where you unravel the knot and reveal your results or findings. In a quantitative study it begins with the hypothesis tests' results, and we find out whether they are supported. Although the resolution is now in sight, we aren't quite there yet; unraveling the knot also involves describing the supplemental analyses, robustness tests, or other post-hoc analyses that round out the initial findings. There can still be moments of tension and surprise as these additional analyses add nuance to your findings, perhaps showing that a hypothesis that was not supported in the primary analysis is supported when you consider additional complicating factors. The Findings section encompasses the falling action in qualitative studies; it unravels the knot by describing the theoretical model you inducted from the data. In both cases the falling action may also spill over into the beginning of the Discussion section, where you summarize your results and findings. In theory papers the falling action is where you develop and present your primary theory deliverable—the theoretical model, typology or synthesis and integration of literatures—because the theory deliverable itself is the solution. By the falling action's end the knot is completely unraveled, and you've fully revealed the answers to the study's central question. Depending on the article's nature and purpose, the rising and/or falling actions could be long or relatively short, even though conceptually the figure presents them equally.

The dénouement occurs in the Discussion section. This is the concluding act that brings all you've revealed during the climax and falling action together and makes sense of it. You integrate the surprise findings and unsupported expectations with the supported relationships and tie them back to theory and practice. It is also where you highlight new insights, make conjectures and discuss the study's limitations. Like many stories, life continues on past the point where your tale ends. The future research directions section is where you describe new adventures the characters in your study can have.

Finally, as Linda Johanson (1994) noted, the article's ending should fix the story in the reader's mind. I think this is probably the hardest part of the paper to write. Indeed, in an interview shortly before his death, Ernest Hemingway confessed that he wrote thirty-nine different endings for *A Farewell to Arms* until he "got the words right." His grandson later discovered forty-seven different endings (Evans, 2017). Johanson suggested that a good ending brings the readers back to the beginning and offers them a fresh perspective on the subject studied. Issuing a generic call for future research, or summarizing the study for the third or more time, is not a satisfying resolution. She recommended using as direct and simple language as possible, and to close with a concrete image, rather than abstract notions.

Treating your research article as a story that unfolds in five acts can provide structure within the article's basic format. When you are lost, or feel that you are rambling and saying the same thing over and over, or aren't sure how to get from one idea to the next, think about where you are on Freytag's Pyramid, and what it will take to get you to the next act in your drama. It can also be useful when using somewhat different story structures, such as presenting a mixed methods study (e.g., Guler, 2007; Uzzi, 1996) or multiple experiments (e.g., Grant, Campbell, Chen, Cottone, Lapedis & Lee, 2007). There will be a clear exposition and dénouement that ties the studies together, but the action rises and falls repeatedly across the different studies.

Applying Freytag's Pyramid to an academic article: an example. To illustrate what this looks like in practice, I will use Freytag's Pyramid to describe the story structure of an article I published in the *Academy of Management Journal* with my co-authors Yuri Mishina, Bernadine Dykes and Emily Block (Mishina et al., 2010)—"Why 'good' firms do bad things: The effects of high aspirations, high expectations and prominence on the incidence of corporate illegality."

The ***exposition*** included the introduction and first sub-section of the theory and hypothesis development section. This is where we laid the groundwork for our study, establishing the paradox at its heart and providing background on our key constructs: illegal actions, internal aspirations and external expectations. We started by noting the many arguments for why high-performing firms didn't need to engage in illegal actions and the costs of doing so, then juxtaposed that with empirical research and recent anecdotal examples such as Enron, Worldcom and Tyco that contradicted this received wisdom. This set up the research question that drove our story, which was why and under what conditions prominent and successful firms would risk engaging in illegal actions. The introduction laid some of the groundwork by establishing that prior research had focused on absolute levels of performance, but had not considered how a firm's relative performance could shape perceptions and decision making. Establishing an interesting paradox in the literature and hinting at the solution was crucial for making the readers want to know more and getting them to read on.

In the first sub-section of the theory and hypotheses development section we explicitly defined corporate illegality as an illegal act primarily meant to benefit a firm by potentially increasing revenues or decreasing costs. This was important expository information because we needed to clearly differentiate illegal acts that benefitted the firm—the focus of our study—from illegal acts like embezzlement that only benefitted the executives personally. We also introduced our other two key constructs and highlighted two key assumptions that we had to make.

Since our study used retrospectively collected archival data, we obviously couldn't assess exactly what was in the minds of the executives or who actually took the illegal actions within the organization. Thus, our first assumption was that the perceptions of a firm's Top Management Team (TMT) matter and will affect the firm's actions. The second assumption was that regardless of whether a firm's TMT members themselves decided to commit an illegal act, or whether it was an individual or group lower in the organization's hierarchy, it was the TMT who established and fostered the organization's culture, its aspiration levels, and the pressure to continue meeting or exceeding aspirations. This is how we began tying the knot that our study would unravel.

Once we established the character introductions, back stories, context and foreshadowing of the problems that lay ahead, we then moved on to the ***rising action***. In developing our hypotheses we needed to establish the theoretical tension we desired, while avoiding some theoretical tension we didn't want. One of the challenges we faced was that there were multiple possible mechanisms that we could theorize drove the relationships we were studying: loss aversion, the house money effect and executive hubris. The first mechanism argues that individuals will take greater risks to avoid sure losses than to protect gains; the second mechanism argues that when individuals are in a gain position they will take more risks because they are playing with the "house's" money (to use a gambling metaphor), not their own; the third mechanism suggests that success will make executives arrogant and begin to believe they can do whatever they want without serious risk of failure. Since they all predicted the same pattern of behavior, and any or all of them could be operative across different firms, we presented all three and developed our arguments irrespective of which mechanism might be operating in a particular instance.

Key to tying our knot was the insight that firms cannot sustain high performance indefinitely; there is always a regression to the mean. Further, performance is assessed relative to individuals' own aspirations and others' expectations; thus they can assess even good performance negatively if it's not as good as hoped for, and these expectations shift upward the longer performance is high, meaning actors evaluate the same level of performance less favorably than before. This led to our argument that the more a firm's performance exceeded their aspirations and others' expectations, the more likely it was to engage in illegal actions to maintain its high relative performance. We then considered how a firm's prominence, and the attention it drew to the firm's actions, would influence these basic relationships. We argued that more prominent firms will feel the pressures to maintain their high performance at all costs more acutely.

Once we established the tension to resolve, the next question was how we were going to test our arguments. This leads to the data and methods section, where we described our sample and how we measured illegal actions, relative performance and prominence. We had a number of challenges—for example, we could only study firms that had been caught doing something illegal, there was a debate in the literature about how to operationalize performance relative to aspirations,[2] and we had missing data for a number of controls that necessitated using a data imputation procedure—that we also had to clearly address. Our analytical approach involved using splines—where we broke our key IVs into separate measures for performance below and above aspirations so that each can generate a different slope—that were not that common when we did the study, and also required additional explanation.

The *climax* occurred in the opening paragraph of the Results section. The knot was fully tied, and we opened this section by discussing some descriptive statistics and the effects of our control variables.

The *falling action* is where the knot unravels. We found good general support for our prediction that the likelihood of corporate illegality went up the more performance exceeded social aspirations, and partial support for our predication about external expectations, where the main effect was only significant when we included the interaction with prominence in the model. The interaction hypothesis between prominence and social aspirations was

---

 [2] We could measure aspirations relative to the firm's own historical performance (historical aspirations), others' prior performance (social aspirations) or a combination of the two. We tried all three approaches and found historical aspirations had no effect, and that social aspirations and the combined measure yielded the same result, so we used social aspirations in our analyses.

not supported—there was no difference between more and less prominent firms—and the interaction effect between prominence and external expectations was supported. We also conducted additional analyses that yielded some surprise findings and a robustness test that assessed how prior illegal actions affected our results. These analyses added some nuance to our findings and helped unravel the knot. Although we did not hypothesize about interaction effects when performance was below expectations and aspirations, we did assess these relationships as part of our empirical analysis. We found that less prominent firms were more likely to engage in illegal actions than prominent firms when their performance was below social aspirations. We also found that less prominent firms' likelihood of illegal actions was unaffected when performance was below expectations, and actually declined the more performance exceeded expectations, which explained the non-significant finding for the main effect alone. Finally, we empirically and logically ruled out the "bad apples" alternative explanation.

The ***dénouement*** comprised the Discussion section and Conclusion. Here we were able to summarize our findings and draw interesting theoretical and practical implications from our analyses. In addition to finding support for our general claim, we also speculated about why more and less prominent firms reacted similarly to performance above aspirations, but differently to performance above external expectations. On the practical side, we drew implications both for those who regulate and oversee companies, and for the investors and others who put relentless pressure on companies for the continually higher performance that led to their illegal actions. Our conclusion wasn't the strongest; we summarized our findings more than we should have, although we did end with a statement about what we know, and not a call for future research.

IDENTIFYING YOUR CHARACTERS

Figuring out who your characters are is as important as understanding the journey they will take. Your characters are who your story is about; they are the ones taking the journey, and interacting with others along the way. They are your protagonist, or hero; the antagonist who may be holding the protagonist back and/or competing with the protagonist, creating the tension in your story; the supporting characters who play important but supplementary roles, perhaps only showing up in one scene, or who provide a necessary boost or create roadblocks along the way; and the ensemble and extras who may have limited or no speaking roles but add richness, filling out the scenes, making them more believable and supporting the action taking place. Because your article is ultimately about the theory explaining the phenomena you are studying, your theoretical constructs are the characters in your drama, not the individuals and organizations that may be experiencing or personifying them.

Main characters. One challenge many academic writers face is that they haven't figured out who the main, supporting and ensemble characters are in their story. Academic articles don't work well when the main and supporting characters are not clearly defined, because the reader doesn't know who to focus on, or what the story is about. In academic writing the central constructs you are theorizing about and measuring as the key independent and dependent variables are your main characters. If you are primarily theorizing about a key construct and the factors that influence its occurrence—for example, if you are interested in what makes some CEOs more likely to become celebrities than others—then the dependent construct CEO celebrity is your main character, and the factors that influence it are your supporting characters.

In contrast, if you are theorizing about the interplay between contextual and personality traits in studying how a climate of safety and individuals' neuroticism influence whether they speak up at work, then the safety climate and neuroticism are your main characters, and voice is a supporting character since it just provides a useful context in this study, rather than serving as the main subject of interest. In other studies where you are theorizing specifically about voice, however, it would be a main character.

Both the independent and dependent variables are the main characters if the influence of one upon the other is your story's focus. For example, in studying the effect of CEO pay on firm performance, both the nature and structure of the pay (e.g., the mixture of short-term and long-term incentive pay, or the use of stock options versus restricted stock) and the type of performance considered (e.g., stock price performance, accounting performance or corporate social responsibility) can receive equal billing. In our "Why 'good' firms do bad things" article, performance relative to internal aspirations, performance relative to external expectations and illegal actions were our main characters, since our focus was on how the former influenced the latter.

Supporting characters. Supporting characters are also critical to your story. They do not necessarily appear throughout the story, and their backgrounds and motivations may not be as thoroughly developed as the main characters', but they play an important role in moving the story along and in tying or unraveling the central knot. They may have direct effects on a main character or be affected by them in some way, as noted above, but supporting characters also frequently serve as moderators and mediators in academic studies, influencing the relationships between the main characters, or how they are affected by the context in which they find themselves. In our "Why 'good' firms do bad things" article, firm prominence was the supporting character; it affected how performance relative to aspirations and expectations influenced the likelihood of illegal actions, but it was not our primary focus.

Ensemble. The ensemble—other characters who play only small roles and help fill out scenes—hold the story together and make it more realistic. In academic studies these characters are typically played by control variables, which help rule out alternative explanations or otherwise flesh out the study's context. In our "Why 'good' firms do bad things" article, our ensemble included a variety of different controls: governance-related variables (CEO/Chair separation, board size, percentage of outside directors and upper-echelon equity ownership), firm size, firm slack (absorbed, unabsorbed and potential slack), year dummies to control for a variety of temporal differences, and environmental munificence and dynamism.

PLOT-DRIVEN VERSUS CHARACTER- OR SITUATION-DRIVEN STORIES

You may be asking yourselves at this point (or not): What about the plot? Shouldn't the plot structure the story? According to Smiley and Bert (2005: 73), "Plot is the organization of materials. It's a pattern of action—the arrangement of scenes, events, description, and dialogue—assembled as a palpable whole." Thus, plot helps shape the specific content and ordering of things within the more general five act structure of Freytag's Pyramid. So yes, plot does provide structure. The question, however, is where the plot comes from. Does it precede the story's creation, or does it emerge from it?

In their memoir/writing guides, novelists Stephen King (2000) and Anne Lamott (1994) are both adamant that plot is emergent rather than formative. King stated their perspective succinctly when he said, "Plot is, I think, the good writer's last resort and the dullard's first choice. The story that results from it is apt to feel artificial and labored" (2000: 164). They both argued that plot emerges from the characters' interactions as you put them into situations and see what happens. They also noted that our lives are not plotted, and the ending, or how we get there, is often difficult to predict. Thus, to try and force a plot onto your characters may feel stilted, strip the story of drama, and create action to get us from one point to the next which is unbelievable, leading to unsatisfying conclusions. If you've ever read an article where the theory and arguments seem forced and ill-fitting, you've read an article where plot preceded story.

At this point I can imagine readers who do qualitative research are nodding their heads muttering "Yep, that's right," while quantitatively oriented readers are exclaiming "Wait a minute! But that's how research is done!" If you are more comfortable with inductive approaches, this emergent process to creating plot seems normal. If, however, you are more deductive in your approach, this may rankle. I argue that a research study, whether approached qualitatively or quantitatively, is an emergent process. We form initial ideas that have, to use King's words, "The stark simplicity of a department store window display or waxwork tableau" (2000: 164), and then we develop and elaborate them over time. That is, at the beginning of a research study we identify our main characters, and perhaps some supporting characters, put them in a situation and start to see how they respond. We may add additional characters and drop others, discover that our main characters have strengths or flaws we were unaware of, or that a supporting character really plays a starring role, ultimately shaping how the story unfolds. For example, in early iterations of our "Why 'good' firms do bad things" article we considered an additional supporting character—the moderating effect of the firm's reputation. However, we ultimately decided to just focus on prominence, dropping the reputation moderator as our story and plot cohered.

Although as scholars we don't necessarily present every twist and turn of this process when we write our stories (Hollenbeck & Wright, 2017), this is how the plot is developed, or—if you prefer King's analogy of stories as uncovered fossils waiting to be found—discovered. Developing a plot beforehand and then forcing it onto your characters is more apt to result in an unfulfilling narrative with logical gaps and leaps that make your readers skeptical, rather than believers in the story you are trying to tell. Plot is important for driving action in your story, but it does not drive how your characters and situations interact—it is driven by them.

STORYLINES AND THEMES

A story's theme, quite simply, is what the story is about. It is the true north of your story that determines what is and is not extraneous; if what you are talking about doesn't contribute to the story's theme, then why are you talking about it? In academic articles the theme is the research question guiding your study. This may be the research question or theme that you started with, or the one that emerged as more interesting and important as the study progressed. Either way, throughout the writing process you should keep returning to the questions: (1) What is this story's theme? and (2) Does everything I've written contribute to and clarify it? If not, then you will need to either revise or delete what you've written, or reconsider what the true theme of your study really is.

Related to plot is the storyline, or storylines, that your characters follow. These are the specific paths that each character takes on their journey. Depending on the number of main characters there may be multiple storylines, as each main character follows its own, but related path. However, every storyline should relate to the story's theme, and ideally the storylines will eventually intersect to give the story a sense of cohesion. One challenge many scholars face is that they spin out too many storylines based on too many different theories, leading their story to lose its coherence and focus, and the plot to become muddled and inconsistent. This problem is not confined to academics. Stephen King (2000) described how he ran into this issue when writing his novel, *The Stand*. By the time he was halfway through writing the first draft he had so many characters and sub-plots that the book was bogging down. His solution? He blew half the characters up, allowing him to simply terminate the extraneous storylines.

Scholars don't have the luxury of bombing their distracting constructs and theories, but we can aggressively use the delete key to take extraneous storylines out and focus on the ones that are the most critical and interesting. If every new construct brings a new theory with it, then you need to reduce the number of storylines. I don't believe that every paper should have just a single theory, because most new theories evolve by integrating parts of other theories. Even if you love the tangent you've gone on, for the sake of effectively structuring your story you may have to kill that particular darling. You can, however, think about whether the tangent might become the basis for an entirely separate study.

The theme is the constant line that runs throughout your story, and the storylines that support the theme should add to the rising action and be resolved in the dénouement. If they don't help answer your research question, go unresolved, or bog down the action in your story then they are good candidates for the cutting room floor. In our "Why 'good' firms do bad things" article, the theme was why high performing firms engage in illegal behaviors given the costs. Our storylines were how internal aspirations and external expectations affected their decisions, and how they were shaped by the attention the firm's prominence drew to their actions. Although our two main characters followed essentially the same storyline in the front end of our paper, an interesting outcome of our findings was that their storylines diverged in the dénouement. Sometimes, because of the journey, our heroes end up following different paths. That's part of what makes the story interesting.

In this chapter I focused on the macro-structure of stories, and how to apply a classic storytelling structure within the framework of academic articles. An excellent exercise you can try is to select one or two articles that you think are really outstanding and engaging pieces of research, and then go through them to identify how they handled the elements of Freytag's Pyramid; character identification and development; and issues of plot, theme and storylines. You can then turn the same lens on your own work and see which structural aspects of your story are strong, and which need improving.

3.   Storytelling tools

My first semester as a doctoral student I took a class called the Classics of Organization Theory. I ended up loving this class; it played a significant role in me becoming an organization theorist and I have taught an OT doctoral seminar myself for over fifteen years. However, as a minty-fresh doctoral student just starting my studies, and having no prior experience with academic prose, reading the work of old dead Germans where the translator seemed to retain the original German syntax was scorchingly painful. Early on, though, we also read excerpts from *The Principles of Scientific Management* by Frederick Taylor (1916). While the book's title does not foretell an interesting read, Taylor used a great story to illustrate his principles: the tale of Schmidt the pig-iron handler.

Taylor described his need for a suitable worker whom he could train to move, on a sustainable basis, four times the amount of pig iron[1] the typical worker could load onto rail cars per day. He identified a man working at the Bethlehem Steel factory he called Schmidt, "A little Pennsylvania Dutchman who had been observed to trot back home for a mile or so after his work in the evening, about as fresh as he was when he came trotting down to work in the morning ... he was engaged in putting up the walls of a little house for himself in the morning before starting work and at night after leaving" (Taylor, 1916: 43–44). He also described Schmidt as "exceedingly close" with his money (i.e., cheap). He then illustrated his conversation with Schmidt using dialogue, including dialect for Schmidt ("Vell, I don't know vot you mean" and "Did I vant $1.85 a day? Vos dot a high-priced man?" are typical examples), and described how Schmidt was paid a premium for hitting his goal each day (the going rate was $1.15) by following his trainer's instructions. He finished by noting that Schmidt continued to move pig-iron at this rate the entire time Taylor was at Bethlehem Steel.

This story struck me, as it did the other students in my class, and was quite a topic of conversation. It never fails to attract similar reactions in my OT seminars. It grabbed us in part because of Taylor's obvious biases towards immigrants and the uneducated (typical of the time), and because of the

---

[1]   A cheap by-product of steel manufacturing that became valuable during the Spanish War. Each "pig" weighed approximately ninety pounds.

ham-handed dialogue. However, it was also an effective story because Taylor employed many storytelling tools in using Schmidt to illustrate his principles of scientific management. He gave his abstract principles a human face; he showed us how they worked, instead of just telling us; he personalized the story by putting himself in it; the full account moved at a good pace so the story didn't become overlong, while still providing adequate descriptive detail so readers got both the flavor of the characters involved in the story and saw how it illustrated his principles in action; and he employed vivid word choices (e.g., "little," "trotted," and "close") that gave Schmidt dimension and were consistent with his story's theme.

Storytelling tools are an essential complement to story structure. They are what move the story from one act to the next, make characters three-dimensional actors instead of cardboard cut-outs, create tension and drama, and help provide the reader with release. Too few academic writers employ these storytelling tools. It is stunning, for example, how frequently social science scholars, who study human behavior, write articles where the human element is all but removed! There are no people doing things, the language is colorless and weak, the story moves either too quickly or not at all, they only tell us what's going on but never show us, and they keep their readers at arm's length with formal and impersonal language. In this chapter I will explain (and hopefully show) how to effectively employ storytelling tools in academic articles. Although the range of techniques is vast, I will focus on four that I think are especially appropriate for academic writing, and that are easy to incorporate: the human face, motion and pacing, showing and telling, and making your writing conversational.

THE HUMAN FACE

In his book *The Elements of Story*, *New York Times* editor Francis Flaherty (2009) led off by discussing the importance of the human face in storytelling. He stated, "Every story, even the driest, has a human face. Draw it well and put it on display, for to readers it is a mirror and a magnet" (Flaherty, 2009: 1). Nowhere is this truer than in the social sciences, where we study human behavior from different perspectives, and at different levels of analysis. The human face should be evident in everything we do, even if we are talking about abstract topics like national deficits, stock buybacks, cycles of poverty, cognitive processes, leader–member exchange or branding techniques. The major criticism leveled against much academic research—that it has no practical or real-world relevance—often results from the lack of a human face in our storytelling. If readers can't see why our studies are consequential for them in a direct, boots-on-the-ground way, they are not going to understand why it's important.

One of the reasons social science research so often lacks a human face is because we are trained and expected to make rational arguments based solely on logic, and the human face has an emotional component. Tapping into the emotional aspects of our rational topics, however, makes them resonate with readers. Another reason is that over-reliance on description and passive constructions (which I cover in Chapter 4) robs the actors of their agency. We need to make greater use of concrete examples that describe people doing stuff and having experiences that illustrate, or are a consequence of, the things we study.

Stephen King noted "[readers] want a good story ... that will first fascinate them, then pull them in and keep them turning the pages. This happens, I think, when readers recognize the people in the book, their behaviors, their surroundings and their talk" (King, 2000: 160). The clumsiness of Taylor's dialogue aside, this is what he did in his Schmidt example. He drew a character that people recognized, and through their interaction illustrated an abstract concept. Direct quotations can have similar effects when they reflect the speaker's actual dialect.

Flaherty pointed out that using examples where an actor is acting is the best way to put a human face on your subject. This can be a direct experience you have had: for example, it could be an illustration like the one I used of myself as a doctoral student to open this chapter; or it could be more in-depth, such as Mike Pratt's description of his experiences joining Amway in his ethnographic study of organizational identification (Pratt, 2000). It could also be a story you've read about in the business press or elsewhere, and repeat. For example, in our article "Master of Puppets: How narcissistic CEOs construct their professional worlds" (Chatterjee & Pollock, 2017), Arijit Chatterjee and I drew on *Mad Money* host Jim Cramer's exposé of Phillip Purcell, former CEO of Morgan Stanley Dean Witter, to illustrate how narcissistic CEOs manage their boards and top management teams differently, using some of Purcell's outrageous behaviors to illustrate our arguments.

A second option is to get someone else to recount a past experience. Any qualitative study is replete with examples from informant interviews; business press articles with direct quotes from individuals describing their experiences are also useful. Flaherty argued that less useful, but also valuable, is to report on a third party's description of the event, particularly if they heard about the story directly from the person who experienced it. Flaherty also noted that you can make up the anecdote, although you need to be clear that it is a fabrication. Helen Sword (2012) refers to these fictional accounts as "scenarios."

A clever example of this approach is Ted Baker's (2007) article in the *Journal of Business Venturing* that was part of a special issue focused on narrative and imagination in entrepreneurship. Contributors were all given the same narrative about two entrepreneurs seeking money to open a toy store. Baker's article "analyzes the 'Toy Store(y)' narrative by imagining the words and perspectives of several participants other than those from whose perspective the original story is told" (Baker, 2007: 694). Baker reimagined the story (originally told from the entrepreneur's perspective) from three other perspectives—the loan officer at the bank, the property owner leasing them space, and the entrepreneur's father-in-law. He created dialogue to illustrate how others perceived the situation and arrived at the decisions they did to "describe and display some ways that ideas about bricolage[2] ... can be applied to the theoretical and practical analysis of entrepreneurial organizations, and to suggest some promising areas for future research" (Baker, 2007: 695).

Whether you are describing your experiences, offering first- or second-hand accounts of others' experiences or creating fictional scenarios, Flaherty (2009) identified three techniques that will help your characters come to life and allow your readers to feel what the people you describe are feeling. The first is to use direct quotations or dialogue. Using colloquial language resonates because it sounds more authentic and "real," making it easier to visualize the people and their experiences. It also allows the emotion to come through. It's why one really good quotation can be so memorable. Just think of your favorite movie quotation. Why does it resonate and stick with you? Odds are it encapsulates the scene where it was uttered, and the emotion employed.

The second technique is to describe the actor's body language. This is subtle, but clenched fists, furrowed brows, shining eyes and sly grins all convey different emotions and give your characters dimension with a minimum of words. The third technique is to describe the physical actions that individuals take. Striding to the front of the room, stopping and kneeling to pet an old dog, and letting the silence hang before answering a question all convey useful information about the character. This is why Schmidt "trotting" to work and back each day and "putting up the walls of a little house for himself" provided important insights about the type of individual Taylor was looking for.

Finally, I add a fifth option to Flaherty's list: let readers put their own face on your story by asking rhetorical questions. This technique can be particularly useful when space is limited or laying out a longer example would derail the article's flow. Rhetorical questions prompt introspection and generate examples that readers are sure to get. For example, in my *AMJ* "From the Editors" (FTE) column with Joyce Bono (Pollock & Bono, 2013) on using storytelling in academic writing, we opened the section on titles with the following rhetorical question: "When you browse through a bookstore, how do you pick which

---

[2]   Bricolage is the process of "making do" by using resources originally intended for some other purpose, and that are available cheaply or for free, to accomplish some end. For example, using the warm water created by a generator's cooling system to grow hydroponic tomatoes (Baker & Nelson, 2005).

ones to buy?" Although we then gave our answer, this hopefully triggered the reader to picture him- or herself shopping for a book, putting their human face on our story. Questions that start "Have you ever known someone who…" or "Have you ever been in a situation where…" also allow the reader to put their own human face on your story.

MOTION AND PACING

A second critical storytelling tool is managing the story's motion and pacing. Stories require both action and commentary—which Flaherty (2009), using a rowing metaphor, referred to as "stroke" and "glide." How you combine them determines your story's motion and pacing. Motion results from actions that move the story forward, taking us from one scene and act to the next. Flaherty described several kinds of action that can create motion. *Natural* actions are the types of action and behavior you'd expect to see in the scene. *Hidden* and *future* action describe actions you cannot see (e.g., social dynamics or cognitive processes) or that haven't happened yet, but could or will happen. *Mental* actions do not involve physical movement, but create change or shifts by injecting a new idea. Finally, *made-up* actions are actions described using similes and metaphors that add motion to the narrative.

Pacing is the rate at which your story unfolds, and results from how you apportion and mix action (stroke) and commentary (glide). Flaherty (2009: 71) stated that "Good stories are a brisk journey, and the reader can always feel the wind in his hair," but he also noted that "Writing requires pacing, an unhurried, uncrowded revelation of facts that allows the reader enough time to pause over an idea, absorb it and reflect on it" (Flaherty, 2009: 86).

Have you ever taken a guided tour where the guide blew through all the key attractions, left no time for questions and provided little insight? Alternatively, have you ever been on a tour where the guide spent so much time yammering about the detail and context of what you are looking at that your back started to ache and you wondered, "Can't we just get on with it?" (There's that rhetorical question!) Articles in which there is too much action and too little commentary are like the former, and articles with too much commentary and too little action resemble the latter. As Joyce and I described (Pollock & Bono, 2013: 630):

> Academic articles with too much action and too little commentary often include rapid-fire statements of findings from other studies (e.g., "Study [1] explored [X]"; "Study [2] found [Y]") but don't discuss how these studies relate to each other or use them to build hypotheses. Descriptions of the data and methods lack crucial details, and there is little interpretation of results or discussion of alternative explanations.

These articles may be short and have motion, but the pace is a forced march, making them difficult to read.

Articles with too much commentary and too little action often have long front ends, extensive literature reviews, detailed descriptions of context, repetitive arguments, and long-winded descriptions of measures. They take us under the hood of statistical techniques (usually with lots of equations), overinterpret results, and report every robustness test ever imagined (footnotes were invented for a reason). Too rich in commentary and lacking action, their pacing is ponderous.

At a macro level, one way to assess whether your article has reasonable motion and pacing is to look at how long each section of the article is. As a general rule of thumb, the corpus of most quantitative manuscripts in management journals—before typesetting and excluding the abstract, references, tables and figures—is about 35 to 40 pages,[3] double-spaced using 12 point Times New Roman font.[4] The introduction should be about 10 percent of the total (3–4 pages), the theory and hypothesis section about 35 percent (12–14 pages), the methods and results sections about 35 percent (12–14 pages), and the discussion section about 20 percent (6–7 pages). Qualitative studies are typically longer (sometimes 20–30 percent longer), with less space typically devoted to the theoretical background, and more of the additional length added to the research context and findings sections. Theory papers are typically shorter (30–35 pages) with more space allocated to elaborating on the new theory and no methods or results sections.

Table 3.1 provides suggested page-length guidelines for each type of article in management. These are just rough guidelines, and you should look at manuscripts in your particular field to assess what percentages are most appropriate.[5] However, if your manuscript's sections, or your manuscript as a whole, significantly deviate from the typical percentages in your field in either direction, you likely have issues with motion and pacing. Sections that are substantially shorter probably need more description and elaboration, and those that are longer could use a good pruning.

At a more micro level, there are several different ways to create motion besides inserting action. Flaherty (2009) suggested employing "*turbo-verbs*"— strong, active verbs that create a sense of motion, even if they describe the

---

[3]   At approximately 350 words per page, that translates into about 12,000–14,000 words.

[4]   Overall manuscript length is therefore typically between 45 and 55 pages, although some journals have shorter page limits.

[5]   These section-length estimates can also change over time as norms change. For example, methods and results sections have generally become longer over the last thirty years as more powerful computers and online databases have increased the availability of sophisticated analytical tools and variables to include in the models.

Table 3.1   *Section-length rules of thumb for management articles*

	Quantitative	Qualitative	Theory
Total length	40–45 pages	45–52 pages	30–35 pages
Introduction	10% (3–4 pgs)	7% (3–4 pgs)	10% (3–4 pgs)
Theory and hypotheses	35% (12–14 pgs)		
Theoretical background		12% (5–7 pgs)	
Literature review			15% (5–6 pgs)
Theory development			55% (16–18 pgs)
Context		7% (3–4 pgs)	
Methods		20% (8–10 pgs)	
Methods and results	35% (12–14 pgs)		
Findings		35% (15–18 pgs)	
Discussion	20% (6–7 pgs)	19% (8–10 pgs)	20% (6–7 pgs)

same things as weaker verbs (e.g., "thrust" instead of "stick" or "put"; "crush" the competition instead of "beat" or "defeat" the competition). Flaherty (2009) also suggested employing "*to and fro.*" Moving between general and specific (or abstract and concrete, or broad and focused) statements also creates a sense of motion. The last two sentences are an example of to and fro. As I discuss in Chapter 4, *varying sentence and paragraph length* can also enhance or retard your motion and pacing. Using *synonyms*, particularly for action words (but never for theoretical constructs!) can also create some motion. Compare "organizations that cannot change their practices will fail to keep up with environmental change and therefore fail to meet customers' changing needs" with "Organizations that cannot adapt their practices will lag behind environmental shifts and therefore fail to meet customers' evolving needs." Which sentence has more motion? (The second one.) Flaherty (2009) also noted that although turbo-verbs and expressive punctuation like exclamation points are useful, they should be employed strategically. Too much of either one results in the breathless prose of a fourteen-year old's text messages.

There are also several techniques you can use to managing pacing, so that readers can understand and absorb your ideas at a reasonable but unhurried rate. Flaherty (2009) noted that authors often pile up words in a rush to get them all out there. He advocates using "*air" words* to create some space around key ideas and terms that are rich in meaning, so that readers can absorb them. Phrases such as "that is," "for example," and "which have," often coupled with punctuation such as semicolons and em dashes (the long ones, like this "—") can provide "the pause that refreshes" (Flaherty, 2009: 86). Another way to add space and mix action and commentary is to use *asides*, such as parentheticals or statements set off in hyphens or by commas, to insert a bit of description into the action. My explanation of the em dash above is one example.

Finally, Flaherty (2009) also suggested using *"right-branching sentences,"* where the action is concentrated at the front, followed by description, to help balance motion and pacing. "They may see executive narcissism as incidental to organizational functioning—annoying to those who must endure it, grist for jokes about self-absorbed CEOs, but little more" (Chatterjee & Hambrick, 2007: 352) is an example. You can also employ a similar structure across a paragraph, with the first sentence providing the action and the subsequent sentences providing commentary. Chatterjee and Hambrick (2007: 352) used a right-branching paragraph when speculating about why scholars had not conducted much research on CEO narcissism:

> First, they may believe that narcissism, derived as it is from Greek mythology, is a fanciful or lay concept, not grounded in good psychological science. But psychologists have extended the psychoanalytic concept of narcissism to the realm of large-sample psychometric analysis; as a result, narcissism passes contemporary, rigorous tests of construct validity (Emmons, 1987; Raskin and Terry, 1988). Research has shown that narcissism is a personality dimension, not just a clinical disorder, and that individuals can be reliably arrayed on this continuum.

The first sentence provides the action and the subsequent sentences provide the commentary.

Ultimately, the best way to identify issues with motion and pacing is to ask readers for feedback. If your reader starts yawning when reading your article or sets it down, the culprit is usually a lack of motion; if they feel agitated and confused, then the pacing is too quick, and more commentary is required. This is why friendly reviews, which I discuss in Chapter 10, are so important. With experience you will develop a good sense for when your storytelling drags or is too rushed, but outside opinions always help.

SHOWING AND TELLING

Helen Sword (2012) argued that stylish academic writing requires both showing and telling. We tell the readers about some abstract idea, process or construct, and then show them what it looks like. The various means described for putting a human face on your article discussed above are all examples of showing. However, Sword also identified simile, metaphor, allusion and personification as other means of showing. These linguistic techniques can make abstract constructs and ideas more vivid and tangible to readers.

Similes make comparisons between dissimilar things, typically using words such as "like" or "as." Briscoe and Safford (2008: 460) used a simile when they talked about the "Nixon in China" effect, stating "Like the effect of

Cold-War President Richard Nixon's surprising visit to the People's Republic of China in 1972, which led other countries to open relations with China, adoption of a practice by activism-resistant firms signaled to mainstream firms that an advocated practice had lost its contentiousness."

Metaphors resemble similes in that they invoke images by making comparisons to other things, but the comparison is implicit rather than explicit; that is, there is no like or as. For example, in my study "(Un)Tangled: Exploring the asymmetric co-evolution of VC firm reputation and status," with Peggy Lee, Kyuho Jin and Kisha Lashley, we used metaphor when discussing the "*co-evolution* of status and reputation" over time (Pollock et al., 2015: 482). Briscoe and Safford (2008: 463) also used metaphor when they said "But over time, and with an accumulation of *waves of movement activity*, certain simple themes, such as resistance or proneness to activism are revived, reinforced, clarified, and *woven* into the socially constructed *fabric* of business culture" (emphasis mine). "Waves of movement activity," "woven" and "fabric" are all metaphors.

Allusions tie abstract concepts to stories and images that are already familiar. For example, Derfus, Maggitti, Grimm and Smith's (2008: 61) use of the "Red Queen" effect[6] to describe competitive dynamics, "whereby a firm's actions increase performance but also increase the number and speed of rivals' actions, which, in turn, negatively affect the initial firm's performance," invoked a well-known scene from Lewis Carroll's *Through the Looking Glass*, about Alice's adventures in Wonderland. Discussions of the "black box" in research (e.g., Hambrick, 2007), where unobserved processes are theorized about but not empirically studied, are another example of allusion.

Finally, personification is the attribution of human characteristics to something nonhuman. Thus, "organizational learning" (Levitt & March, 1988) is an example of personification. Briscoe and Safford (2008: 463) also employed personification when they claimed that "media accounts of Exxon's response to activism on a range of issues have tended to characterize it as 'recalcitrant,' 'adversarial,' and rooted in a culture of 'digging in their heels'."

Thus, showing does not require extended examples or anecdotes. It can be as simple and subtle as the adjectives and verbs used to describe your actors and their actions. If you only tell your reader about your ideas, they are destined to be buried in a desert of arid prose (metaphor!); show them what your ideas look like through examples, similes, metaphors, allusions and personification.

---

[6]   Originally coined by evolutionary biologist Leigh Van Valen, this allusion references a scene where Alice is running as fast as she can but is not getting anywhere, and the Red Queen says, "Here, you see, it takes all the running you can do, to keep in the same place. If you want to get somewhere else, you must run at least twice as fast as that!" (Carroll, 1960: 345, quoted in Derfus et al., 2008: 61).

MAKE YOUR WRITING CONVERSATIONAL

Which situation feels more engaging to you: chatting over coffee with a friend, or listening to a lecture in a 500-person lecture hall? Unless the lecturer has the rare, Oprah Winfrey-like ability to make audience members feel she or he is talking just to them, I'll hazard a guess it's the former. Personalizing your writing by using first person pronouns like "I" and "we" and second person pronouns like "you" and "your," making small jokes and asides, and otherwise pulling your readers closer rather than pushing them away, enhances the story-telling qualities of your writing. And yet, academic writers frequently stiff-arm their audiences, keeping them at a distance by creating an impersonal voice via third person constructions, using abstract nouns—or no nouns at all—as subjects, and offering no anecdotes, asides or humor to lighten or enlighten their arguments (Sword, 2012). Indeed, Sword (2012) found that natural scientists were better at personalizing their writing using first person pronouns than social scientists, who actually study people!

What does this look like? Rather than saying "I studied," "we studied" or "we found," writers depersonalize what they say by employing phrases like "This study considers," "research explores" or "it has been shown." "I identified 200 companies for my study" becomes "two hundred companies were identified for this study"—by whom we know not. Take ownership of your ideas and actions and clearly identify who is acting: you, your reader, a company, a research participant or an informant. Writers will sometimes try to refer to themselves but not quite make it, using phrases like "this writer," or the one I hate most of all, "the present author." Argh! Shoot me now! Please, please never do this. Just say "I."

So why do academics do this? Sword offered two reasons: the first is a lack of confidence, which leads writers to try and sound more "scholarly" or "scientific"; the second reason is that at some point they were scolded by their advisors, editors or other more senior gatekeepers for trying to be more conversational. I'll add a third reason: we (and I include myself in this) do it because we read so much work written this way that it infuses our subconscious and we don't even realize we're doing it. So how do we combat it? The first step, as with any good recovery program, is acceptance. We all do it, it's all around us. The second step is awareness. Pay attention to what you are writing, particularly when you are rewriting, and inject yourself back into your work, making it more conversational. The third step is to actively try and change your behavior. Experiment. Consciously try to be more informal in your writing. Say I and we. Add some small jokes or asides.[7] Academic research isn't stand-up comedy, but a little levity personalizes your work and can be useful in making your larger point. Read what you've written out loud and see if it sounds like something you'd say. If it sounds stilted and awkward, change it to be more conversational. And make your reader part of the conversation. Address your readers directly, at least from time to time, perhaps using some of the techniques I discussed above. Making your writing conversational doesn't make it any less scholarly (although a few tight-asses may complain during the review process), but it does make it more accessible and easier to get your message across, which is the point.

In this chapter I described some storytelling tools you can easily apply in academic articles: creating a human face, motion and pacing, showing and telling, and making your writing conversational. As the varied examples I provided illustrate, these techniques are frequently used to make academic articles more engaging and readable. I encourage you to reread your favorite articles and look for examples of these tools, and to experiment with them in your own writing.

---

[7]   This can be particularly difficult in cross-cultural contexts. One of my former international students said that watching comedies and reading memes and blog posts helped her get a better sense of what's funny to Americans.

4. The building blocks of storytelling: words, sentences and paragraphs

When I was a kid, my weekly highlight was Saturday morning cartoons. They started at 7:00 am on all three major television networks (ABC, NBC and CBS) and ran until noon. I'd drag my bean bag chair in front of the TV, grab one of the special "Saturday morning donuts" my Mom bought each week, and plant myself until *American Bandstand* started, signifying the cartoons were over.

Like many kids who grew up in the US during the 1970s, watching Saturday morning cartoons was also where I learned math, English and civics, courtesy of *School House Rock*. *School House Rock* was a set of short, interstitial cartoons ABC ran during its Saturday morning programs that used catchy tunes and stories, along with groovy '70s animation, to teach kids multiplication (My Hero Zero, Naughty Number Nine, Little Twelve Toes), grammar (Verb: That's What's Happening, Lolly, Lolly, Lolly. Get Your Adverbs Here; Conjunction Junction), American history (The Shot Heard Round the World, The Preamble) and civics (I'm Just a Bill). As a result, everyone of a certain age can sing the preamble to the constitution, knows three is a magic number, and remembers that "'and', 'but' and 'or' can get you pretty far."

The grammar basics I learned from *School House Rock* still serve me today. Writing is much more than grammar, but understanding grammar—the purposes different words fulfill, and how to order words into sentences, sentences into paragraphs and paragraphs into stories—is critical for clear and effective writing and storytelling. *School House Rock* also taught me that the sound and rhythm of words are critical to enhancing their understanding and influence. This is not going to be a pure grammar chapter, however. The technicalities of grammar can get esoteric pretty quickly, and to be honest I still have trouble keeping many of the terms straight.[1] While I do provide a list of stylistic and grammatical dos and don'ts based on common mistakes I've seen students and authors make, I prefer to weave discussions of grammar into a broader discourse on clear writing, active writing, and the importance of sound, cadence and rhythm in your writing.

---

[1]   For excellent and accessible treatments of grammar and punctuation I recommend *Sin and Syntax* (Hale, 2013), *Eats, Shoots & Leaves* (Truss, 2003) and *The Best Punctuation Book, Period.* (Casagrande, 2014).

CLEAR WRITING

What is "clear" writing? Let's start by defining its antithesis: "cluttered" writing. Writing expert William Zinsser (2006: 6–7) stated,

> Clutter is the disease of American writing. We are a society strangling in unnecessary words, circular constructions, pompous frills and meaningless jargon ... Every word that serves no function, every long word that could be a short word, every adverb that carries the same meaning that's already in the verb, every passive construction that leaves the reader unsure of who is doing what—these are the thousand and one adulterants that weaken the strength of a sentence.

Clear writing, then, is the opposite of cluttered writing. It is concise, with no extraneous words or phrases; it uses the simplest, most direct words possible; it is active and vivid; and it moves readers along without them even noticing it. It is transparent, free from obscurity and ambiguity, and thus easily understood. Clear writing is neither boring nor dumbed down; it is rigorous and stylish, but lacks the excessive flourishes that retard motion and impede understanding.

If, as the old adage goes, clear thinking equals clear writing, then why is so much academic writing so cluttered? Are academics' thought processes that hopelessly muddled? Or, are they intentionally or unintentionally muddling their clear thinking with their cluttered writing? While in some cases it's the former, I think in most cases it's the latter. Given how much time academics spend clarifying their insights by conducting carefully designed research grounded in precise argumentation, why then do they sabotage themselves when presenting their ideas to the world? The primary reasons writing experts offer for cluttered writing are fear, arrogance and the desire to show off (King, 2000; Sword, 2012; Zinsser, 2006). Scholars are afraid their ideas will appear too simple and self-evident, so they try to pad them and make them appear bigger and more important. Or, they use jargon and long, obscure words to show how much smarter they are than their audience, and rhetorical fireworks to demonstrate their skill.

So, does this mean if we just get over ourselves and our insecurities our writing will magically become clearer? No. There are other, more insidious, processes at work that also contribute to cluttered writing. First, we are confronted with supposed cultural norms about what sounds "scholarly"—often reinforced at crucial points in our development by well-meaning but misinformed mentors, editors and reviewers—that become self-fulfilling prophecies the more they are repeated. Even worse, we marinate in cluttered prose through our daily interactions with academic writing. This creates cognitive entrenchment (Dane, 2011), infiltrating our psyches to such a degree that we no longer recognize how cluttered the writing is. Indeed, as a new doctoral student, one of the biggest challenges I faced was learning how to "read" academic articles. In becoming skilled at deciphering cluttered prose, we slowly sink into its swamp.

Clear writing isn't simple and it requires a lot of hard work and rewriting, hence the famous aphorism "I would have written a shorter letter, but I didn't have the time."[2] William Zinsser wrote eloquently about clear writing in his book *On Writing Well*, and Harold Evans wrote a fantastic book on the subject, *Do I Make Myself Clear?* This book not only provides great insights into what clear writing looks like, it is also chock full of examples where Evans—a former editor of British newspapers *The Sunday Times* and *The Times*—rewrites published prose to make it clearer. I encourage you to read both books for full treatments of the whats and hows of clear writing. Here I identify five pathologies that afflict academic writing in particular, and I offer some remedies. I do not include the passive voice in this list because I think writing actively is so important it deserves its own section.

THE FIVE PATHOLOGIES OF ACADEMIC WRITING

The Fat Suit

I'm a fan of superhero movies, and the most memorable meme generated by *Avengers Endgame* was "Fat Thor." As the film opened, the previously ripped and confident God of Thunder had become a bloated, self-pitying drunkard. To accomplish this visual feat, the chiseled actor Chris Hemsworth had to stuff himself into a prosthetic fat suit. Like Fat Thor, many otherwise fine sentences are turned into bloated caricatures by encasing them in fat suits of unnecessary words. Extraneous verbiage inflates manuscripts and dulls the contours of otherwise sharp-edged prose. Removing excess words takes the fat suit off your sentence and addresses many other pathologies of cluttered language.

In explaining their famous "Rule 17: Omit Needless Words," Strunk and White (2000: 23) stated, "A sentence should contain no unnecessary words, a paragraph no unnecessary sentences, for the same reason a drawing should have no unnecessary lines, and a machine no unnecessary parts." This doesn't mean every sentence has to be short; long complex sentences are fine, and can even become an economical substitute for a series of shorter sentences.

---

[2]   This phrase has been attributed variously to Mark Twain, George Bernard Shaw, Voltaire and Winston Churchill, among others. According to Google Answers (http://answers.google.com/answers/threadview?id=177502) it originated in a letter Blaise Pascal wrote in 1656. His original statement was not as pithy as the aphorism; translated into English it said, "I would not have made this so long except that I do not have the leisure to make it shorter."

But every word must be necessary and serve a purpose. For example, the last sentence of the prior paragraph originally read, "Removing excess words not only takes the fat suit off your sentence, it is also the key to dealing with the other pathologies of cluttered language" (26 words). Removing "not only," and substituting "addresses" for "it is also the key to dealing with," saved nine words—reducing the sentence's length by a third while increasing its clarity.

Unwanted flab sneaks into sentences in all sorts of ways. Take the sentence "Research suggests that attaining positions of high status is a universal motive." Where's the fat here? Is "Research suggests that" necessary for enhancing our understanding? What about "positions of"? Nothing is lost, except unwanted bulk, when this sentence is shortened to "Attaining high status is a universal motive." The revised sentence is also more declarative and active. While you don't want to be caught out making unsubstantiated assertions, if you have citations or other evidence to back up your declarations there's no reason to be mealy-mouthed and equivocal.

There are plenty of other examples that crop up in academic writing. The phrase, "consistent with the tenets of resource orchestration theory" would be fine without "the tenets of." "In order to" can always be shorted to "To," and "the reason for that is" can be replaced with "because." "Extant" is another academic favorite that can be excised. "Extant research suggests" always puzzles me, because nonexistent research can't suggest much. Another academic favorite is the clarification, where something is defined, and then defined again following phrases such as "or," "that is," and "in other words." Clarifying technical jargon is fine; otherwise you really need to consider why you need the "other words," and whether the clarification's words are the ones you should be using in the first place.

Hale (2013) noted that prepositional phrases are another source of clutter. Prepositional phrases consist of a preposition, its object (a noun or verb) and other words used to modify the object (Hale, 2013). The most frequently used prepositions are *to, of, about, at, before, after, by, behind, during, for, from, in, over, under*, and *with*. Hale offered this simple test to identify prepositions: if you put the word in front of "the log" and the phrase makes sense, it's a preposition. While prepositions serve an important purpose, prepositional phrases are frequently unnecessary, appear in passive constructions, and are often weaker than single adjectives and adverbs. Always consider whether you can delete the prepositional phrase or replace it with a single, more elegant word. Strunk and White (2000) also noted that putting statements in positive form ("He agreed" rather than "He did not disagree"; or "The results fail to support the hypothesis" rather than "We cannot disconfirm the null hypothesis due to a lack of empirical support") always shortens sentences.

Take this sentence from a famous article in economics,

> Control of agency problems in the decision process is important when the decision managers who initiate and implement important decisions are not the major residual claimants and therefore do not bear a major share of the wealth effects of their decisions. (41 words)

Can you find the wordy negative forms and unnecessary prepositional phrases? "Are not the major residual claimants" and "do not bear a major share" are in the negative; "of agency problems," "in the decision process" and "of the wealth effects of their decisions" are unnecessary prepositional phrases. The last phrase is actually a pile-up of two prepositional phrases. Rewriting this sentence as "Controlling agency problems is important when outcomes create no financial consequences for decision makers" results in 14 words instead of 41, and it addresses both problems. Remove the fat suit and show off your sentences' bulging biceps and six-pack abs.

Burying the Lead

Burying the lead is another academic favorite. Journalists use the term to describe stories where the subject is buried deep in the article. I use burying the lead to describe sentences where the subject is buried by a long opening clause, what Harold Evans (2017) called "predatory clauses." These clauses are typically lists of qualifications or additional facts that the writer is trying to squeeze into the story. As Evans (2017: 52) noted, "It's alright to set up the main clause with a concise introductory subordinate element, say a prepositional phrase, to give it context, but you don't want to ramble on to the point that the reader loses interest, or doesn't notice, when you finally get to the sentence's subject."

What's often happening, particularly in academic articles, is that the writer is justifying their conclusion before offering the conclusion itself. In the following example from a highly cited sociology article, the lead is buried under two sentences:

> These ideas are familiar from observations of premodern cultures (e.g., Durkheim 1915; Douglas 1966; Berger and Luckman 1966) and are responsible for the image of stasis that we frequently ascribe to such societies. It is thus interesting to note that the idea that actors are constrained by accepted models represents an important but underrecognized thread that runs through much thinking on modern organizations and markets. (65 words)

What's the main idea here? That the lack of change created by accepted mental models, observed in both pre-modern and modern societies, is underrecognized. We don't learn this until we're 54 words in, though. I combined these two sentences into a single sentence, "Underrecognized is that the barriers to change created by adherence to accepted mental models exist equally in modern and premodern societies." That's 21 words (30 if you add back the references) and the main point is back in the lead.

Sentence Stuffing

Have you ever been coated in word splatter by a child excited to tell you about what happened to them, or to explain why they aren't at fault for something bad that just happened? In both cases the kids try to cram as many different ideas and explanations into a sentence as possible, sometimes with multiple asides and tangents. Academics do it, too, typically offset by commas, parentheticals and dashes. If your sentence has multiple "ands", "furthers," "in addition tos" and the like, you may be stuffing too many ideas into one sentence.

Take this sentence from our old friend Frederick Taylor's *The Principles of Scientific Management* (1916: 9):

> In the same way maximum prosperity for each employee means not only higher wages than are usually received by men of his class, but, of more importance still, it also means the development of each man to his state of maximum efficiency, so that he may be able to do, generally speaking, the highest grade of work for which his natural abilities fit him, and it further means giving him, when possible, this class of work to do.

This 78-word sentence is a whopper; it's chock full of blubber, it combines the ideas maximum prosperity and maximum efficiency in a single sentence, and it buries the lead about maximum efficiency. You can de-stuff sentences by breaking them up, so each idea gets its own sentence in which to shine. For example, "Maximum prosperity means paying men higher than average wages for the highest grade of work they are best suited to perform. It also requires developing their natural abilities to their maximum efficiency by regularly assigning them such work." These two sentences contain just 38 words, convey the same meaning, and treat each idea separately.

Tangents and asides are not always bad things. As you may have noticed, I really like them. The challenges are making sure the asides are relevant, advance the idea in the sentence, and are brief. If the aside fails to meet the first criterion, then it is a candidate for the cutting room floor. If it is relevant but isn't brief, or is brief and relevant but doesn't advance the sentence, then it's a candidate for a footnote. I disagree with editors and reviewers who say there should be few if any footnotes in an article, and that if it's important enough to say you should include it in the main text. Including necessary information in the main text that doesn't advance the sentence's main idea can derail motion and pacing. Examples include information on additional models run where the results were the same, or additional measures used to operationalize the same construct that either yielded similar results or were not significant. They are also useful when something needs additional explanation, to point readers towards additional information (like footnote 1 suggesting further reading on grammar and punctuation) or when you just can't resist providing an interesting factoid (like footnote 2 about Blaise Pascal).

Read my Mind

A fourth common pathology is that authors leave out key information readers can only obtain by reading their minds. This pathology also hinders your ability to create a human face because necessary detail and examples are missing, and it results in motion and pacing that are too quick and abrupt. It also makes your paper feel more like a lecture than a conversation, where you are being talked at, instead of with.

In her essay on clear writing, former *Academy of Management Review* editor Belle Ragins (2012) identified unfamiliar jargon, undefined acronyms and poorly elaborated concepts as instances requiring mind reading. I would add to her list: unarticulated underlying assumptions; the "connective tissue" that takes readers through your argument so they can see how you get from A to B to C; how you measured key constructs and why you included particular control variables; how and why you identified your sample or interview informants; what particular tables and figures or graphs illustrate; and even why your study is important and needs doing. Thus, this pathology is the opposite of the fat suit; rather than too many words there are too few, at least of the right sort.

Ragins (2012) noted that this pathology results from writers' closeness to their work. Because they live and breathe their study, they simply cease to notice when they are assuming knowledge on the reader's part. The connections and information are all there in their head; they just haven't made it from their head into their writing. Linda Johanson (2007) wrote a very useful article on being more empathetic with your readers. She argued that many failures during the review process resulted from failing to understand the reviewers' sensemaking processes (Weick, 1995) as they interacted with the article. She suggested that by putting yourself in the reader's chair and understanding how they read your article, you can do a better job at "sensegiving" (Gioia & Chittipeddi, 1991), providing them the information needed to interpret your article in the way you want.

As we will discuss further in Chapter 10 on the writing process, both Ragins and Johanson advocated getting friendly reviews and listening carefully to journal reviewers' critiques as ways to address this pathology. They both also emphasized paying serious attention to the reviewers' and editors' comments. Johanson further recommended avoiding acronyms, particularly if you are introducing a new concept or theory. While repeating the words may seem redundant, it also embeds them in readers' minds, making them easier to recall. I always spell out acronyms the first time I use them, and almost always define a construct the first time I mention it. More difficult, but just as necessary, is anticipating your readers' questions and where they are likely to have challenges, and providing the information necessary to answer their question or explain whatever they are likely to stumble over.

Both recommendations require reading your paper like a reviewer. Some people are better at this than others. One way to develop this skill is to review a lot for journals and conferences. By critiquing others' work and offering suggestions on how to improve it, you develop skills you can apply to your own work. Turning a reviewer's eye to your own writing is essential for catching the omissions and assumptions that require readers to develop their psychic abilities. The parts of the paper that were the most difficult for you to write and understand yourself are also likely culprits.

For example, in writing my article on the co-evolution of status and reputation mentioned in Chapter 3 (Pollock et al., 2015), I knew that describing the complex analytical approach we employed would be challenging, because I had trouble fully understanding it initially. My co-author Kyuho Jin—the stats wiz behind the analysis—and I iterated on this section until it was understandable to someone without a deep, technical grasp of the method and all the important technical aspects were still correctly described.

Pompous Prose

When I was a doctoral student we read about Crozier's study of a French cigarette manufacturing plant where the instructions for repairing the manufacturing equipment were "accidentally" destroyed in a fire, and the mechanics who fixed the machines never wrote new instructions, instead passing down the knowledge orally, and only to those they trusted to keep them secret. In this way they exercised considerable power beyond their official standing in the organization's hierarchy.

Technical jargon serves the same purpose. While it is often useful for conveying specific information and meanings among those who speak the language, it also keeps "outsiders" at arm's length and is a source of power for the insiders who can divine its meaning. Long, complex and obscure words do the same. Fearful that our ideas will seem too simplistic, or out of a desire to show off, scholars frequently succumb to pompous prose, larding their sentences with unnecessary jargon and overly complex words. If your goal is to make your writing more conversational and engaging, this isn't how to do it. Further, in an intriguing study of the inferences readers make about writers' intelligence, Oppenheimer (2006) found simple writing was easier to process, enhances ease of understanding and leads to a variety of beneficial outcomes. He also found that even if larger vocabularies are associated with greater intelligence, from the reader's perspective using more complex language led to perceptions that the writer was *less* intelligent.

The obvious solutions to pompous prose are to limit jargon when equivalent common language terms are available, and to use shorter rather than longer words when possible. I also suggest avoiding words and phrases that sound pompous (e.g., "to wit," "inter alia,") and presumptuous (e.g., "obviously," "as everyone knows," "of course," "merely"); also avoid obscure references (Like the Emperor Huang Ti ...) and "insider" references (As everyone who attended EGOS last year knows ...) that make your reader feel like a low-status outsider. And do not use foreign languages, particularly as quotes, unless you know your audience speaks the language, or the foreign word or phrase is the accepted construct label (e.g., Guanxi).

For example, I once received a review where the reviewer wrote, "Julius Caesar claimed, 'Julius Caser Malo hic esse primus quam Romae secundus.'" That's not helpful. Although the reviewer then translated the quote (it is better to be first in the countryside than second in Rome), the Latin version created the impression—at least as I, the reader, perceived it—that the reviewer was trying to demonstrate their intellectual superiority. Just going with the English translation feels less demeaning.

ACTIVE WRITING

The passive voice is the biggest bane of academic writing. You can pick up any academic journal and I guarantee it's awash in passive constructions. As Evans (2017: 83) stated, the passive voice "robs sentences of energy, adds unnecessary words, seeds a slew of wretched participles and prepositions, and leaves questions unanswered: *It was decided to eliminate the coffee break.* Which wretch decided that?" Everyone writes passive constructions, including passive voice haters like me. I'm constantly going through my drafts removing passive constructions that slip in. The keys are to recognize and eradicate them when found; however, not everyone recognizes them easily, particularly if English isn't your first language. Here's how you do it:

Sentences using the active voice have a subject doing something to an object via an active verb; thus, the subject typically appears early in the sentence and the object appears later, with the active verb in between. The Writing Center at the University of North Carolina-Chapel Hill[3] noted that sentences using the passive voice employ passive verbs (varieties of "to be") and a past participle, and that the object appears early in the sentence (i.e., the object of an action becomes the grammatical subject of the sentence) while the subject appears later, or not at all. Verb forms of "to be" include *is, are, am, was, were, has been, have been, had been, will be, can be, will have been,* and *being.* A participle is an active verb usually ending with an -ing (present participle) or -ed (past participle) that is used as an adjective (i.e., to modify a noun, as in "laughing man" or "haunted eyes"). Not all past participles have -ed endings though; for example, drunk, driven, woken, spoken and thought are the past participles of irregular verbs where the -ed endings don't work (e.g., drinked, drived, woked, spoked, thinked).

So, "We surveyed 500 managers" is active: there is a clear subject early in the sentence (the pronoun "we"), an active verb (surveyed) followed by the action's object (managers). "Five hundred managers were surveyed" is passive: the object (managers) appears early in the sentence followed by the "to be + past participle" combo (were surveyed) and the subject is nowhere to be seen. Sentences that start with "It" also typically employ the passive voice ("It can be seen that...," "It is well known that...").

One of the reasons passive constructions slip into so many papers is that authors are loathe to take credit for their ideas and actions because some misbegotten soul told them it wasn't scholarly; so, they revert to the subjectless passive voice. International students from countries whose cultures prize humbleness have also told me they revert to the passive voice because it's less "aggressive." Thus, "we hypothesized" becomes "it was hypothesized that" and "we explored how sleep influences managers' openness" becomes "the influence of sleep on the openness of managers was explored." It's okay to take ownership of your ideas and actions; and active constructions need not be aggressive or self-aggrandizing. Like I said in Chapter 3, please, please use personal pronouns. Another way to make your writing more active is to use possessives. For example, whenever you see a prepositional phrase starting with the word "of," consider whether you can replace it with a possessive statement, as I did when I replaced "the openness of managers" with "managers' openness."

This doesn't mean that the passive voice is always bad. Evans (2017) identified four circumstances where the passive voice is appropriate: (1) When the doer of the action is not known (86 percent of the surveys *were returned*); (2) When the action's receiver merits more prominence than the doer (the cannabis dispensary owners *were raided* by the government); (3) When the

---

[3]   See: https://writingcenter.unc.edu/tips-and-tools/passive-voice/

action's doer is known but tact or cowardice imposes reticence (Your paper *was rejected* because it was impossible to wade through all the passive constructions); (4) When the subject's length delays the verb's entry (Surveying the homeless, who do not have fixed home addresses, phone numbers or email addresses, *was accomplished* by sending doctoral students into homeless encampments).

THE "SOUND" OF WRITING

The "sound" of writing is critical, and we "hear" writing even when reading silently. According to Yellowlees Douglas (2015), author of *The Reader's Brain*, this is in part because of how we learn to read—sounding out unfamiliar words and breaking them down into parts—and also because the visual, speech and auditory centers of our brains are linked. Thus, thinking about the sound, rhythm and cadence of your writing is a critical tool for facilitating understanding, managing motion and pacing, and moving your story from one act to the next.

How words sound. How words sound can support and enhance your sentence or paragraph's theme and create physical reactions in your readers. In her classic *Sin and Syntax*, Hale (2013) identified five common devices often employed to achieve these outcomes: assonance, consonance, alliteration, rhyme, and onomatopoeia. Assonance repeats vowel sounds across words (start, march); consonance echoes the initial consonant later in the same word (tabletop, coca cola); alliteration uses the same initial sound created by a letter or combination of letters across words within a sentence or phrase (nattering nincompoop, fresh fish); rhyme sets up an exact correspondence between the final syllable or syllables of words (bop 'til you drop);[4] and onomatopoeia refers to words that sound like what they name (sizzle, barf, wham).

Adjectives and verbs can also sound like the themes you are trying to invoke. For example, when I described the fat suit earlier, I employed words like "bloated" and "stuff," which evoke images consistent with my theme. When describing motion and pacing, words like "slog" and "meander" sound slow, while "race" and "sprint" sound quick. Thus, saying "the strategic alliance blew up" suggests a different circumstance than "the strategic alliance dissolved," and both are more interesting and informative than "the strategic alliance ended." While we shouldn't get too carried away with this in academic writing, particularly given the precise usage many words have, choosing words that sound like what you mean and create melody make them memorable. That's why the preamble to the US constitution could be set to music.

---

[4]   This one is probably best left unused in academic writing.

Cadence. Cadence is the rhythm and pattern of words and sentences created by patterns of long and short, up and down, and in and out. As Hale (2013) noted, these patterns exist within words and phrases and have specific names, such as iamb (short-long, as in "exist'), trochee (long-short, as in "started") and amphilbrach (short-long-short, as in "specific"). If you are interested in these details, linguists have lots to say on the subject; however, I simply want to emphasize that patterns matter. Varying long and short words, and words with different emphases, creates variety and rhythm.

Vary sentence structure. Douglas (2015) offered three cadence principles. Her first principle is to create cadence by varying sentence structure. She identified four general sentence structures. Sentences can be simple. They consist of one major clause that stands on its own, like the preceding sentence. Complex sentences consist of a major and a minor clause. The major clause can stand on its own and doesn't sound like a fragment (this is the major clause); the minor clause cannot (this is the minor clause). A compound sentence is comprised of two major clauses, and the major clauses are connected by a coordinating conjunction ("and," "but" and "or" can get you pretty far, but "for," "nor," "yet" and "so" are also helpful coordinating conjunctions). In a compound-complex sentence, like this one, there are two major clauses and a minor clause is embedded within one of the major clauses. Vary the mix of simple, compound, complex and compound-complex sentences within each paragraph.

Although Douglas focused on variation, this doesn't mean you shouldn't also use repetition—another powerful tool for employing cadence. Look no further than Martin Luther King's "I Have a Dream" speech for a powerful example. However, you must use repetition intentionally. Consider the following excerpt from Leblebici, Salancik, Copay and King's (1991: 334) article on institutional change in the radio industry:

> Broadcasting evolved uniquely in the U.S. into a privately owned and operated commercial enterprise. As Waller (1946) found, other countries organized it in a variety of ways, but public ownership or supervision was their standard. In Iceland, the state owned and operated all broadcasting equipment and maintained and rented receivers to listeners. In Italy, Turkey, and the U.S.S.R., the state also owned broadcasting equipment and did all programming and broadcasting. In Sweden and Switzerland, the state retained ownership and technical operations but left programming to a state-controlled society. The United Kingdom created and franchised the BBC, an independent public corporation, to own, program, and broadcast its country's radio. Government involvement was least in The Netherlands, where an association of listeners was established to own and run radio (Waller, 1946). That the United States stood alone in successfully evolving a private broadcasting industry is remarkable.

Leblebici and colleagues created an interesting cadence by using similarities and variations in sentence structure to illustrate the differences in nations' approaches. The third and fourth sentences are both simple sentences beginning with "In," as the countries identified followed the simplest approaches. The fifth sentence about Sweden and Switzerland also begins with "In," and the first major clause of this complex sentence is similar to the simple sentences, but the minor clause illustrates a slightly more complex difference. The next sentence about the UK is a compound sentence with the minor clause embedded in the major clause, which also reflects the quasi-embedded nature of a centrally controlled system within a public corporation. They used a compound sentence to describe the Netherlands's different and more decentralized but still public approach; and the final simple sentence opening with the determiner "that" highlights the uniqueness of the US's approach.

Punctuation as vocal inflections and breath marks. Varying your punctuation can also create cadence. Some sentences require no punctuation. Others, well, they need to be broken up a bit. There are lots of rules for employing punctuation correctly, and I urge you to learn them. Conceptually, though, I think it's easiest to think of punctuation as the means for adding vocal inflections and breath marks.

When words are spoken the speaker can add inflections—pauses, changes in pitch and rate, emphases—that add variety and rhythm to the words. When we read words silently we still "hear" the words being spoken inside our heads, and punctuation is the writer's primary tool for adding these inflections. If you've ever sung off sheet music you probably know what I mean by breath marks; they are the indicators that tell the singers when to take a breath. Punctuation serves the same purpose in writing. As an example, take a breath as you begin to read the next sentence. If you run out of air and have to take another breath but there has been no punctuation indicating that you should then some punctuation should be added. You may also consider breaking the sentence into two or more sentences. Conversely, if you feel like you are going to hyperventilate because the writing asks you to take lots of short breaths in quick succession, you can remove some punctuation and perhaps combine two short sentences into a single compound or complex sentence. Reading sentences out loud can help you determine whether you have too much or too little punctuation, and whether it's in the right place. Many times, I've encountered an oddly placed comma disrupting the sentence's flow that the writer could have caught had they read the sentence aloud.

Vary sentence and paragraph length. Douglas's second cadence principle is to vary the length of your sentences. If every sentence is short your writing will take on the rat-a-tat-tat (onomatopoeia!) of machine gun fire; and it will have a similar effect on the reader. If all your sentences are long, compound-complex sentences, your reader will feel like they are drowning. This is why sentence length also plays such a critical role in shaping your story's motion and pacing. Mixing long and short sentences can create a sense of motion, while also providing readers the opportunity to pause and catch their breath. It also facilitates shifts between exposition and action. The previous example from Leblebici and colleagues (1991) provides a nice illustration.

Varying paragraph length is as important as varying sentence length. Stephen King (2000) noted that you can figure out whether a book or article is going to be easy reading or not just by looking at the paragraph structure. Lots of long paragraphs that fill entire pages mean you are in for a slog, while many short paragraphs suggest a brisk but perhaps uninformative trip. Mix up your paragraph lengths, and if you find you're writing one long paragraph, consider breaking it into shorter paragraphs. If you cover two or more main ideas in the paragraph, this is easily done; just give each idea its own paragraph. Another good candidate for splitting is when you follow an idea with an extended example. The example can be the start of a new paragraph. If a paragraph takes up a half-page or more, I always give it a hard look to see if I can split it into two paragraphs. If I don't, then I try to make sure the next paragraph is short.

Go from simple to complex. Douglas's third cadence principle focuses on ordering. She recommended that in complex sentences, and particularly in lists, place the item with the fewest words and least syntactic complexity first, and the longest, most complex item last. She offers two reasons: (1) items ordered by size, importance or complexity create an organized flow; and (2) starting with the more complex items creates more cognitive load, because the reader has to try and keep more items in working memory as they complete the sentence. So, "We obtained data from proxies, annual reports, the Center for Research on Securities Pricing (CRSP), and a custom survey of executives and directors of Fortune 500 companies" has better cadence than "We obtained data from the Center for Research on Securities Pricing (CRSP), annual reports, a custom survey of executives and directors of Fortune 500 companies and proxies." The Leblebici and colleagues example also moves from simpler to more syntactically complex sentences, but then moves back again to simpler structures.

MY IDIOSYNCRATIC LIST OF STYLISTIC AND GRAMMATICAL DOS AND DON'TS

Every writing book has a section where the author describes his or her idiosyncratic list of what they consider the most important dos and don'ts with respect to grammar, word usage, and such. This is mine. I won't repeat the points I've already made, but assume they are on the list, too. I can't cover everything in detail so I've also identified other writing books that I recommend at the end of this chapter. Now, I will get on my soapbox and lecture you a bit about my stylistic and grammatical dos and don'ts.

1. *Get rid of dingleberries at the ends of paragraphs.* When the last line of a paragraph only has a couple of words, I call that a dingleberry. They should be wiped off whenever possible, particularly if you face page rather than word limits. My rule of thumb is if the paragraph's last line is less than one-third of a line long, rewrite the paragraph until you remove the line.

2. *Use parallel construction and signpost your transitions from section to section.* You are trying to make your writing as easy to follow as possible. Although parallel construction (i.e., using the same sentence structure repeatedly) may seem less creative at times, it can make it easier for readers when they skim your paper looking for specific things. For example, when discussing your results start with a reminder of what the hypothesis was, tell us what the results were, and finish with "Thus, Hypothesis X was supported/not supported/partially supported." Clear transitions and signposts similarly help readers to find things in your paper and know when you've moved from one section to the next.

3. *Never use synonyms for your key constructs.* As I discussed in Chapter 3, one way to create motion and make your article more interesting to read is using synonyms to create variety. However, in academia similar terms can represent different constructs; thus, synonyms can also create confusion. Keep your language consistent when talking about your theoretical constructs and use synonyms to create variety elsewhere.

4. *Use citations to support your arguments, definitions and claims, but use them judiciously.* Don't over-cite by providing a reference for every other word, and don't feel you have to cite every study ever written on a topic. Be thorough but judicious, and have a purpose for citing each article. If you cite an article only once and have at least two other citations for the same point, drop the extra citation. This is a great way to shorten papers, when necessary.

5. *Do not use "we" to refer to just yourself (the royal "we").* You may be tempted to mask the fact that your paper is sole-authored during the review process by using "we" instead of "I." Don't. You'll inevitably screw it up. Never refer to yourself in the plural (if there are multiple co-authors, "we" is fine, though).

6. *Use the right tenses in the right places.* Use past tense when describing others' previous research and in the methods section when describing what you did in conducting your own research; use the present tense when discussing your results and the conclusions you've drawn from them.

7. *Managing nouns and pronouns for sex and gender.* I recognize this is a tricky and evolving topic, but here's what I currently do. I use the plurals "individuals" or "people" (versus "individual" or "person") whenever possible; that way I can avoid the whole gender pronoun thing by using "they." Although we refer to an individual using "they" in everyday speech, and it is becoming more accepted by some in formal writing as our understanding of gender identity evolves, "they" typically should not be paired with a singular (e.g., "when an individual is surprised, they might jump in their seat"). When I use "individual" or "person," I use him or her, he or she or even s/he or him/her; using just him isn't politically correct, and always using her results in the same problem: it negates the existence of the other gender. Another option is to alternate genders; use "her" the first time and "him" the next time, etc. If the group you are referring to is all, or virtually all, male or female, though, I just use him or her, respectively. I usually point this fact about the group out, though, before I do it.

8. *Do not refer to individuals participating in a study as "subjects."* Call them what they were (students, mothers, birthday party clowns), or call them participants, respondents or informants, depending on the type of study conducted.

9. *Write out numbers one through ten unless they are in a sequence (our scale ranged from 1–5) or part of a hypothesis label (e.g., H1) or a value from a table or other statistical result.*

10. *Don't start sentences with numbers or acronyms.* If you do need to start the sentence with a number, spell it out (like my favorite sentence I heard touring Graceland: "One third of all people in Sweden own an Elvis Presley album. That's one in three."). Same for acronyms. Spell them out, even if you've used the acronym previously.

11. *Avoid starting sentences with adverbs.* I do it occasionally, and it's typically something like "similarly" or "conversely" when I'm trying to avoid being wordy (e.g., instead of saying "In a similar vein" or "The alternative is" or "On the other hand"), or "finally" when I get to the end of a list. Most sentences starting with adverbs just sound clunky, though. And I hate the adverb "importantly" more than any other sentence opener. Please never use it. I don't want to have to hunt you down.

12. *Avoid redundant modifiers (adverbs and adjectives).* Adverbs and adjectives are of course valuable aspects of storytelling, but they can be overused. Use adverbs sparingly, in particular, as they are more likely to clutter up your sentences. Avoid using adjectives and adverbs that have the same meanings as the nouns and verbs they modify, and don't use multiple, redundant adjectives when one good one will do.

13. *Data is a plural, datum is singular; phenomena is plural; phenomenon is singular.*

14. *Know the difference between Affect, Effect and Impact.* Affect[5] is a verb (e.g., affect the outcome); effect is a noun (e.g., the interaction effect was); and impact is also a noun (e.g., that story had a real impact on me), so you can "have an impact," but "A is a moderator impacting the relationship of B with C" is bad grammar, no matter how many times others say it or write it. A affects or influences B's relationship with C, it doesn't "impact" it.

15. *Use recursive and non-recursive correctly.* This is one that, until recently, I got wrong myself. It's counter-intuitive, but recursive models are unidirectional, even if the same rule is being applied repeatedly, and non-recursive models have one or more feedback loops or reciprocal effects. So, if you are arguing that something feeds back on itself, or two things mutually influence each other, they are non-recursive.

16. *Failing to find support for a hypothesis beyond a particular level of statistical significance means the results are "not significant," not "insignificant."* Results are not significant when they fail to disconfirm the null hypothesis at a statistically meaningful level of probability. Insignificant means something is trivial or doesn't matter—this is an issue of effect size, not statistical significance. There can be many reasons why a result is not statistically significant that have nothing to with effect size, and even small effect sizes can be important.

17. *Since vs. because.* Since means "after that," because means "why."

18. *That vs. which.* That and which are used to introduce restrictive and non-restrictive clauses, respectively. You use "that" when a clause is necessary to understand the meaning of a sentence ("she opened the book *that* had all the answers"; you need the clause to know what book she opened), and "which" when the clause adds additional information, but could also be left out of the sentence ("She could find all of the answers in her book, *which* was published last year.).

19. *Use "the" correctly.* "The" is the most commonly used word in the English language, and native English speakers are never really taught how to use it. We learn it intuitively. A former student who is Indian once told me that there is no equivalent to the word "the" in Hindi. This is true of other languages, as well. So, this point is to help all non-native English speakers. "The" is an article used to identify a singular noun. It references "old" information. "The results suggest" assumes the reader already knows what results you are talking about; "the street" refers to a specific street, whereas "a street" does not assume you know what street

---

[5]   Although spelled the same, I am not referring to the noun "affect," defined as a set of observable manifestations of a subjectively experienced emotion.

is referenced, and the street's identity doesn't matter. "The" is also used to identify something unique (the universe), and classes of actors referred to in the plural but that have a common identity (the social sciences), along with a few other exceptions.

20. *Their vs. there*. The former is possessive, the latter is positional (e.g., Their house is over there, next to the woods).
21. *While vs. although, but and whereas*. While means at the same time; although, but and whereas are used to modify or qualify prior statements or make comparisons.
22. *Understand the difference between i.e. and e.g.*: i.e. is "in other words" or "that is," e.g. is "for example." Do not use either of these in the main body of the sentence, only within parentheses (e.g., like this). Another, lesser-used abbreviation that is sometimes employed instead of "i.e.," is "c.f.," which means "compare." If you use "c.f.," make sure you're really making a comparison and not just providing an example.
23. *Learn how to use apostrophes*: 's is the appropriate singular possessive, even on names and words ending in s's (e.g., the Stevens's house); s' is the plural possessive (e.g., students' grades).
24. *Do not use contractions*. I'm using contractions (like I'm) in this book because I want to make it as informal and readable as possible. However, in academic journal articles the norm is to avoid using contractions unless you are quoting someone who used them.
25. *Only use ampersands (&) within parentheses for citations*. So "Pfeffer and Salancik's (1978) resource dependence theory" and "resource dependence theory (Pfeffer & Salancik, 1978)" are okay; "Pfeffer & Salancik's (1978) resource dependence theory" is not.

RECOMMENDED BOOKS ON WRITING

Casagrande, J. (2010), *It Was the Best of Sentences, It Was the Worst of Sentences*, Berkeley, CA: Ten Speed Press.

Casagrande, J. (2014), *The Best Punctuation Book, Period*, Berkeley, CA: Ten Speed Press.

Douglass, Y. (2015), *The Reader's Brain: How Neuroscience Can Make You a Better Writer*, Cambridge, UK: Cambridge University Press.

Evans, H. (2017), *Do I Make Myself Clear? Why Writing Well Matters*, New York: Little Brown.

Flaherty, F. (2009), *The Elements of Story: Field Notes on Nonfiction Writing*, New York: HarperCollins.

Forsyth, M. (2013), *The Elements of Eloquence: Secrets of the Perfect Turn of Phrase*, New York: Berkley Books.

Hale, C. (2013), *Sin and Syntax: How to Craft Wicked Good Prose*, New York: Three Rivers Press.

Huff, A.S. (1999), *Writing for Scholarly Publication*, Thousand Oaks, CA: Sage.

King, S. (2000), *On Writing*, New York: Pocket Books.

Lamott, A. (1994), *Bird by Bird*, New York: Anchor Books.
Strunk, W. and E.B. White (2000), *The Elements of Style 4th Edition*, Needham Heights, MA: Allyn & Bacon.
Sword, H. (2012), *Stylish Academic Writing*, Cambridge, MA: Harvard University Press.
Truss, L. (2003), *Eats, Shoots & Leaves: The Zero Tolerance Approach to Punctuation*, New York: Gotham Books.
Zinsser, W. (2006), *On Writing Well*, New York: HarperCollins.

5.   Introductions, titles and abstracts

When my wife Sarah and I do outdoor art shows we are allocated a ten-foot square space in which to set up our booth. That means we have the amount of time it takes someone to walk about ten feet (roughly five seconds at the slow, shuffling pace most patrons adopt at crowded art shows) to capture their attention and lure them into the booth. Once through the door, the next step is getting them to engage with the art, and then with Sarah (or sometimes me), hopefully leading to a sale. If they are looking the other way, talking to someone or staring at their cell phone we can't grab their attention. The opportunity to sell them something, then, is lost.

To attract their attention we spend a lot of time positioning the most colorful and interesting pieces in the most visible spots. Sarah also places short blurbs by each piece explaining what she found interesting about the scene and where it's located. Once in her booth, these blurbs make patrons spend more time looking at each piece and increase the likelihood they identify some connection with it or the locale. Sarah also greets each person who comes into her booth (many artists don't). She tries to solicit personal information about individuals who show more than a cursory interest in the work so she can make them feel comfortable and find points of common interest or experience, because people buy the artist as much as the art.

Attracting readers' attention and getting them to read your article requires similar steps. When browsing a journal's table of contents, another article's reference list or online search results, an interesting and informative title helps snag readers' attention so that they don't just walk on by, and instead look at your abstract. It is then your abstract's job to intrigue readers enough that they come through the door and read your Introduction, which then has the task of setting the hook sufficiently to draw them into the rest of the article. If you can't get them beyond your abstract or Introduction, then all your gripping storytelling techniques and lyrical prose will be for naught. The Introduction also creates the interpretive frame through which readers assess the rest of your article. This is critically important during the review process. If your Introduction grabs reviewers' interest, they will read the rest of the paper looking for reasons to give you a revision; if it doesn't, then they're more likely flipping to the end to see how long the paper is (and thus how long the torture is going to last), and reading the paper with a focus on reasons to recommend rejection. This is why, even though it only represents about 10 percent of your article, the Introduction is the section most critical to your success, and authors spend more time writing and rewriting it than any other section.

In this chapter I explore how to effectively attract readers' attention and set the hook so that they read the rest of your article. I first discuss what comprises an effective Introduction, because it's the largest and most important part of setting the hook. I then discuss how to grab readers' attention with interesting titles, and lure them in with succinct, informative abstracts.

THE INTRODUCTION

When we were associate editors for the *Academy of Management Journal*, Adam Grant and I wrote a "From the Editors" column on writing effective Introductions (Grant & Pollock, 2011). We analyzed *AMJ* Best Paper award-winning articles and surveyed their authors about what they thought were the key aspects of effective Introductions and their process for writing them. We also surveyed *AMJ* Outstanding Reviewer award winners about their thoughts on Introductions, how much weight they put on them in their decision making, and common errors authors make. I relied on this work and the insights we drew from it, along with other scholars' advice and my own experiences as an author, reviewer and editor in developing this chapter.

I define the Introduction as the first few pages of the article before the Theory and Hypotheses section (what some call the "opening"). Although psychologists often refer to the whole front end of the paper before the data and methods section as the Introduction, I avoid this terminology because it diminishes the importance of theory development, instead privileging the empirical portion of an article. The Introduction provides the exposition that situates your study, introduces your theme and main characters, and foreshadows the knot you'll tie in the rising action. An effective Introduction is typically about three to four double-spaced pages, and answers three sets of questions: (1) Who cares? (2) What do we know, what don't we know, and so what? and (3) What will we learn?

Who Cares?

Like any good story, yours needs to grab the reader's interest early. If it doesn't capture their interest, or they find it tedious, they are unlikely to go further, instead moving on to other articles. Thus, the Introduction's first task is to "hook" the reader, so that their answer to the question "Who cares?" is "I do!" Your Introduction has the best opportunity to capture a broad range of readers' interests if it positions your article in "Pasteur's Quadrant," (Stokes, 1997);

that is, if it has both theoretical and practical relevance.[1] Good hooks also begin introducing your main characters. Based on our analysis of *AMJ* Best Paper winners, Adam and I identified two primary hooks: *the quote* and *the trend*. Because of space limitations we described a third hook that really merits its own category, *the anecdote*, as an extended form of quote. There is also a fourth type of hook, *the rhetorical question*, that we didn't discuss because it didn't emerge in that analysis. Rhetorical questions are also effective for grabbing readers' attention, establishing what your study is about and why it's interesting.

The *quote* engages readers in the intriguing and practical nature of your question. Also known as an epigraph, quotes are typically presented at the very beginning of the paper, right before the Introduction's first paragraph. To be effective, the quote must capture your article's theme. For example, in my article "Master of Puppets: How narcissistic CEOs construct their professional worlds," Arijit Chatterjee and I (Chatterjee & Pollock, 2017: 703) opened our article with the following quotes from a biography of narcissistic CEO "Chainsaw" Al Dunlap:

> During his twenty-month stay at Scott, Dunlap generated more self-celebrating publicity than any other business executive in the world, with the possible exception of Microsoft's Bill Gates.
> Other top executives at Sunbeam were fearful of Dunlap's "torrential harangue," and their knees trembled and stomachs churned. (Excerpts from Byrne, 1999: 30, 154).

These quotes about Al Dunlap's behaviors and their effects on others illustrated the two competing needs driving narcissists—the need for acclaim and the need to dominate others—that figured centrally in our theorizing.

Although opening quotes often come from books or the mass media, qualitative scholars also use quotations from their data. For example, Mike Pratt (2000: 456) opened his study, "The good, the bad and the ambivalent: Managing identification among Amway distributors," with the following quote:

> People say that we brainwash people. That's true. We are talking about brainwashing—to help make you all more positive people!—A speaker at a meeting of Amway distributors.

---

[1]   Stokes argued research high in theoretical and low in practical relevance is part of "Bohr's Quadrant" (named after the chemist Neils Bohr, who developed the Bohr model of molecular structure), and studies high in practical relevance and low in theoretical relevance part of "Edison's Quadrant" (named after the inventor Thomas Edison).

This quote captured his study's focus on how and why organizations promote strong attachments among their members by increasing their identification with the organization and weakening external linkages.

While quotes can be very effective at hooking readers, there are also plenty of bad examples of opening quotes. If you use a quote as your hook, make sure it really fits your study's theme, and try to reference the quote in some way—either in the Introduction or later in the paper—to highlight its relevance to your study.

The *trend* highlights trends in the real world or in academic literature that are important or represent some puzzle or paradox. Real-world trends describe changes in workplaces, industries or the broader social environment that relate to or exemplify your study's theme and suggest or provide evidence that the changes are not isolated incidents. Academic trends highlight that your topic is important because it has attracted scholarly attention, but it hasn't been resolved or the studies yield contradictory conclusions. Authors using the academic trend often provide either dense citation lists to illustrate the trend exists or refer to review articles or meta-analyses on the topic. Michael Johnson and his colleagues (Johnson, Hollenbeck, Humphrey, Ilgen, Jundt & Meyer, 2006: 103) used an academic trend to open their study, "Cutthroat cooperation: Asymmetrical adaptation to changes in team reward structures":

> In response to the increased use of team-based structures in organizations, research on work groups has expanded a great deal. Along with the increased attention devoted to work groups has come an emerging conceptual consensus that teams embedded in organizations are best viewed as complex, adaptive, and dynamic systems that perform over time (McGrath, Arrow, & Berdahl, 2000).

Jason Davis and Kathy Eisenhardt (2011: 159–160) used a real-world trend in their study, "Rotating leadership and collaborative innovation: Recombination processes in symbiotic relationships," when they stated:

> Technological innovation is central to how organizations create value for themselves, unleash gales of creative destruction on competitors, and enable progress for society. Product development and acquisition have long been significant strategies for innovation (Brown and Eisenhardt, 1997; Ahuja and Katila, 2001). But in increasingly open and dynamic industries in which resources are highly distributed and frequently changing, it is unlikely that single organizations can consistently develop or acquire the best innovations. Instead, technology collaboration has become an essential innovation strategy (Teece, 1986; Mowery, Oxley, and Silverman, 1998).

They went on to provide several examples of technology collaborations among companies such as Microsoft and Intel, and Apple and Google.

The *anecdote* uses a narrative example to introduce or highlight the article's main theme and/or the paradox at its heart. Anecdotes can be real-world examples or they can be fictional (i.e., a scenario). Anecdotes are effective because they put a human face on the paper's theme right away. For example, Adam Grant and David Hofmann (2011: 1494) opened their study, "It's not all about me: Motivating hand hygiene among healthcare professionals by focusing on patients," with the following anecdote:

> In 1847, Ignaz Semmelweis required health care professionals at the Vienna General Hospital to wash their hands, and death rates due to childbed fever decreased from 18.3% to 1.3%. Since then, extensive research has demonstrated that hand hygiene plays a critical role in preventing the spread of infections and diseases (Backman, Zoutman, & Marck, 2008). Nevertheless, it is common for health care professionals to wash their hands less than half as often as recommended, and many interventions for improving hand hygiene among health care professionals have proven ineffective (Gawande, 2004; Whitby et al., 2007).

You can also employ longer anecdotes. My opening paragraph to this chapter is one example; and Donde Plowman and colleagues' study, "Radical change accidentally: The emergence and amplification of small change" (Plowman, Baker, Beck, Kulkarni, Solansky & Travis, 2007), provides a great example. They opened their Introduction with a synopsis describing Mission Church—their study's subject—and its decision to start feeding the homeless on Sundays, which eventually culminated in

> Full-scale dental, medical and eye clinics ... and, within a few years, a 501(c)(3) spin-off (a tax-exempt organization) of the church was receiving city grants, providing a "day center" for several thousand homeless people and serving over 20,000 meals a year. Legal assistance, job training, laundry services, and shower facilities are a few of the programs, in addition to the clinics, that emerged from the initial idea of a hot breakfast. (Plowman et al., 2007: 515–516)

The *rhetorical question* stimulates thinking about or illustrates the study's main theme or paradox by prompting the reader to generate examples from their own lived experience. Although it isn't used as frequently as the other types of hooks, it's effective when used properly. For example, in our study "Crossed wires: Endorsement signals and the effects of IPO firm delistings on venture capitalists' reputations," Dave Gomulya, Kyuho Jin, Peggy Lee and I (Gomuyla et al., 2019) opened our Introduction with the following rhetorical question:

> How do you decide whether to try a new restaurant, see a new doctor, or stay at a new hotel? Odds are that you look for different clues, or signals, that you are likely to have a good experience—chief among them the organization's or individual's reputation. (2019: 641)

We used this question to connect with readers' everyday experiences, illustrating the practical relevance of our study. By answering the question, we also illustrated the two main constructs in our study—signals and reputations. We drew on this opening question later in the paper to continue the analogy and again put the readers' human face on our theoretical arguments.

What Do We Know, What Don't We Know, and So What?

In addition to setting the hook, your Introduction must identify what ongoing theoretical conversation you are joining (Huff, 1999), what's missing in this conversation, what you're bringing to the party, and why it's relevant and important. This is where you clearly introduce the main characters and your story's theme. It's also where you engage in active sensegiving, because you need to identify an unaddressed, or inadequately addressed puzzle, and convince readers that it exists, and it's an important puzzle to solve. I prefer the terms "puzzle" and "paradox" to "gap," which evokes a minor or incremental issue. Readers are rarely intrigued by gap filling, and gaps often exist for a reason: because the issue simply isn't relevant or important to address. Just identifying the puzzle is not enough, and neither is simply being "the first" to address some issue—you need to explain why it's important. Karen Locke and Karen Golden-Biddle (1997) referred to the conversation you are joining as "the intertextual field," and identified two process—(1) establishing, and (2) problematizing the intertextual field—involved in answering the questions what do we know, what don't we know, and so what? While their insight that the author constructs the conversation he or she contributes to is profound, for the sake of clarity I will use the term "conversation" instead of intertextual field.

    Establishing the conversation. This is where you answer the question "what do we know?" Establishing the conversation involves identifying and bringing together the literature or literatures that form the conversation you are contributing to, identifying where the conversation hasn't gone, and explaining why it needs to go there. The answer may be located compactly within a couple of paragraphs, or it may spread out across the Introduction. Locke and Golden-Biddle identified three different approaches to establishing the conversation. The first approach is called *synthesized coherence*. With this approach, you draw connections among different conversations that share a common, but unrecognized interest; thus, you build a bridge across different conversations that should be talking to each other. Locke and Golden-Biddle noted this requires first formulating general characterizations of each conversation using terms like *common, general, shared* and *underlying*. Next, you identify common linkages across the conversations, often employing words like *in each, both* and *as did*. Finally, you reinterpret the work to show that an underlying commonality exists, frequently employing phrases like *implicitly*, *make the implicit explicit* or *in both*.

The second approach is called *progressive coherence*. Here, you identify a single conversation and show how it needs to move forward. Studies employing progressive coherence often reference time and create a chronology of how the theoretical conversation has evolved (thus you often find they also use trends as their hook). You see phrases like *recently, over the last xx years, early studies ... more recent studies ...*, and *over the years*. They also demonstrate the conversation's maturity by providing dense lists of citations and demonstrate consensus within the conversation using the commonality words mentioned above.

The third approach is called *non-coherence*. Here, rather than demonstrating consensus within or commonalities across conversations, you highlight the conflict or disagreements that exist within or across conversations and explain how you'll adjudicate among them. The conversation or conversations are thus described using more contentious terms such as *on the one hand, inconsistent, conflicting, lack of agreement, disputes, lack of consensus* and *controversy*, or are put in direct opposition using terms like *conversely* and *in contrast*. Authors using non-coherence identify different scholars or groups of scholars associated with the opposing camps, and frequently describe competing findings that nullify each other.

Problematizing the conversation. Once you've established the conversation, you then need to "problematize" it by establishing how it's deficient—a deficiency that your study addresses. This is how you answer the questions "What don't we know?" and "So what?" It's also how you identify the knot you'll be tying. Locke and Golden-Biddle identify three increasingly critical means of problematizing the conversation: (1) incompleteness, (2) inadequacy and (3) incommensurability.

The *incompleteness* problematization doesn't criticize the prior literature; rather it stipulates that while the preceding insights are all fine, there is still more to know or understand and thus the conversation needs further development. Authors employing this approach identify the omission, explain its importance and then foreshadow how their study addresses the omission and contributes, "politely ... somewhat tentatively and with humility" (Locke & Golden-Biddle, 1997: 1042–1045). For example, in their study "Helping other CEOs avoid bad press: Social exchange and impression management support among CEOs in communications with journalists," Jim Westphal and colleagues (Westphal, Park, McDonald & Hayward, 2012: 218) stated,

> While this literature has yielded important insights about the tactics that executives and other spokespersons use to manage the impressions of external audiences about a firm's leadership and performance prospects, it has not addressed a major limita-

tion to the effectiveness of impression management that has been identified in the larger literature on social influence.

The *inadequacy* problematization is slightly more antagonistic. Rather than just suggesting we have more to learn, it suggests the conversation is inadequate: either it fails to sufficiently incorporate different perspectives and views of the phenomena, or it has overlooked different and better explanations. It more directly illuminates the conversation's oversights, introduces and cites literature to support an alternative perspective, and directly (rather than tentatively) points out how the study contributes by addressing the oversight. Thus, it is moderately critical of the conversation thus far. For example, in their article "Institutional entrepreneurship in mature fields: The Big Five accounting firms," which explored how central institutional actors—who benefit most from the status quo—can initiate major changes, Royston Greenwood and Roy Suddaby (2006: 27) stated:

> The notion of change, however, "poses a problem for institutional theorists, most of whom view institutions as the source of stability and order" (Scott, 2001: 181). If, as institutional theory asserts, behavior is substantially shaped by taken-for-granted institutional prescriptions, how can actors envision and enact changes to the contexts in which they are embedded? Seo and Creed (2002: 226) referred to this as the "paradox of embedded agency." A central challenge for institutional theory, therefore, is to show how and why actors shaped by (i.e., embedded within) institutional structures become motivated and enabled to promote change in those structures.

The most aggressive and antagonistic problematization approach is *incommensurability*. Authors who employ incommensurability not only claim the conversation overlooks different and relevant perspectives, they also claim the conversation is wrong, and they directly advocate alternative theses they regard as superior to the existing conversation. They employ provocative and confrontational language to directly criticize the current conversation and directly state how their study contributes. Paul Hirsch and Mike Lounsbury (1997: 408) provided a good example of this approach in their essay on reconciling "old" and "new" institutional theory:

> A major purpose of the article to follow is to restore action to institutional theory's increasing focus on structure and to better relate action to structure in deconstructing DiMaggio and Powell's new institutionalism ... We believe that if taken literally, however, the dichotomous contrast they set up between the old and the new is a false and misleading one. It is inappropriately pejorative toward proponents of the more action-oriented old institutional school as well as the new institutionalists interested in studying generative processes.

Each problematization approach can be effective, but they also have risks. While the incompleteness problematization is the most inoffensive, the claimed contributions can also seem like incremental gap filling. Conversely, incommensurability makes the strongest contribution claims but runs the risk of becoming too strident and polemical, stimulating an aggressive backlash. Inadequacy problemitizations may strike the best middle ground but can also come off as over-claiming if incompleteness is more appropriate, and as too wimpy and waffling if incommensurability is warranted. Thus, be sure to choose a problematization that best fits your situation and potential contribution. In deciding, consider the level of consensus or conflict on the topic, and whether you think there's something wrong, or just more to know.

What Will We Learn?

To answer the final question "what will we learn?" you need to tell readers how your contribution changes, challenges or advances the conversation. Although it sounds straightforward, this is one of the hardest things to do, and is a principal reason most studies get rejected. Indeed, when I was an editor this was far and away the most frequent issue I listed in decision letters. Even for papers that received revisions, it was typically one of the primary issues identified. Sometimes this problem arose because the authors didn't adequately problematize their study, and sometimes it was because their study didn't actually change, challenge or advance the conversation in any meaningful way. However, it also sometimes happens when authors think their contribution is so obvious everyone will see it without them having to point it out.

When I'm working on my introductions and trying to figure out and explain what my study contributes and readers will learn, I frequently turn to Murray Davis's (1971) classic article, "That's Interesting!" Everyone who has taken a research design course in the last 40 years has probably encountered this article. In it, Davis systematically laid out the ways a study can be interesting. I've summarized Davis's "Index of the Interesting" in Table 5.1. When trying to assess what makes your study interesting, peruse this list and assess which types of interestingness (and it can be more than one, but it must be at least one) your study invokes. It also provides you with the language necessary to explain why your contribution is interesting, and what your readers will learn.

John Hollenbeck (2008) noted that Davis's approach is effective because it "shifts the consensus" about what we think we know, showing that what we think is good is actually bad, what we think is random is actually systematic and structured, what we think is simple is actually complex, etc. Thus, consensus shifting involves identifying widely held assumptions, challenging or putting boundaries on them (e.g., demonstrating why they may work in one context or time period, but not another), and describing their implications for

Table 5.1   Davis's Index of the Interesting

Type of Interestingness	Why it's Interesting
Order from Chaos	What seems disorganized and unstructured is really organized and structured
Chaos from Order	What seems organized and structured is really unstructured and disorganized
Simplicity in the Complex (Invisible Structure)	What seem like heterogeneous phenomena are really a single phenomenon
Complexity in the Simple (False Structure)	What seems like a single phenomenon is really heterogeneous phenomena
The Psychological is Social	What seems like an individual phenomenon is really holistic
The Social is Psychological	What seems like a holistic phenomenon is really individual
The Social-Psychological	What seems holistic or individual is really a property of the relation between the two
Local is General	What seems like a local phenomenon is really generalizable
General is Local or Contextual	What seems like a general phenomenon is really local or context-dependent
Unobserved Dynamism	What seems stable and unchanging is really unstable and changing
Unobserved Regularity or Periodicity	What seems unstable and changing is really regular and repeating
Unobserved Functionality	What seems ineffective for achieving an end is really functional
Unobserved Dysfunction	What seems functional for achieving an end is really ineffective
Unobserved Good	What seems like a bad phenomenon is really good
Unobserved Bad	What seems like a good phenomenon is really bad
Unobserved Correlation	What seem like independent phenomena are really interrelated
False Correlation	What seem like interrelated phenomena are really independent
False Coexistence	What seem like phenomena that can exist together really cannot exist together
Surprise Coexistence	What seem like phenomena that cannot exist together can really exist together
False Positive	What seems like positive covariation is really negative covariation

False Negative	What seems like negative covariation is really positive covariation
Other False Variants of Shape	Incremental is continuous, continuous is incremental, curvilinear is linear, linear is curvilinear
False Similarity	What seem like nearly similar phenomena are really opposite phenomena
False Difference	What seem like different phenomena are really the same
Dependent Variable is Independent Variable	What seems like the predictor is really the outcome
Independent Variable is Dependent Variable	What seems like the outcome is really the predictor
One-Way Relationship is Complex	What seems like a direct relationship is really a mutual non-recursive relationship

the conversation going forward. For example, this is the approach Greenwood and Suddaby (2006: 27) used when they noted

> Contrary to extant theory, according to which the network centrality of elites embeds them within prevailing logics of action and dulls them to the possibilities of change, we show how such a network location can sharpen awareness of alternatives.

Hollenbeck argued that "consensus creation" is another powerful way to contribute. He noted that with consensus creation "the authors show that there are two (or more) clear lines of discrepant thought simultaneously existing in the literature" (Hollenbeck, 2008: 20) and how their study either clarifies the lines of debate or resolves the conflict. For example, Hirsch and Lounsbury (1997: 408–409) claimed this approach when they stated

> DiMaggio and Powell's (1991) recasting of the action-structure debate calls for reconciliation. They selectively present both sides, but without addressing sufficiently the advantages and disadvantages of each or how they can meet. In this article, we add these and invite the field to embrace and distinguish both.

The award-winning authors and reviewers Adam and I surveyed said that, on average, 30 percent of their decision to recommend rejection or revision was based on the Introduction. So, put in the effort to develop a focused Introduction that sets a compelling hook; establish and problematize a theoretical conversation so that readers understand what we know, what we don't know and why it's important; employ Davis's index to assess what makes your study interesting, and consider whether you are engaging in consensus shifting or consensus creation, and thus what the reader will learn. This will increase the likelihood your decision letters will lead with something other than "Your study doesn't currently make a clear theoretical contribution."

LURING READERS WITH TITLES AND ABSTRACTS

Before you can hook readers, you need to attract their attention and lure them to nibble at your offering. Effective titles and abstracts play these roles. Borrowing an earlier analogy that Joyce Bono and I used (Pollock & Bono, 2013), think about how you browse for books in a bookstore (yes, people still go to bookstores). Odds are that when you are looking at a display table or shelf, a book's title is the first thing to grab your attention and get you to pick the book up. If it seems sufficiently intriguing, the next thing you probably do is scan the book's synopsis on the flyleaf or back cover. In academic articles, titles and abstracts play these roles.

Titles

Helen Sword (2012: 63) said, "Like a hat on the head or the front door to a house, the title of an academic article provides a powerful first impression." An effective title is your first and best opportunity to attract readers' attention and lure them to your abstract, and then the Introduction. An effective title stirs the reader's curiosity and acts as a mini-abstract, providing, with an economy of words, essential information about the article's theme, theoretical orientation and sometimes its context. I also think the best titles stick in readers' minds, which is essential to aiding recall, and thus making your article more influential and highly cited. Think about how you decide on references to use when writing a paper. Do you keep stopping to search the Internet for the perfect reference, or do you cite the papers that come to mind? While we sometimes go searching, in most cases it's the latter, and a memorable title makes the paper easier to recall.

So what does an effective title look like? They can take a variety of forms. They can be a single direct statement or phrased as a question followed by an answer. One of the most common phrasings is the "two-piece" title, with the two pieces separated by a colon. The part before the colon actually has a name: it's called the antepone. Some people use the antepone for a catchy phrase related to the paper's topic, while others use it to provide more descriptive information. The main mistake authors often make is making both pieces of the title really long—akin to the sentence stuffing I discussed in Chapter 4—and packing them with all kinds of jargon. While the intent—to convey the maximum amount of information—is laudable, the result is a turgid and ungainly title that no one remembers. Following my discussions of pacing and cadence in Chapters 3 and 4, if you have a long antepone, the second piece should be short; if your antepone is short, the second piece can be longer. Greenwood and Suddaby's (2006) title "Institutional entrepreneurship in mature fields: The Big Five accounting firms" is an example of the former; my title (Chatterjee & Pollock, 2017) "Master of Puppets: How narcissistic CEOs construct their professional worlds" is an example of the latter. Also try to manage the number of polysyllabic words in your title, particularly in the longer piece. Too many long words bog down a title.

Although some people find them corny, and I've seen (and written) some bad ones, catchy antepones that evoke your study's theme can grab attention and stick in readers' minds. One approach is to use plays on words. Two of my favorites are "'She'-E-Os: Gender effects and investor reactions to the announcements of top executive appointments" (Lee & James, 2007) and "How golden parachutes unfolded: Diffusion and variation of a controversial practice" (Fiss, Kennedy & Davis, 2012). Plays on well-known movie titles are also effective, such as Mike Pratt's (2000) "The good, the bad and the ambivalent: Managing identification among Amway distributors," and my article with Kisha Lashley (Lashley & Pollock, 2020) "Waiting to inhale: Removing stigma in the medical cannabis industry." You can also use song titles and lyrics. "Master of Puppets" is the name of a kick-ass Metallica song. Other examples are "Time for me to fly: Predicting director exit at large firms" (Boivie, Graffin & Pollock, 2012) and "Born to take risk? The effects of CEO birth order on strategic risk taking" (Campbell, Jeong & Graffin, 2019). Finally, you can also employ unusual juxtapositions. A good example of this approach is "The bedside manner of homo economicus: How and why priming an economic schema reduces compassion" (Molinsky, Grant & Margolis, 2012). In addition to attracting attention with clever phrasing, these titles are well-paced, have good cadence and tell you key things about the studies' themes and contexts.

Abstracts

Although they are the most-read part of papers after the title, abstracts typically receive little attention when discussing academic writing. Abstracts are your Introduction in miniature, providing enough detail so readers have a better sense of what the paper's about, but also leading them to want to know more, so that they move on to the Introduction.

Abstract lengths vary by journal. I've seen some journals require abstracts as short as 50 words, which really limits how much you can say. These abstracts are just teasers. Most journals keep abstracts between 100 and 200 words, which is plenty of space to accomplish your goals. Because of these limits, your sentences need to be short and direct. A good abstract provides the following information: (1) The research question; (2) The theoretical domain;

(3) The type of study (e.g., qualitative, quantitative or theory); (4) The empirical context (if not a theory paper); and (5) A synopsis of your major findings. It should also at least tease at what's interesting, and why. Take, for example, Mike Pratt's (2000) abstract:

> An ethnographic study of distributors for Amway, a network marketing organization, examines the practices and processes involved in managing members' organizational identification. It shows that this organization manages identification by using two types of practices: sensebreaking practices that break down meaning and sensegiving practices that provide meaning. When both sensebreaking and sensegiving practices are successful, members positively identify with the organization. When either sensebreaking or sensegiving practices fail, members deidentify, disidentify, or experience ambivalent identification with the organization. A general model of identification management is posited, and implications for both theory and practice are offered.

In 95 words Pratt tells us what kind of a study it is (ethnographic), the context (Amway, a network marketing organization), what the research question and theoretical domain are (the practices and processes involved in managing members' organizational identification), and summarizes his major findings, which also tease at why it's interesting. He uses clear, direct sentences, providing the key information with a minimum of words.

As when Sarah and I do art shows, you have five seconds or less to attract readers' attention with your title, and only slightly longer to lure them with your abstract and hook them with your Introduction. In this chapter I've provided guidance on what good titles, abstracts and Introductions look like, but I'm sure you have your favorites. And as always, norms can vary by field. I encourage to you reread and break down some of your favorite titles and Introductions, and look at whether and how authors capture essential information in their abstracts.

6.   Theory and Hypotheses

"Your arguments are under-theorized." "Your hypotheses seem obvious." "What's new here?" At some point in our careers we've all received similar feedback on the papers we've slaved over. There are probably no more important, or maddening, comments. They're important because they cut right to the heart of your study and say you did an inadequate job tying the knot. At the same time, they're maddening because they're hugely subjective statements, particularly if they aren't followed up by specific reasons why the reviewer thinks your paper is under-theorized, your hypotheses are obvious, or you aren't offering anything new.

Regardless, what they say is you didn't adequately define and present each of your main characters, supporting characters and their storylines in a way that creates a coherent and persuasive narrative. These are the Theory and Hypotheses section's primary roles. In this chapter I discuss the major components of the Theory and Hypotheses section and the most common challenges writers face: developing theoretical arguments, construct clarity, developing clear hypothesis statements, and structuring the section's narrative in a logical and effective way. Although much of what I discuss also applies to theory papers and the theoretical background section of qualitative studies, there are also some differences. I address these differences in Chapter 9.

WHAT THEORY IS AND IS NOT

The Theory and Hypotheses section is the portion of a quantitative empirical article that lies between the Introduction and the Data and Methods; it is the section that comprises the bulk of your paper's "front end." This section builds on your Introduction by elaborating on the conversation or conversations you are participating in and what's incomplete, inadequate or incommensurable in them; presenting your theoretical arguments and insights that address these deficiencies; and clearly stating the hypotheses you logically derived from them. This is where most of the rising action occurs, and where your knot gets tied. Key to developing an effective Theory and Hypotheses section, then, is developing your theoretical arguments. However, what constitutes theory development, and whether it's adequate, is a subjective assessment that ultimately depends on readers buying your story, which depends on you making a persuasive argument. To that end, it is important to understand what does and does not make for persuasive theoretical claims.

There are several classic articles on what theory is (e.g., Van Maanen, 1995; Weick, 1989; Whetten, 1989), but at its most basic level, theory is an explanation of *why*. If you get feedback that your paper or hypotheses are under-theorized, then you aren't doing a compelling job explaining why you expect the relationships you do. Theory provides a story about the connections between phenomena, and why actions, events, structures, thoughts or feelings occur. It emphasizes the nature, direction, context and timing of relationships, and delves into underlying processes to understand the systematic reasons things occur or do not occur.[1]

A good theoretical argument has both simplicity and interconnectedness (Sutton & Staw, 1995). It often starts with one or two conceptual statements and then proceeds to build a logically detailed case. According to former *Academy of Management Journal* associate editors Ray Sparrowe and Kyle Mayer (2011), a good theory development section cites relevant work, focusing on their arguments as well as their findings. It avoids dragging in extraneous or peripheral studies, and takes head-on studies that seem to make a similar contribution, elaborating on their differences. It weaves new ideas with existing theory and findings to substantiate the hypotheses, so that the formal hypothesis statement isn't a surprise by the time the reader gets to it.

However, many scholars mistake different theory-building tools for theory itself. In their classic essay on this issue, Robert Sutton and Barry Staw (1995) provided some useful insights into what theory is not, as a means of understanding what theory is. They identified five common tools important to developing theory, but that do not constitute theory or theoretical arguments: references, data, lists of variables and constructs, diagrams, and hypotheses.

References are necessary to develop and distinguish new theory but are not substitutes for theory itself. Individuals falling into this trap engage in "argument by citation," making statements followed by long lists of citations rather than saying what these different studies argued and found, and weaving these arguments and findings into their new theoretical claims about why something occurs. Argument by citation reflects the mind-reading pathology discussed in Chapter 4, because it assumes readers have an intimate knowledge of each study and can connect the pieces themselves. The reader shouldn't have to be familiar with the reference to know what it says. It is up to you, the writer, to

---

[1] Theorizing doesn't just mean invoking specific theories (e.g., institutional theory, transactions cost economics theory or job characteristics theory). For example, mechanism-based theorizing (Davis & Marquis, 2005) doesn't necessarily invoke a specific theory, but it does explain why certain relationships and phenomena exist and how they affect each other. This is theorizing, too.

summarize the concepts, constructs, logic, relationships and causal mechanisms the references describe, and how they are linked to the theory you are developing.

Like references, *data* are necessary for providing theoretical insights because data and empirical findings can confirm, discredit or lead to revising a theory. However, data is not theory, because it doesn't explain why something did or didn't occur; it just illustrates what happened. Similarly, simply presenting another study's findings doesn't constitute theory and cannot be solely used to justify your hypotheses, because a summary of findings alone again doesn't explain why the findings occurred, only that they did. You must blend them with the theoretical explanations for the findings in developing your arguments. So, either before or after summarizing what a study found, you should also provide some insight into why the authors believed this result occurred, and what its implications are for your arguments. How does it add to your story, and help you tie your knot?

Lists of variables and constructs alone also do not constitute theory, because you need to place them within a context and articulate the relationships among them. If you've ever reviewed a paper (you are unlikely to see one in print) that simply lists and defines constructs and then follows the definitions with hypotheses, you are witnessing the use of variable lists as theorizing. Whenever you list a construct you need to discuss its relationships to other variables in your study. You may also need to discuss its relationships to other, similar constructs, and explain why this construct and not others are the most relevant to your story.

Diagrams are helpful tools for illustrating your theoretical arguments but they are not theory themselves, because again they do not provide the explanation *why*. Unlike variable lists, they do at least (I hope!) indicate the relationships among constructs; however, without a verbal explanation of what's happening—and again, *why* it's happening—they do not constitute theory. As I've noted in Chapter 4, if you include a diagram or figure in your paper you better explain it; they do not speak for themselves.

Hypotheses also are not theory, because they describe *what* the relationship looks like, not why it will occur. Hypotheses summarize predictions based on the theory and provide the bridge between theory and data; they make explicit how you'll operationalize the relationships and variables that flow from your logical theoretical arguments. Thus, they are an outcome of theory, not a substitute for it.

In building your theoretical arguments and presenting your hypotheses, always pay attention to whether you are clearly defining your main and supporting characters—your key constructs. You must justify their importance, articulate the relationships among them, and explain why these relationships exist and what the consequences are. The first order of business, then, is construct clarity.

CONSTRUCT CLARITY

Former *Academy of Management Review* Editor Roy Suddaby wrote a useful essay (Suddaby, 2010) on construct clarity that applies equally to theory, quantitative and qualitative studies. Suddaby (2010: 346) stated "Clear constructs are simply robust categories that distill phenomena into sharp distinctions that are comprehensible to a community of researchers." Construct clarity is important because it facilitates communication among researchers. It ensures they are talking about the same or different things, reducing the unnecessary construct proliferation that results from calling the same thing different names. Construct clarity also helps scholars develop better measures (i.e., it enhances construct validity), facilitating knowledge accumulation about the phenomena. Finally, Suddaby argued that construct clarity enhances creativity and innovation, because the ability to capture essential characteristics and distinguish among different phenomena "not only serves as a useful means of description but can stimulate insights into additional possible relationships, related constructs, and often related theories" (Suddaby, 2010: 353).

Clear constructs have coherent definitions and scope conditions, and an identifiable lineage and relationship to other constructs. The newer the construct, the more important it is that you provide this information. Regardless, you should always define your constructs. Good *definitions* capture the construct's key characteristics, avoid tautologies (i.e., defining the construct in terms of itself), exclude the construct's antecedents and consequences from the definition, define the construct as narrowly as possible while still allowing for generalizability, and strip "surplus meaning" that may have accreted on the construct over time and through misuse. If you are using an existing construct, then one or more definitions also often exist. You will therefore need to explain why you chose the definition you did. Being explicit about your definition also helps identify the conversation you are joining. For example, Violina Rindova and colleagues (Rindova, Williamson, Petkova & Sever, 2005) noted that economists and sociologists define reputation differently: economists define it as expectations about a firm's ability to deliver quality products and services in the future, whereas sociologists define it as a global impression reflecting how a particular group or groups perceives the firm. These definitions emphasize different theoretical assumptions about how the construct functions. Clearly explaining your definitional choice situates you in the appropriate conversation.

Scope conditions refer to when the definition will and won't apply. They can be temporal, geographic, industry or age specific, and tied to level of analysis or an organization's form (e.g., public or private, for profit or non-profit, etc.). And since most constructs derive from pre-existing constructs, a construct's *lineage* describes the related constructs that the construct has emerged from. For example, in a clever study of how the direction of changes in reward structure (i.e., from cooperative to competitive or competitive to cooperative) affect teams' abilities to adapt to the new structure (Johnson et al., 2006; mentioned in Chapter 5), Johnson and his colleagues introduced a new construct—cutthroat cooperation (nice alliteration)—that they linked to other constructs such as centralization and decentralization, cooperative and competitive rewards, and friendly competition.

It is also important to identify the focal construct's relationships to other, often similar constructs, not just those they emerged from. For example, when Violina Rindova, Mat Hayward and I introduced the construct firm celebrity (Rindova et al., 2006), which we argued was one of several different types of "social approval assets," we had to differentiate firm celebrity from the related constructs reputation, status and legitimacy.

It's important to define new constructs the first time you mention them—whether that's in the Introduction or in the Theory and Hypotheses section—and elaborate on their scope conditions, lineage and relationship to other constructs in the theory development section. If a construct is well known you can probably get away without defining it in the Introduction even if you first mention it there, and just define it where you elaborate on it in the Theory and Hypotheses section. Confine detailed discussions of why you chose one definition over others, scope conditions, etc., to the theory development portion of your article; including them in the Introduction would derail your problematization and ruin your motion and pacing from the get-go.

HYPOTHESIS STATEMENTS

Hypotheses are the logical outcomes of your theoretical arguments.[2] Although they only represent a few lines in your paper, they explain *what* the relationships will look like based on the whys you established in your theorizing, and they guide your empirical analysis. I know some editors who, before reading a paper, examine just the hypotheses to see if they can figure out what the story is likely to be. Like constructs, your hypotheses must be clear and coherently organized. At a minimum, all hypotheses must specify the *nature* of the relationship; that is, distinguishing which are the independent (IV) and dependent (DV) variables. They must also specify whether the *direction* of the relationship is positive or negative. Thus, saying that "X is associated with Y"

---

[2]   Hypotheses are distinct from propositions, which I discuss in Chapter 9.

is inadequate because it fails to specify which variable is influencing the other, and whether that relationship is positive or negative.

Hypotheses should also capture other relationship characteristics. If the relationship is anything other than linear, the hypothesis should specify its *shape*. Is it fully curvilinear, where low levels of the IV have a positive relationship with the DV, and high levels of the IV have a negative relationship with the DV (or vice versa)? Or is it partially curvilinear (e.g., positive but diminishing) or cubic? You also need to specify *intervening variables* (i.e., mediators or moderators) and the *strength* and direction of their effects. It's also important to specify the strength and direction of the effects when making relative comparisons between constructs (e.g., X will have a greater positive effect than Z on Y).

It's critical that your hypotheses accurately reflect the type of relationship you both theorize and test. Hypotheses generally take one of three forms. *If-then* statements suggest that if some specific condition holds, a particular outcome will occur: if X, then Y. "Female CEOs with equivalent experience will be paid less than male CEOs" is an if-then hypothesis: if female, then less pay. Interaction hypotheses can also be if-then statements: the positive(negative) effect of X on Y is weaker(stronger) if Z occurs. For example: "The negative effect of gender on CEO pay is weaker when the company is headquartered in a more egalitarian country" conditions the effect of our first if-then hypothesis on a characteristic of the company's home country.

Hypotheses can also be *Continuous* statements: the greater(lesser) the value of X, the greater(lesser) the value of Y. "The higher the firm's stock performance, the higher the CEO's total compensation" is an example of a continuous hypothesis. "The longer a CEO's tenure in the position, the weaker the effect of their firm's stock performance on CEO pay" is an example of a continuous interaction hypothesis. Curvilinear hypotheses are also generally continuous statements (e.g., firm performance will have a positive but diminishing relationship with CEO pay). Do not use continuous hypothesis statements, however, unless your constructs are also continuous. You cannot use continuous hypotheses if the constructs are dichotomous or categorical, because binary and categorical constructs can be non-ordinal (e.g., female/ non-female) or have discontinuous effects across states (e.g., low, medium and high status).

Finally, Hypotheses can also be *Difference* statements that make relative comparisons. They can be either main effect or interaction hypotheses and can incorporate either if-then or continuous relationships. For example, "X will have a greater (lesser) effect on Y for category A than for category B" compares the effect of the same IV on the same DV across different contexts (e.g., firm performance will have a more positive effect on male CEO's total compensation than on female CEOs' total compensation). In contrast, "X will have a greater(lesser) effect on Y than Z will have on Y" compares the relative influence of different IVs on the same DV in the same context (e.g., gender will have a greater effect than firm performance on a CEOs' total compensation). And "X will have a greater(lesser) effect on Y when Z is high(low) than when Z is low(high)" compares the effects of an IV on the DV at different levels of a moderator (e.g., the relationship between gender and CEO pay will be stronger the lower the firm's performance). As you craft your Theory and Hypotheses section, make sure you pay as much attention to hypothesis clarity as you do to construct clarity.

STRUCTURING THE THEORY AND HYPOTHESES SECTION

All Theory and Hypotheses sections must accomplish certain tasks, but you can structure them in a wide variety of ways. Although the following list isn't exhaustive, I argue that how you structure a Theory and Hypotheses section depends on (1) The number of theoretical domains identified in your conversation and your problematization approach; (2) Whether you introduce a new construct; (3) The number of main characters and their roles; (4) The number of supporting characters and their roles; (5) How you introduce the context, use it to move the story along and to provide a human face; and (6) Where you put your model figure. In the remainder of this section I discuss each of these contingencies and offer some rule of thumb suggestions about their implications for structuring your Theory and Hypotheses section. Table 6.1 summarizes my recommendations. While, as with most of my recommendations, I'm confident you can find effective examples that violate them, these rules of thumb provide you a starting point for making reasonable choices, and from which you can depart and experiment.

Number of theoretical domains. One key structural factor is whether you focus on one primary theoretical domain or work with multiple literatures. Studies that employ progressive coherence with an incompleteness or inadequacy problematization generally focus on a *single theoretical domain*. Thus, their Theory and Hypotheses section typically starts with a literature review that both establishes what we know about the literature and its limitations. This sets the stage for developing specific arguments about what's needed, including perhaps new constructs, and what the new relationships look like and why. Hypotheses are typically introduced towards the end of each section as you develop each part of your theory.

For example, in their study "Impact and the art of motivation maintenance: The effects of contact with beneficiaries on persistence behavior," Adam Grant and his colleagues used progressive coherence and an incompleteness problematization to argue that scholars had neglected the relational aspects of job

Table 6.1   *Structuring the Theory and Hypotheses section*

Factor	Positioning
Single theoretical domain	Theory review first, hypotheses following later after new theory supporting each one
Multiple theoretical domains	General overarching framework early, then specifics on theories introduced and integrated or contrasted. Theories and hypotheses can be sequential, or theories presented first with hypotheses following
Existing constructs	Can introduce them together; early, or after context. Can also introduce them sequentially as hypotheses are developed
New construct	Typically introduced early
Single main character	Introduce early **If IV:** After defining it, explain how it affects supporting character DVs **If DV:** After defining it, explain how it's affected by supporting character IVs
Multiple main characters	**Both IVs and DVs:** If a single DV and multiple IVs, DV first followed by IVs If single IV and multiple DVs, IV first followed by DVs If multiple IVs and DVs, either can come first or they can be interspersed as story unfolds **All IVs:** Can be introduced sequentially with hypotheses, or as a group if relative comparisons are made, followed by hypotheses
Single supporting character	**If DV:** Often introduced early **If IV:** As story unfolds
Multiple supporting characters	As story unfolds
Context	**Early:** If integral to introducing your characters **After theory:** If not integral to introducing characters but helps tell story **Late:** If lab study or more generical context not critical to story (e.g., S&P 500)
Figures – general illustration	Where relevant theory is discussed
Figures – summarizing model	After hypotheses are developed

design (Grant et al., 2007). They argued that designs which bring the job holder into contact with the beneficiaries of their actions increase the job holders' motivations to persist in their tasks. Since they focused on a single theoretical domain, they opened their Theory and Hypotheses section by introducing their key construct—motivation maintenance—in the first paragraph, and then situated it within the job design literature beginning in the second paragraph, building towards their first hypothesis. As this was a two-experiment study, they followed each hypothesis with the methods and results of the experiment testing it; but they followed this same general structure when developing each hypothesis.

Studies that use synthesized or non-coherence with inadequacy or incommensurability problematizations draw on *multiple theories*. To create a coherent narrative, you often need to place these theories within an overarching framework of some sort that introduces and discusses their relevant aspects, and then integrates or contrasts them. You typically present your general integrating framework at or near the section's beginning, and then get into the more specific details of each theory and develop your associated hypotheses. Depending on whether you are contrasting or integrating theories, and how you integrate them, you can introduce the different theories and their associated hypotheses sequentially, or you may introduce and integrate all of the theories first, with the hypotheses based on the integrative arguments following.

For example, in their cutthroat cooperation study discussed earlier, Johnson and colleagues (2006) started by reviewing structural contingency theory and social interdependence theory, integrating them along with a novel use of the second law of thermodynamics to create their new theoretical framework, structural adaptation theory. They then used this framework to develop their key constructs and hypotheses.

New or existing constructs. *Existing* constructs typically require less development than new constructs. You want to make sure you define each construct, identify the relevant literature and explain how it relates to the arguments you are building. However, you can introduce the constructs together before developing your hypotheses, or sequentially as you develop each hypothesis. You may also decide to discuss some other things, such as your context, before introducing existing constructs.

On the other hand, you generally introduce *new constructs* early on. They are typically your theoretical contribution's main focus and require more elaboration than existing constructs. In addition to providing a clear definition and describing the construct's scope conditions, you must also pay significant attention to distinguishing the construct from other, related constructs and establishing the need for, and unique value-added of, the new construct. One approach is to have a whole section dedicated to defining the construct, where you start with the definition and then proceed to review the relevant literature, then explain and justify the construct. Another is to build to the construct definition by starting with a literature review that identifies some missing piece—your construct—which you then introduce. Both approaches are effective, although the latter approach risks burying the lead and losing your reader's interest if you take too long to get to the punchline introducing your new construct.

Number of main characters and their roles. As I discussed in Chapter 2, you should introduce your main characters in your exposition and then elaborate on their story and the path they travel in the rising action. Discuss a *single main character* at the beginning of the Theory and Hypotheses section, and clearly establish its relationship to your study's theme. Thus, it may be the subject of your literature review, or may follow immediately after it. If your single main character is an IV, then how it affects supporting character (DV) outcomes should follow its definition. If it's a DV, then after introducing and defining it you should identify the supporting IV characters that influence it. For example, as mentioned above, Grant and colleagues (2007) introduced their main character, motivation maintenance, in the first paragraph of their theory development.

You have a wider variety of options with *multiple main characters*, depending on whether they are IVs and DVs or all IVs (multiple DV main characters only are rare). Which comes first depends on the storylines you develop and how you want to tie the knot. If there's a single DV main character and multiple IV main characters the DV typically comes first, since most of your story will be about how the IVs influence the DV. However, if there's a single IV and multiple DV main characters you'll likely introduce and discuss the IV first, since most of your story will be about how this IV affects different outcomes. If you have multiple IV and multiple DV main characters you can pursue either option, or you can intersperse the IVs and DVs as your story unfolds; it really depends on your story. If your main characters are all IVs, you can introduce them sequentially followed by their relevant hypotheses, or if you are making relative comparisons among them, in a group followed by your hypotheses.

Number of supporting characters and their roles. You typically introduce and discuss supporting characters when their role in the story becomes relevant. Thus, they are introduced as the story unfolds, particularly if they are IVs that serve as mediators or moderators. However, if you have a *single DV* supporting character you may want to introduce and discuss it early, so that you can develop and discuss the IV main character(s)'s relationship with the DV. You typically introduce *multiple supporting characters*, whether IV or DV, as the story unfolds.

For example, in my study with Mike Pfarrer and Violina Rindova, "A tale of two assets: The effects of firm reputation and celebrity on earnings surprises and investors' reactions" (Pfarrer et al., 2010), our main characters were the IVs firm reputation and celebrity, and our supporting characters were the DVs positive and negative earnings surprises, and investors' reactions to earnings surprise announcements. Although earnings surprises were supporting characters, we couldn't tell our story until the readers knew what they were; so, we opened our theory development by defining and reviewing the literature on earnings surprises. We then introduced our main characters and developed theory supporting our first set of hypotheses about how reputation and celebrity influenced the likelihood firms would experience positive and negative earnings surprises. After that we introduced the second supporting character, investors' responses, and developed theory supporting our second set of hypotheses about how possessing reputation and celebrity would affect investors' responses to positive and negative earnings surprises. Thus, we introduced one supporting character at the beginning and the other later, as the story unfolded.

Context. You can introduce your research context early to set up your story, introduce it throughout the Theory and Hypotheses section to provide illustrations, or introduce it at the end to set up your empirical analysis. For example, if your research context is integral to describing key characters in your story, you'll want to introduce it early on. In our study of the effects of firm reputation and celebrity on earnings surprises (Pfarrer et al., 2010), earnings surprises were our research context, as well as a supporting character. Describing earnings surprises right away made developing our theoretical arguments much easier.

In contrast, in my study with Jung-Hoon Han, "The two towers (or somewhere in between): The behavioral consequences of positional inconsistency across status hierarchies" (Han & Pollock, 2021), we didn't introduce our research context—Hollywood performers—until after we had reviewed the literature and developed our basic theoretical framework. In this instance we used our research context to create a human face for our study, and we used examples from our context to "show" the theoretical arguments supporting each hypothesis we "told" readers about. This approach also helped our motion and pacing by creating some breathing room for readers before plunging into the next complex, and more abstract, theoretical argument.

You may also choose to avoid mentioning your research context at all, or to present it only after you've developed all your hypotheses. This approach is most effective if you are conducting an experiment or simulation (e.g., Grant et al., 2007; Johnson et al., 2006), where you create an artificial context for your study, or if your context is something general, like S&P 500 firms. As I discussed in Chapter 3, context-free theorizing is generally pretty boring to read so you'll want to be sure and work other real-world examples into your theory and hypothesis development so that it has a human face and you can show readers what the relationships look like, rather than just telling them.

Introducing theoretical figures. My general rule of thumb is to introduce figures that review or develop a general theory where you develop theory, and to introduce figures summarizing hypothesized relationships at the end of the Theory and Hypotheses section. If you introduce your summarizing figure early, readers tend to forget what it looks like, particularly if it's complex. Even if you reference it along the way, readers must flip back repeatedly to remind themselves. Johnson and colleagues (2006) provide a nice example of the former when they used a three-dimensional figure to illustrate how they integrated rewards into structural contingency theory. Baum and colleagues (Baum, Rowley, Shipilov & Chuang, 2005) provide an interesting three-dimensional example of the latter. If you employ a summarizing figure, please label each link in your model with the associated hypothesis.

In this chapter I discussed the three key tasks the Theory and Hypotheses section fulfills as it propels the rising action in your story and ties the knot: (1) Introducing and clearly delineating your key constructs; (2) Establishing the theoretical conversation you are joining, how it's deficient and what you're contributing (i.e., how your theory explains unexplored or under-explored whys); and (3) Justifying and presenting the hypotheses capturing your expected relationships among the main and supporting characters. I've also discussed how the number of literatures you draw on, whether you rely on existing constructs or introduce a new construct, the number and roles of your main and supporting characters, and how you employ your research context influence how you structure this section. I encourage you to return to your trove of favorite articles and study when and how the authors introduced their main and supporting characters, and how they structured their rising action to explain why they think whatever they're studying happens, and how they effectively tie their story's knot. Hopefully they'll help you structure your work so that you'll never again be told your hypotheses are under-theorized.

7.   Methods and Results

As a doctoral student, what was the first section of a paper you were responsible for drafting? For many it's the Methods section, and maybe the Results section. Many consider the Methods section the "easiest" section to write because it's heavily descriptive: this is how we collected our sample; this is how we measured our variables; and this is how we analyzed the data. Faculty also ask doctoral students to write the Results section because they were likely the ones who ran all the analyses. Reporting whether the results support the hypotheses also seems more straightforward than making complex theoretical arguments.

However, like the Introduction and Theory and Hypotheses sections, the Methods and Results sections must also persuade readers. The Methods section has to persuade readers that your empirical study is well designed and you did everything correctly. The Results section must persuade readers that your results support (or fail to support) your hypotheses and that you've ruled out alternative explanations. That is, your results are valid, reliable and hopefully replicable. In this chapter I briefly review the four major types of validity that the Methods and Results sections address, and the tradeoffs facing all empirical research. I then discuss each section's purpose, the challenges in writing the Methods and Results sections, and how they are generally structured. I focus just on quantitative studies in this chapter, and I address the Methods and Results sections for qualitative empirical studies in Chapter 9.

THE FOUR MAJOR TYPES OF VALIDITY

The Methods and Results sections must persuade readers that you've adequately addressed the four major types of validity: Internal Validity, External Validity, Construct Validity, and Statistical Conclusion Validity.[1]

Internal validity is the degree to which there is no plausible alternative explanation for the causal relationship between changes in an independent variable and changes in the dependent variable. Thus, if you are making causal

---

[1]   For an exhaustive discussion of validity, I suggest *Experimental and Quasi-Experimental Designs for Generalized Causal Inference* by Shadish, Cook and Campbell (2002). For a less exhaustive and more accessible primer, I recommend Don Schwab's (2005) *Research Methods for Organizational Studies*.

claims your Methods and Results sections must persuade readers that you've ruled out the plausible alternative explanations that threaten internal validity. If you aren't making, or can't make, causal claims (e.g., the relationships are cross-sectional and correlational), you need to make sure your language is appropriate to the claims you can make and test (e.g., are "associated with," rather than "cause"). Using causal language when testing correlational relationships is one of the most common mistakes in Methods and Results sections.

External validity is the degree to which the relationships between the independent and dependent variables hold across different entities, settings, measures and times. In other words, the extent to which your findings are generalizable to other contexts and construct operationalizations. Thus, describing your research context is critical for persuading readers of your study's external validity, because how you describe your context helps readers see similarities with other research contexts. Providing specific examples from other contexts can also help. And as with internal validity, you need to demonstrate that you've ruled out contextual, temporal and measurement validity threats, and/ or bounded your theory and claims so that you don't try to generalize your findings more widely than is defensible.

Chapter 6 covered one aspect of *construct validity*—the degree to which operationalizations of the independent and dependent variables accurately reflect the theoretical constructs of interest and not alternative constructs. The Theory and Hypotheses section focuses on clearly defining the constructs and the expected theoretical relationships among them. The Methods section focuses the second aspect of construct validity: the extent to which the empirical measures reflect the construct definitions. Here you need to persuade readers that your measures capture all the constructs' salient characteristics and aren't contaminated by other constructs' characteristics. Your measures must also demonstrate face validity—that is, they seem reasonable to an intelligent individual or expert informant. The Results section captures the third aspect of construct validity, as it establishes whether the empirical relationships between the measures reflect the theoretical relationships among the constructs.

Finally, *statistical conclusion validity* is the degree to which the statistical tests used to evaluate the relationships between the independent and dependent variables accurately reflect the relationships in the population at an acceptable probability level. Thus, your sample descriptions, measures and analytical techniques need to persuade readers that your sample is sufficiently large and free from obvious biases, and that your measures are accurate, unbiased and do not contain large amounts of error. You also need to establish that the analytical techniques you employed are appropriate given your data's distributional and other properties, and do not bias your results towards finding false positives (i.e., Type I errors) or false negatives (i.e., Type II errors).

THE THREE-HORNED DILEMMA

The psychologist Joe McGrath (1982) noted that all research designs have strengths, and all are also fatally flawed. This is because the different designs are arrayed across three dimensions—measurement precision, generalizability and contextual realism, portrayed in Figure 7.1—which are a function of the design's obtrusiveness and context dependence. Obtrusiveness is the degree to which a design requires direct researcher involvement and behavioral manipulation of an artificial context, and the level of reactivity to the researcher's actions. Context dependence is the degree to which the design seeks to explain behaviors that are universally observed regardless of context, or particular behaviors in particular contexts. To the extent that you maximize a study's measurement precision, generalizability and/or contextual realism you must necessarily minimize the other dimensions. At best a design can be somewhat strong on two dimensions and really weak on the third. This is why McGrath argued all designs are fatally flawed.

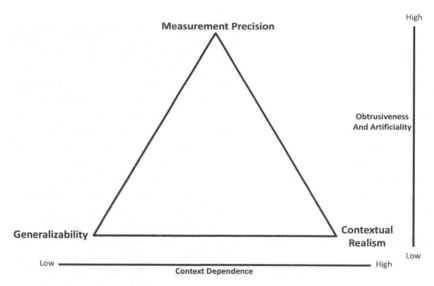

Figure 7.1　　*The three-horned dilemma*

Thus, laboratory experiments—which are high on measurement precision and very low on contextual realism—are the most obtrusive and contextually artificial; the participants know that they're being studied and that the researcher has artificially created the situation, and the results may be fairly context dependent and not generalize to other groups, or to field settings. Archival studies using secondary data are the least obtrusive, because the subjects are unaware that they are being studied and therefore have good to very good contextual realism. However, that can also make them more context dependent, limiting their generalizability, and they have lower measurement precision because the measures used may be crude or contaminated. Random-sample population surveys are highly generalizable, but they are also obtrusive and artificial, and provide limited control over the respondent's experience and response conditions compared to an experiment. In describing your methods and interpreting and drawing conclusions from your results, it's important to recognize and acknowledge the strengths and flaws of your research design. They also provide the basis for discussing your study's limitations, which I'll cover in greater detail in Chapter 8 on the Discussion section. Demonstrating you are aware of your study's weaknesses, as well as its strengths, enhances your credibility.

The preceding lays the basic groundwork for writing about your research methods and results. In the remainder of this chapter I discuss each section's purposes in more detail, describe the writing challenges each section poses and how to overcome them, and present each section's basic structures.

METHODS SECTION

Purposes

The Methods section is the end of the rising action, where you finish tying the knot. This section has three main purposes. Its first purpose is to *describe*. You describe your research context if you haven't already done so. You also describe how you created your sample and measures. If you conducted an experiment or survey, you describe how it was designed and carried out. Finally, you describe how you analyzed your data. These descriptions should include enough detail that readers could replicate your study if they wanted. Thus, the Methods section is like a good recipe; it not only lists the ingredients, it describes the amounts of each ingredient, the order in which they are combined, and the techniques used to combine and cook them.

The Methods section's second purpose is to *explain*. You explain the choices you made in creating your sample and measures, and why they were appropriate. You also explain how you addressed the different challenges that came up, such as missing data or sample attrition due to participants dropping out or firms being acquired. And you explain how you addressed threats to interpreting your results, such as collinearity and endogeneity.

However, it's not enough to just describe what you did and explain why you did it; you also need to *justify* why your choices were appropriate. Explaining and justifying your actions and decisions are thus the persuasive heart of your Methods section. Justifying involves providing the evidence supporting your explanations, such as identifying the alternative measures you considered and why you rejected them, or providing evidence that the steps you took to address endogeneity were effective. Explanations without justifications are declarations; explanations with reasoned justifications are persuasive arguments.

Challenges in Writing the Methods Section

AMJ Associate Editors Anthea Zhang and Jason Shaw wrote a "From the Editors" column (Zhang & Shaw, 2012) on effective Methods and Results sections. In it they identified the three Cs necessary: Completeness, Clarity and Credibility. I use their three Cs to highlight the challenges in writing each section.

Completeness. Completeness requires that you put yourself in the reader's chair (Johanson, 2007) and think about all the things they need to know. The biggest completeness challenges authors typically face are mind reading, motion and pacing, sentence stuffing, and burying the lead. Completeness requires providing enough detail about what, how and why you did what you did that readers can assess your responses to the different validity threats your study faced. Readers also need enough detail to replicate your study or employ your approaches and measures in other studies. At the same time, you can't describe every twist and turn, or the hundreds of individual decisions you had to make as you collected, coded and analyzed your data. Since you have lived with your study for so long, you may have difficulty discerning between too little and too much information.

If you provide too little information, readers need to employ mind reading to capture essential information, and your motion and pacing is likely to be a choppy forced march. For example, if you said, "Our index was composed of six measures, such as financial leverage and several intensity measures using various balance sheet items," it would be impossible to replicate your measure. Conversely, if you provide too much detail, such as describing the ten different potential intensity measures in detail, and explaining one by one why you did or didn't use each measure, you'll have little motion as readers slog through the mire of overstuffed sentences and buried leads. As I'll discuss in Chapter 10, this is where friendly reviewers can help. They'll tell you when they need more information, or less. Co-authors who weren't intimately involved in the data collection and analysis can also help you see when more, or less, detail is needed.

Clarity. It is possible to be complete in your descriptions, and readers may still have no idea what you did. Although clear writing is always important, as discussed in Chapter 4, what I'm referring to here is having empathy for readers who may not be technical experts; they need information that is accessible, as well as complete and technically correct. Indeed, the more technically complex the measure or technique, the more important it becomes to explain it clearly using non-technical language. The biggest challenge to clarity is pompous prose. Employing only technical jargon and treating formulas as self-evident are two examples of pompous prose. If you provide a formula, make sure you define each term in it using words, and explain the relationships. And do your best to minimize technical terminology when more accessible labels are available. If you're doing network analysis, for example, call the connection between two actors a tie, not an "edge," even if that's the term mathematicians inexplicably use.

Additional ways to enhance your Methods section's clarity are to use simpler sentence structures, show as well as tell, and employ cadence to your advantage. Breaking your sentences into shorter sentences makes it easier to follow the steps you took. After describing a complex and/or abstract technique or method for constructing a measure, provide an example to illustrate it. Summary tables and figures are also useful ways to show as well as tell. And use the same organizational structure when describing each variable to create a cadence that makes the descriptions easier to follow. For example, for each measure you could name the variable, define how you operationalized it, and then provide any additional detail required to flesh out how the variable was constructed and justify why it's better than possible alternatives.

Credibility. The reader must ultimately trust that you did all the things they can't see correctly. The biggest challenges to your credibility are mind reading and failing to show as well as tell. If you leave out key information and don't illustrate that you know what you're doing, readers are more likely to question whether all the other assumptions and choices you made but don't discuss were correct. One way to establish your credibility is by demonstrating your knowledge of the processes you employed. This doesn't mean showing off or using lots of technical jargon; rather, it means providing examples and clearly walking your readers through them. This is where the details matter. Explain where you obtained your data and how you collected and coded it. Provide your scales' items, and if you adapted a measure from another scale, explain why the adaptation was necessary and provide the items in an appendix or table, along with the relevant statistics demonstrating the measure is still valid and reliable. Explaining your choices and demonstrating that you considered alternative approaches also help establish your credibility, because they show you aren't just cherry-picking results or employing the one technique that provides your predicted outcomes. Reading your paper like a reviewer, anticipating likely issues readers will raise, and addressing them proactively also helps enhance your credibility. Finally, you can enhance your credibility by demonstrating that you are cognizant of the three-horned dilemma. Avoiding language inconsistent with your design's strengths, and restricting your claims to things your research method can support, gives readers more faith that you understand your study's strengths and weaknesses.

Methods Section Structure

Context and sample selection. If you haven't already described your research context elsewhere, this is the first thing you should do. If you've already described it, you may want to provide a little more detail, or at a minimum restate the context and time period (e.g., all firms included in the S&P 500 between 2005 and 2015). If you are focusing on a specific industry or industries, explain why. If you are creating a matched sample, explain why, describe and justify your matching criteria, and provide descriptive statistics or other data that show they are good matches. If you're conducting a lab experiment, this is where you describe your participants, including relevant demographic breakdowns.

After describing who you're studying, the next task is to walk readers through how you arrived at your final sample. You'll essentially create a funnel that takes readers from the initial group considered down to your final sample size and observation structure. Start at the highest level and identify the number of actors you considered, and then explain any reasons for attrition and how many actors you lost along the way for each reason. Once you've identified your final sample of actors, identify the total number of observations in your sample based on your observation structure. For example, in Chatterjee and Hambrick's (2007: 361–362) study of narcissistic CEOs, they explained,

> We started by identifying all software and hardware companies listed in Execucomp, which consists of roughly the 1,500 largest public U.S. firms, between 1992 and 2004 ... We identified the CEO for every firm-year in this time frame and then imposed two filters. First, we only considered those CEOs who started their tenures (which we designate as year t) in 1991 or later. Second, we included only those CEOs who had four or more years of tenure within our study period. These two filters generated 111 CEOs in 105 unique firms ... Our dependent variables were measured annually for each of the subsequent years of the CEO's tenure (t + n, where n > 2), yielding a total of 352 firm-years for testing the effects of narcissism.

Depending on the reasons for the attrition, you may also want to provide descriptive statistics that demonstrate that your final sample reflects the larger group from which it's drawn. You can also rule out bias by comparing the actors you excluded to those in your sample, and show they are similar along relevant dimensions.

Dependent variables. One of the ways to enhance your Methods section's clarity is to use a consistent ordering structure. Variables are typically presented in the order they are described in an equation. Thus, with rare exceptions, you should describe your dependent variables first (even if they aren't main characters), the independent variables that test your hypotheses next, and your control variables (the ensemble) last. If you have multiple dependent variables, list them in the same order they appear in your hypotheses. You can also enhance clarity by identifying the variable name using italics, bolding or some other highlighting technique. Don't make your readers hunt for them. Define the measure, and then provide the additional detail that explains how you constructed the measure.

For example, if you had to transform or manipulate the raw data to create your final measure (e.g., standardizing multiple indictors and combining them into an index, or adding a decay function to a measure that accumulates events over time), walk the reader through the steps so that they understand what you did and provide an example so that they can do the same thing in their own studies. If you are using a scale or index, describe the items and dimensions, and provide the relevant statistics to demonstrate their construct validity and reliability. If this is a new measure, readers will require more information confirming the measure's reliability and construct validity; it's also helpful to include the actual items in an appendix. If you are using a measure someone else developed, make sure you cite where it comes from and explain why it's a good measure to use. If your measure was manually coded by raters, describe the procedure (including a basic description of the raters), explain how you assured reliability, and provide the relevant statistics. If there are other popular alternatives for your measure that you also tried, you can either note the results in a footnote here or discuss it in the robustness tests section of your Results. You enhance your credibility if you can anticipate your readers' questions and provide answers at the point their questions are most likely to arise, or at least note the answers are forthcoming.

Independent variables. The most effective way to order your independent variables is to start with the main characters and then list the supporting characters, listing them in the order they first appear in the hypotheses. All the other issues I described above for presenting your dependent variables also apply to presenting your independent variables.

Control variables. List your control variables in the same order they will appear in the tables. If you are controlling for different kinds of issues that you can group together, organize them by topic (e.g., industry-level controls, firm-level controls, governance characteristics, big five personality traits, etc.). Reviewers are increasingly sensitive to the risks that arise from including unnecessary controls (Atinc, Simmering & Kroll, 2012), so for each control variable it helps to clearly describe the measure and explain why you needed to control for it, preferably with a supporting reference. "Because all my good results go away if I don't include it" isn't an acceptable justification.

Analysis method. The final part of the Methods section typically describes your analytical approach. Clearly describe the analytical approach you used (e.g., MANOVA, hierarchical linear modeling, random effects regression, negative binomial regression, etc.), including the name and version of the software employed and the specific commands run (e.g., we employed random effects regression using the *xtreg* command in STATA 16.0, and controlled for serial correlation by calculating robust standard errors). Different algorithms make different assumptions, and these can change over versions of the same software, as well as across different programs. Providing this information makes it easier to assess your findings and enhances your credibility because it shows you took the appropriate steps.

In addition to identifying the statistical tool used, identify the assumptions that make it appropriate for analyzing your data. This enhances the three Cs, and statistical conclusion validity. If there are specific choices you made about distributions, link functions, etc., with the analytic approach, explain your choices and justify why they are appropriate. If there are tests (e.g., the Hausman test, Hansen's J test, etc.) used to determine the right approach to employ, state what the results of that test were to help justify your choice. Finally, if you used multiple analytical methods to test different hypotheses, describe them all. If you also considered alternative methods, you can mention them here in a footnote, in the robustness tests section, or in an appendix if the description is extensive. If you are going to address alternative approaches in the robustness tests section, foreshadow that here so the reader knows it's coming.

RESULTS SECTION

Purposes

The Results section is where the falling action occurs, and you unravel the knot you tied in the preceding sections. It *describes* the results of your hypothesis tests, and whether your hypotheses were supported; it *interprets* the effect sizes and practical importance of your findings; it *explores* potential reasons behind unexpected findings, which can lead to new theoretical insights in the Discussion section; it *confirms* the robustness of your findings to a variety of validity threats; and it *considers* other issues and questions using post hoc analyses.

Challenges in Writing the Results Section

Completeness. Just as you needed to put yourself in the reader's chair to provide all the information they need to assess your methods, you must also do so with respect to what readers need to assess the veracity of your results and understand their implications. Thus, the major challenges are once again mind reading, showing as well as telling, and motion and pacing.

Readers will want to expeditiously rule out the most routine issues, so provide them with the basic analyses (e.g., variance inflation factors [VIFs] and the condition number to rule out collinearity) and data (e.g., descriptive statistics) they need to do so. When presenting data such as descriptive statistics, make sure you present them in easily digestible and interpretable forms. At a minimum you should provide a table that includes means and standard deviations for the untransformed versions of your measures (e.g., if you transformed total assets into its natural log, just use total assets) and the correlations among each measure. This makes it easier to get a better sense of what your data looks like.

You may also provide other descriptive statistics that are interesting and help provide insight into your context. For example, in my study, "The role of power and politics in the repricing of executive options," Harald Fischer, Jim Wade and I (Pollock et al., 2002) provided descriptive statistics to show that when CEOs' stock options were repriced (i.e., their "strike" prices were lowered, making it easier for them to make money on the option) the market was not down (the primary justification for repricing the CEOs' options), and that the vast majority of CEOs still would have been "in the money" at the end of the year, even without the repricing. This helped rule out the stated explanations for most repricings.

In addition to providing diagnostic information, make sure you clearly test all your hypotheses and state whether they are supported, partially supported or not supported. This seems basic, but you'd be surprised how often it's hard to tell which hypothesis is being tested, and what the outcome was. Provide tables illustrating all your primary results, and graph all significant interactions. You cannot test interaction hypotheses by assessing the direction and significance of the coefficients alone. Another good habit is to include the coefficient and exact p-value for each hypothesized relationship in the text of your paper when discussing the hypothesis test (e.g., $\beta = .78$, $p = .012$). That way readers don't have to stop and flip to your table to try and find the result, disrupting your readers' focus and the Results section's pacing.

Clarity. This section is where you untie the knot so it's necessary to help readers keep track of your findings. However, findings patterns can become complex, particularly if you have a lot of hypotheses and/or there are multiple tests for each hypothesis with a mix of support. In addition, it has been a while since readers encountered Hypothesis 1, and they may not remember exactly what it was. The biggest inhibitors of clarity, then, are the cadence of sentences and paragraphs, the fat suit, and failing to show as well as tell.

One way to enhance the clarity of your findings is to consider the cadence of this section and use a repetitive structure when presenting your results. For each hypothesis test, begin the paragraph by restating the hypothesis (e.g., "Hypothesis 1 argued that ..."), so readers are reminded what it was. Then clearly identify which table and model or models in the table test the hypothesis (e.g., "Model 2 in Table 3 tests this hypothesis"). Next, describe the test's results (including the coefficient value and p-value, as I noted above[2]). If different model specifications provide different results, clearly note this and say what each suggests (e.g., "Although the moderating effect of network size is positive and significant at $p = .012$ when entered by itself in Model 3, it is only significant at $p = .07$ when all the interactions are included in the fully saturated Model 7"). If you decide to discuss some alternative robustness or other tests you conducted, state what you did and what you found. You should also provide examples of effect sizes, or the practical effects of the independent variable on the dependent variable. For example, in our study, "How much prestige is enough? Assessing the value of multiple types of high-status affiliates for young firms" (Pollock, Chen, Jackson & Hambrick, 2010), my colleagues and I used our regression models to estimate how much the market valuation of newly-public firms increased with the addition of each type of high-status affiliate (executives, directors, venture capitalists and underwriters) the firm had when it went public.

Finally, make sure you clearly state whether these results support, partially support or fail to support the hypothesis. Employ the same structure for each hypothesis. If the findings are complex, and/or post hoc tests reveal some additional wrinkles, such as specific boundary conditions, you can enhance clarity by including a table at the end of the results section that summarizes your hypotheses and the results.

You'll also enhance clarity by discussing your hypotheses in order. The one exception to this is if testing the hypotheses in order requires the reader to jump back and forth between different tables. In that case you may want to discuss all the hypotheses tested in one table first, before moving on to the next table. Of course, you should also consider whether it makes more sense to reorder your hypotheses when you develop them so that this doesn't become an issue.

In addition, how you organize and show your findings in tables affects clarity. Clarity is greatest when you list all your independent variables in the

---

[2]   Some journals also request confidence intervals. Make sure you are aware of and follow the journal's reporting norms.

same order you present them in the Methods section, keep them in the same order across tables, and label them clearly and consistently. Don't use the abbreviations you gave them in your dataset; spell them out so readers don't have to guess. Include just the control variables in your first model, then add all the independent variables in the second model, followed by additional models testing your interactions, etc. This makes it easier to follow your results. You can put all your results testing the hypotheses either above or below your control variables. I prefer below, because I think it's easier to follow, but tastes vary. Finally, make sure you've clearly labeled your tables with good descriptive names, note what symbols you are using to indicate different significance levels at the bottom, and clearly label the columns if you have different dependent variables in the same table. And if your sample size varies across models, make sure you list the N for each model, as well.

Credibility. Readers also must trust that you've done everything correctly, and that you've thought about and ruled out alternative explanations. They can't do that unless you tell them you addressed the issues and show as well as tell them what you did. Don't just consider coefficients' positive/negative signs and p-values. Show them that you understand what your results really mean by calculating effect sizes and showing the practical implications of your results. Find some way to convert probabilities and percentages into meaningful numbers, and interpret them so that your readers understand what they imply. Even a small effect size can have big implications (Cortina & Landis, 2009). You also demonstrate your credibility by engaging in best practices for interpreting your results. For example, plot all significant interactions and test their slopes for significance. When testing interaction hypotheses, base your claims about hypothesis support on the graphs, not just the coefficients in the tables. Assess whether the slopes are significant; don't just guess based on how the graph looks. Further, make sure you determine inflection points for curvilinear relationships and the points where the lines cross for interactions, and assess whether they are within the feasible range of your data.

Readers will also have more faith in your abilities if you conduct and report robustness tests and explain how they rule out alternative explanations and validity threats. This may involve using different measures, different analytical approaches, assessing endogeneity, decomposing indices or conducting other comparisons to show that one index component isn't driving all your results. More journals are starting to use supplemental online files for these kinds of analyses. Even if you put the actual models in an online file, make sure you discuss the findings in your paper. Your results may also yield unexpected findings or suggest other interesting issues you can explore. Addressing this in a post hoc analyses section shows that you haven't engaged in HARKing (hypothesizing after the results are known) (Hollenbeck & Wright, 2017).

Results Section Structure

Descriptive statistics. The first sub-section typically presents and discusses the descriptive statistics. It is comprised of one to two paragraphs that introduce the descriptive statistics table, highlight anything unusual and explain how to interpret values readers might misinterpret. This is also where you comment on the correlations and report the results of the collinearity tests, if you haven't done it in the methods section, as well as any other descriptive statistics that you decide to provide. Try to keep it succinct, though, because you are just delaying the unveiling of your hypothesis tests.

Hypothesis tests. In this section you provide the primary results and your conclusions regarding each hypothesis. Try to use simpler sentence structures and, as I discussed under clarity, take each hypothesis in order, restate the hypothesis, relay the relevant results and say whether and to what extent it's supported. You may do some additional robustness or other tests here, but it may be better to save them for a subsequent section if they are longer and will disrupt your motion and pacing.

Robustness tests. You often need to establish the robustness of your findings in the face of different validity threats or alternative explanations. If the discussion is short (e.g., "We re-ran our analyses operationalizing firm size as sales and total employees, instead of total assets, and the results were unchanged") they may be intermixed with the hypothesis test discussions, or included as footnotes in the Methods or hypothesis tests sections. If they require more than a sentence or two, however, or if there are several issues to address, it's generally better to include them in a separate robustness tests section following the hypotheses tests. This allows you to deal with them in a more systematic way and avoid bogging down the flow of other sections. This section is typically organized by threat; state what the issue is, why it's a potential problem, what tests you did to address it, what the results are, and what the implications are for interpreting your findings. Save assessing any theoretical implications or limitations they suggest for the Discussion section.

Post hoc analyses. Post hoc analyses differ from robustness tests, which assess the veracity of your results. This section is where you explore unexpected and non-findings further, or consider relationships you didn't hypothesize about but that are interesting and worthwhile to explore. They often emerge from the primary analysis, or result from reviewer comments and requests. For each post hoc analysis, clearly explain the reason for the analysis, what you did and what you found. Depending on the issue, you may need to provide the same kinds of detail you did for the hypothesis tests. You may or may not include results tables, depending on the extensiveness of this section and what you find. Again, these analyses may also be candidates for an online supplement. You can foreshadow any relevant theoretical implications these analyses suggest for the Discussion section, but don't get into detailed assessments of their theoretical implications here.

Although the Methods and Results sections are more descriptive than the Introduction and Theory and Hypotheses development sections, they still play a critical role in persuading readers that your empirical analyses actually answer the research questions you've set for yourself by explaining and justifying your choices, and being as complete, clear and credible as possible. By the end of the results the knot should be untied, and the stage should be set for the dénouement in the Discussion section.

8. Discussion section

Marta Geletkanycz and Ben Tepper (2012) employed a clever hook in opening their *AMJ* "From the Editors" column on Discussions:

Afterthought (noun):
1. a reflection after an act
2. something secondary or expedient
3. an action or thought not originally intended

By the time authors begin to craft a Discussion section, a long, sometimes arduous journey has been traveled. Study design and execution are normally well advanced, and the prospect of submission for publication consideration looms large. Thus, it is perhaps not surprising many authors view the Discussion as a perfunctory exercise—a final, obligatory hurdle to be overcome with dispatch so as not to delay a manuscript's transition to "under review" status. In approaching their Discussion as a technical formality (i.e., an afterthought in the mold of definitions 2) and 3) rather than as a forum in which to explore more deeply the significance of their work (definition 1), authors forego a number of valuable opportunities.

I really like this opening because it succinctly captures the challenges facing the Discussion section.

There are two primary reasons authors so frequently blow off the Discussion section and treat it as perfunctory, or "something secondary or expedient." First, authors are frequently fried by the time they get to it, and tired of working on the paper. You can't really write the Discussion until you've collected and analyzed your data, drafted the rest of the paper and have a good handle on your results. By then you just want to get it out of your cognitive space and move on to other things. Second, it's hard to end stories well, and many authors don't really know what to say. You've already spent a ton of time laying out your theory, talking about what you expect, and discussing your results and how you've tortured the data to make sure your findings are robust. Now, it seems, you're supposed to do it all again. That's why so many Discussion sections often end up as results rehashes that conclude with a half-hearted call for future research on the subject. Combined, these reasons make the Discussion section the hardest part of the paper to write well.

However, if you can gird your loins, dig deep and make the effort, a good Discussion section can also be the source of your most insightful theoretical contributions. Because you now have results to work with, you can place them, along with speculations about the implications of your unexpected results and post hoc analyses, back within the broader conversation. In this chapter I explain the Discussion section's purposes, offer a playbook for how to approach and make the most of it and provide some guidelines for how to structure it effectively. I discuss the differences in qualitative and theory article Discussions in Chapter 9.

PURPOSES

The Discussion section is your story's dénouement—it's where you make sense of what happened during the falling action and bring your story to a close. Your main character (or characters)—the hero or protagonist—is in a different place than where it started. The main character's story isn't over, but this part of their journey has come to an end. If you have multiple main characters who to this point have been on the same journey, you may discover that their paths now diverge, and they will take separate journeys going forward. Thus, as Geletkanycz and Tepper (2012) noted, the Discussion section is both an ending and a new beginning. As such, it fulfills a variety of purposes.

First, the Discussion section is where you *remind* readers what your research question was and *answer* the question by summarizing what you found in the Results section. It's where you *place* your findings in the broader context of the conversation you constructed in the Introduction and Theory and Hypotheses sections, and describe how the conversation has changed as a result of what you found. The Discussion is also where you *speculate* about unexpected findings (i.e., non-significant relationships and relationships that were in the opposite direction) in ways that create new theoretical insights and directions for future inquiry. And it's where you *identify* the practical implications of your theory and findings, *acknowledge* your study's limitations and their implications for future research and finally *conclude* the story. Thus, a strong Discussion section really is a reflection after the act. Weak Discussion sections, however, share several common flaws.

TYPICAL DISCUSSION SECTION FLAWS

Geletkanycz and Tepper (2012) identified three common Discussion section flaws: (1) rehashing results, (2) meandering and (3) overreaching. To this list I add a fourth: superficial interpretations.

Rehashing results. Probably the most common flaw in weak Discussion sections is that they do little more than rehash the study's results for the second or third time, rather than drawing implications from them, linking them back to broader theoretical contributions, or identifying practical implications. As I noted above, it's important to remind readers what your research question was and answer the question by summarizing the results, but that shouldn't be the sum total of what you do in the Discussion section.

Superficial interpretations. Discussions that primarily rehash results do frequently make some half-hearted attempts to draw insights from the findings, but they tend to be superficial rather than reflective. The authors usually don't get beyond restating their general theoretical arguments from their hypothesis development, they fail to tie these arguments back to the limitations in the broader conversation they identified in the Introduction, and they don't discuss the implications of their non- and surprise findings for the conversation moving forward.

Meandering. Discussions that meander are also usually superficial, but in a different way. Instead of simply repeating their earlier arguments, these Discussions go all over the place, spending a sentence or two touching on topics and introducing theories that have not made an appearance in the article until now. They try to go wide but fail to go deep enough into any one topic to offer genuine insight. Thus, they are unfocused and don't take the reader to an ending with a satisfying sense of resolution.

Overreaching. Finally, some Discussions overreach, claiming contributions to the literature that far outstrip what their data and findings can support. Overreaching can go hand in hand with meandering, as authors try to show their study's wide-ranging implications, or it can be more focused but still involve far too much hand waving and bluster. Overreaching often occurs when the authors have completed their study, and perhaps received some friendly reviews, only to find that what they've "discovered" isn't really that novel or interesting. In attempting to save their study, or in response to comments about "obviousness," or "what's new here?" they furiously try to make their study seem more novel and "important" than it actually is.

So, what does a good Discussion section do? It articulates your study's theoretical contributions to the conversation you are joining. It also discusses other methodological contributions your study makes, if any, and its practical implications. At the same time, it demonstrates you are cognizant of your study's limitations, and of the future research directions your findings, and these limitations, suggest. Finally, it brings your story to an effective conclusion.

THEORETICAL CONTRIBUTIONS

Go back to the beginning. One lament I've heard from people who struggle with the theoretical implications portion of the Discussion section is that beyond summarizing their results, they don't know where to go with it. One answer is to go back to the beginning—specifically, the Introduction. The Discussion section should match the Introduction with respect to the research question posed, and by answering the questions "What do we know, what don't we know, and so what?" and "What will we learn?" It may have been some time since you read your Introduction, so reread it and refresh your memory about what you promised readers early on that made them interested enough to get to this point. It's now time to deliver the goods.

Your Introduction identified several contributions your study was going to make. You can use these to structure the theoretical implications sub-section of your Discussion. That way, you can make sure they match. All too often the theoretical contributions in the Discussion, particularly Discussions that meander, don't match the contributions identified in the Introduction. If you have more theoretical contributions in the Discussion than in the Introduction, either you need to revise the Introduction or drop tangential contributions in the Discussion. If you have fewer theoretical contributions than the Introduction, either you need to add contributions to the Discussion or drop them from the Introduction. You can tie these contributions back to the conversation identified earlier by talking about them in the same way you problematized them—show how your results address issues of incompleteness, inadequacy or incommensurability, and how you are shifting or creating consensus.

Remember what scholars do. The Methods and Results sections present the whats, whens and wheres. Your Discussion section should return readers to the main focus of the Theory and Hypotheses section: the *whys*. That's how you avoid just rehashing results. However, you don't want to offer superficial interpretations by simply repeating your hypotheses. While you need to revisit your theoretical arguments for the supported hypotheses, and briefly summarize them to remind readers what your new theory is, you also need to tie them back to, and show how they change or advance, the conversation you identified. Within the conversation there may also be alternative explanations for your findings that you'll have to address. If you've already ruled some out empirically or logically, remind the reader of that. Address any other potential alternative explanations that you can, and for the ones you can't address, discuss the implications for future research.

You also need to discuss your unsupported hypotheses. If the results were not significant, speculate about the reasons why. The reasons could be theoretical, or empirical features of your measures or context. Even the empirical explanations can create boundary conditions for theorizing about the phenomenon. For example, there might be characteristics of your study's time period (e.g., social norms, a recession, or regulatory actions like Sarbanes–Oxley) or cultural context (e.g., a US sample, or a Chinese sample) that affect the relationships you studied or mechanisms at work. You should also discuss your surprise findings, why you think they occurred, and the implications they have for theory and future research. Your post hoc analyses also may have yielded some potentially novel theoretical insights. Speculate about them and their implications for the theoretical conversation going forward. In all these instances, move the discussion up a level of abstraction from your specific findings to more general theoretical claims—discuss how they apply to other contexts besides your own, and/or what boundary conditions your context may put on your theorizing. Finally, use examples and interpret the implications of the effect sizes presented in your results to show readers what your results mean; don't just tell them.

OTHER CONTRIBUTIONS AND IMPLICATIONS

Methodological contributions. In addition to theoretical contributions, your study likely makes other contributions. For example, you may have created a new measure, developed a new methodological approach, or employed a method used in other fields that hasn't been employed in your field. If you make a methodological advance, highlight it. Review past measures' or approaches' limitations, including how they may have led to inappropriate theoretical conclusions; identify how your approach addresses these limitations; and discuss the implications for future research, and how it can employ your approach or measure.

Practical implications. Even if you don't make a methodological contribution, your study should have some implications for practice or public policy. Identifying the practical implications of your study demonstrates its relevance and importance. Most journals in business disciplines, particularly management, expect you to give some attention to your study's practical significance in the Discussion. *AMJ* editor Lazlo Tihanyi (2020: 329) has noted, however, that "this section in many recent articles has been reduced to a short paragraph that often repeats the required theoretical implications in more practical terms. Moreover, practical implications often address short-term profit motives rather than socially responsible management practices with long-term benefits for the broader society." A useful, practical implications section could employ Davis's (1971) index of the interesting but apply it to non-academics' interests. Implications that are somewhat non-obvious or counter-intuitive may be particularly interesting. Consider your study's implications for how managers actually do their jobs, and also consider the implications for other stakeholders beyond the actors you immediately studied (e.g., customers, investors, the government) and what your findings mean for them. As Tihanyi (2020) advocated, this can help you identify longer-term implications and benefits that are *important*, as well as interesting.

For example, Johnson and colleagues' (2006) cutthroat competition study, discussed in Chapters 5 and 6, included an extensive section on the practical implications where they described several scenarios and the implications of different changes in reward structures. They also tied their discussion back to an earlier example about the challenges of intelligence sharing across federal agencies and changing entrenched reward structures, illustrating both the importance and interestingness of their study, and the life and death consequences that can result from their findings.

LIMITATIONS AND FUTURE RESEARCH

Limitations. As I discussed in Chapter 7, all studies have weaknesses, and you enhance your credibility when you acknowledge and show you tried to address them, when possible. The Discussion section is a useful place to do so. Ideally, you can acknowledge them but also demonstrate they aren't a big issue for your study. Any empirical evidence you can provide is better than pure logic and argumentation. If you addressed the issue earlier in the Methods or Results sections, remind readers of what you did. If you can do something that you haven't reported previously, now's the time to mention it. And if there isn't anything you can do empirically, making a logical argument for why the problem isn't a problem in your case is better than nothing at all. Don't be overly defensive, though. If it's an issue you can't address, then acknowledge that, discuss its implications for interpreting your findings, and suggest how future research can address it. For example, Johnson and colleagues (2006) identified five clear limitations that bounded their study based on the characteristics of their sample and their experimental design—using undergraduate participants, their task's generalizability, using only two time periods and ad hoc teams, conducting the study in a western culture only, and using a task that could affect the likelihood of cutthroat competition.

Future research. Your Discussion section should also highlight the future research directions your study suggests. These may result directly from your theoretical implications and contributions, your limitations, or more generally from your study's context, methods or elsewhere. Identifying future research directions is useful because they highlight avenues for additional contributions that you either intend to make yourself in subsequent work, or that others interested in the same topic can pursue. Make sure, however, that your suggestions for future research do more than signal "this is an issue a reviewer raised, we didn't want to/couldn't do it, so we'll say someone else should." Demonstrating viable future research directions inspired by your study makes your contribution more explicit.

CONCLUSION

Finally, you'll need to include at least a short paragraph at the end that brings your story to a close. Try to avoid just rehashing your results again or calling for future research. These are the most common kinds of conclusions (and I've written many such conclusions myself), but they're unsatisfying. Like

Linda Johanson (1994) suggested (as I mentioned in Chapter 2), return to your Introduction and end your story on a more elevated plane. Tie back to your research question somehow and show that the conversation is now in a different place than where it started. This is easy to say, and really hard to do. Huseyin Leblebici and his colleagues (1991: 359–360) provided an excellent example of what a good conclusion looks like:

> These conjectures return us to the questions we posed about how institutions change, and provide some tentative answers in broadcasting: Fringe players were instrumental in generating new practices; subsequent adoption and legitimation of their innovations by established players produced new patterns of transactions; and, these new organizations of the field transformed the new conventions into institutionalized practices by eroding the relevance of the previously core resources. Yet once institutionalized, the new institutions created new competitive pressures to seek alternatives outside their bounds. The cycles of transformations in the conventions, organization, and institutionalized practices in broadcasting show that institutional change is the product of endogenous forces that are associated with the historical evolution of the field itself. Though they are products of practical consciousness, institutions produce unintended consequences that define the ends and shape the means by which future economic and political interests are determined and pursued. This is the duality of all institutional practices.

While they reviewed some of their findings, they did so in the context of tying them back to their research question and answering their more general question about how institutions change. Beginning with the sentence "The cycles of transformations …" Leblebici and colleagues did exactly what Johanson suggested, ending their story on a more elevated plane. The final sentence, "This is the duality of all institutional practices" was a fantastic declarative statement that brought their study's journey to a satisfying end.

DISCUSSION SECTION STRUCTURE

The preceding lays out the Discussion's major sections: recapping the study's purpose, research question and results; theoretical implications; methodological (if any) contributions and practical implications; limitations and future research directions; and conclusion. Many studies follow this Discussion section structure. However, while in almost all cases the Discussion opens with a recap of the study's purpose and research question, and at least a brief summary of the major findings, the components of the other sub-sections may be combined in different ways.

For example, in our study on the co-evolution of reputation and status (Pollock et al., 2015), mentioned in Chapters 3 and 4, we gave only a very brief summary of our findings, interweaving the more specific recap of each main set of findings with their theoretical and practical implications. In each sub-section we summarized a set of findings and then discussed their more general theoretical implications, ending with a practical example. We used the VC firm Benchmark Capital for two of the examples, first using their early experience to illustrate the importance of building a reputation for performance rather than just chasing high-status affiliations, and later using them to illustrate how associating with big hits (i.e., blockbuster IPOs) affected the trajectories of their reputation and status differently over time. To illustrate how lower-status actors can still benefit even if high-status actors get more credit, we used Elevation Partners, once dubbed the "the world's dumbest VC investor," and how they benefitted when their early investment in Facebook was later valued at $1.3 billion dollars. We described some future research directions along with our discussions of the theoretical and practical implications of our findings, and when discussing our limitations.

Johnson and colleagues (2006) also employed a somewhat different structure in their Discussion section. They started with a section that interspersed the recap of their findings with some theoretical implications, and they followed it with a longer than typical practical implications section. They separated their limitations and future research directions into distinct sub-sections, and then closed with a long "concluding remarks" section that introduced additional theoretical implications before concluding the paper. Although non-traditional, it was very effective in highlighting both the theoretical and practical importance of their study.

Deviating from established templates has risks as well as benefits. Reviewers have certain expectations, and non-standard formats and approaches violate them. This can create negative reactions, even if reviewers don't know what exactly is bothering them. I cannot say how Johnson and colleagues' Discussion came to be, but our Discussion structure evolved from the more standard format in our initial submission to its final shape over the course of the review and revision process. Like the old story about boiling a frog in a pot of water by turning the heat up bit by bit so it doesn't notice the change, it may be easier to adopt unique structures incrementally, as reviewers start to buy into and become committed to your manuscript.

This chapter concludes my discussion of the main parts of a quantitative empirical article. However, that is only one kind of article we write. While the Introduction's role is consistent across article types, qualitative and theory articles differ substantially in the other sections. I discuss these differences in Chapter 9.

9. What's different about qualitative articles, theory articles and book chapters

My family were not world travelers. The only time I ever left the US while growing up was for a fishing trip to Canada when I was thirteen. Even then, we flew into and out of the lake from Ely, Minnesota on a pontoon plane, so I never met a Canadian. My first "real" international trips as an adult were again to Canada, for the Academy of Management annual meetings in Vancouver and Toronto. My next international trip was to Ireland, for a vacation with my wife. All of these trips were to places where English was (mostly) the predominant language, so there was some level of familiarity. At the same time, I continually noticed differences, large and small, that reminded me I wasn't in the US.

If your experience primarily is with writing quantitative empirical articles, trying to write a qualitative or theory article will be like visiting a foreign country where you might speak the language, but so much else is different and just a little off-kilter. And if your primary experience is with qualitative empirical studies, the last four chapters may have felt like reading a travel guide about a country you haven't been to but might visit some day. Some of the chapters, like Chapter 5 on Introductions, are universal, and apply equally to whatever type of article you are writing. Others, like Chapter 7 on Methods and Results, may bear little resemblance to the world you know.

In this chapter I focus on what's different about writing effective qualitative empirical and theory articles, compared to quantitative empirical articles. I will also spend a little time talking about additional differences between journal articles and book chapters. I haven't given qualitative and theory articles a separate chapter because I think they are less important or "easier" than quantitative studies, and thus don't require as much discussion. Although my research is primarily quantitative, I have published multiple qualitative and theory papers, and have found that in some ways qualitative empirical and theory articles are harder to write effectively than quantitative articles. I decided to focus on qualitative and theory articles separately because I believe that although there are many aspects common to writing all three types of articles, there are also some important differences. I want to highlight these differences. I also hope that this chapter provides those of you who don't do quantitative research with a little touch of home in this section of the book—kind of like an American finding a McDonald's or Starbucks (an unfortunate comment on what makes for American cultural familiarity, I know) in an otherwise very foreign land.

WHAT'S DIFFERENT ABOUT QUALITATIVE ARTICLES

Inductive vs. Deductive Research

To understand what's unique about qualitative articles, you need to first understand the difference between inductive and deductive research. I will not go on a long philosophical discourse here; but in a nutshell, deductive research uses theory to develop testable hypotheses, and then compares the hypothesized relationships to empirical data (i.e., the "real" world) to assess whether the hypotheses are supported by empirical reality or not. Thus, deductive research goes from the general to the specific, and is "theory testing," because the theory and hypotheses are largely developed before the empirical data is analyzed and the hypotheses are tested, as discussed in Chapter 6.

Inductive research, in contrast, starts with empirical data about a specific phenomenon and analyzes it to discern more generalizable inferences. Scholars induct more generalized theory from the specific situations and individuals they study. Inductive research is therefore "theory building," because the theory does not exist before the data is analyzed; rather, it emerges from the data analysis.

Although I have seen a few inductive quantitative studies (Feldman, Ozcan & Reichstein [2019] and Guldiken, Mallon, Fainshmidt, Judge & Clark [2019] are recent examples), they are relatively rare; and while I've heard qualitative scholars claim you can use qualitative data for theory testing, these claims aren't accompanied by examples. Thus, for the most part quantitative research is deductive theory testing, and qualitative research is inductive theory building. These fundamental differences in how the research design creates new insights also affect how quantitative and qualitative articles are written. To make these differences more concrete, I will use the article "Assessing creativity in Hollywood pitch meetings: Evidence for a dual process model of creativity judgements" by Kim Elsbach and Rod Kramer (2003) to illustrate the unique differences in qualitative articles. This study won an *AMJ Best Paper* award and explored how experts (Hollywood executives and agents) use different cues to assess the creative potential of unknown screenwriters by associating them with different creative and uncreative prototypes. Keep in mind, however, that this is just one example used for illustrative purposes.

Qualitative studies can vary widely as a function of the qualitative methods employed.

Storytelling Structure Differences

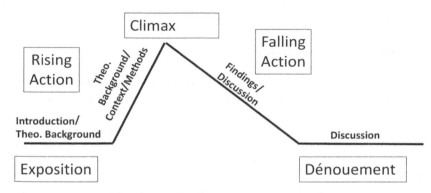

Figure 9.1   Proportional Freytag's Pyramid for qualitative articles

AMJ associate editors Tima Bansal and Kevin Corley (2012) wrote a "From the Editors" column about the differences between qualitative and quantitative articles. Their discussion highlights some of the structural differences. First, they noted that qualitative papers have a shorter front end because you aren't building your theoretical arguments up front. Although, as in quantitative studies, the front end establishes the research question's importance, situates the study within an ongoing conversation, and highlights what the conversation is missing and where it needs to go, it does not then develop theoretical arguments or hypotheses. Instead, it turns to the research context and methods employed, followed by a long Findings section where the data analysis is presented in narrative form (with accompanying data tables and figures) followed by a Discussion—which is also longer than in quantitative studies—where the new theory is developed and tied back to the ongoing conversation. Thus, when mapping the storytelling structure using Freytag's Pyramid (see Figure 9.1), the exposition is about the same length as in quantitative studies, but the rising action will be taller and steeper, and the falling action will be much longer, because the theoretical model is the outcome of the falling action, not part of tying the knot. The dénouement will also be longer, as explaining what the unraveling means for the literature and the new paths the main and supporting characters will traverse requires more space. As I discussed in Chapter 3, qualitative studies are generally longer than quantitative studies; however, most good journals recognize this and provide qualitative authors more leeway when it comes to page limits.

Elsbach and Kramer's article (2003) reflects this structure. Their front end (Introduction and Theoretical Background) was about 15 percent of the paper, the Methods were approximately 20 percent, the Findings (including tables) were 50 percent, and the Discussion was approximately 15 percent of the paper. These percentages roughly match the percentages I gave in Chapter 3 for qualitative studies.

Front End Differences

The Introduction is basically the same as for quantitative studies because it fulfills the same purposes. The one significant difference is that qualitative studies typically also justify why using qualitative methods are appropriate. Whereas quantitative scholars rarely if ever have to justify why they are using quantitative methods, qualitative scholars more frequently have to either explain why sufficient theory doesn't already exist about the topic, and thus why qualitative methods are appropriate, or they have to explain why what they are studying (e.g., processes that are hard to observe, or that play out over months, years or decades; decision making processes that cannot be captured quantitatively for a variety of reasons) is difficult to study quantitatively.

The biggest front end difference is that there is no hypothesis development. Thus, the Theoretical Background section is primarily used to further establish the research question's importance and set the stage for the empirical analysis. In contrast to quantitative studies, the theoretical background section is also generally written later in the process, because the theoretical framing, and even the research question, can change over the course of the qualitative study, depending on what the data collection and analysis reveal. Thus, the literatures used to set up the study may also evolve, and rather than predicting the study's outcome this section foreshadows what you eventually found. Getting the balance right on how much to say and how much literature to review can be challenging, though I've found that if you review the literature too extensively then reviewers think that the theory is driving your analysis, rather than reflecting what you found. If you say too little, and fail to position your study and its contribution clearly, your study is perceived as "too broad." Whereas quantitative studies have more latitude to be broader but shallower in their insights, qualitative studies tend to be more focused, and thus are narrower but deeper.

Elsbach and Kramer's (2003) Introduction was consistent with the guidelines I described in Chapter 5. It's interesting to note, though, that they didn't justify the appropriateness of their qualitative methodology in the Introduction. Rather, they critiqued the creativity literature's heavy reliance on lab studies in their Theoretical Background section (which they called Existing Theory and Research on Creativity Assessment), and then made the case for using a qualitative approach in the beginning of the section describing their research context and method. Overall, they kept the background section pretty short and focused. The creativity literature is vast, and they only discussed creativity assessment, primarily emphasizing the limitations in the prior work that their study addressed.

Methods Differences

Like quantitative methods sections, qualitative methods sections must also strive for the three Cs of completeness, clarity and credibility that I discussed in Chapter 7 (Zhang & Shaw, 2012). However, Bansal and Corley (2012) noted that qualitative methods sections differ in significant ways from quantitative methods sections. Whether in the Data and Methods section or in a separate section dedicated to the research context, qualitative studies must provide a clear and detailed description of the research context that typically goes beyond what quantitative studies provide. Doing so is important, since understanding the nuances of the context is key to interpreting the data and findings.

Further, although both quantitative and qualitative studies have a variety of methods available, it usually takes more explanation to justify the qualitative methodological approach employed because there are fewer standardized and widely understood labels and analytical tools in qualitative research than there are in quantitative research, providing quantitative scholars with a somewhat more convenient shorthand. Qualitative Methods sections also reveal more of the researcher's personal journey. It's common that as the research unfolds the research question evolves or changes, the researchers seek out other types of actors for interviews, and they collect different data than they originally anticipated. The researcher features prominently throughout the narrative—using lots of first person pronouns, describing all the twists and turns they took, and the reasons they took them. Qualitative methods sections also spend more time describing how the researchers analyzed their data.

To understand why these descriptions are important requires understanding the way qualitative scholars establish trustworthiness. Lincoln and Guba (1985) laid out four criteria necessary to establish the trustworthiness of qualitative findings: (1) Credibility, (2) Transferability, (3) Dependability and (4) Confirmability.[1] Credibility is based on whether the researcher gives voice to

---

[1]   Also see Pratt, Kaplan and Whittington (2020) for a discussion of the issue, and the dangers of foisting a quantitative, deductive perspective on qualitative, inductive research.

the different perspectives they encountered, and enhances the likelihood readers will perceive that the findings accurately represent the data. Transferability means the researcher demonstrates they don't simply accept assumptions that the people and context they are studying must represent the population; rather, they question how similar other contexts are to their context. Dependability refers to the consistency of the findings. Variations across data sources or accounts should be due to contextual factors, not the inquiry process. Thus, researchers must account for how the study itself, and their own interactions with respondents, might introduce inconsistencies by influencing behaviors. Finally, Confirmability refers to the neutrality of the findings. Reflecting on how credible the interviewees—or your own—perceptions are, and showing that you can triangulate on them through other sources, such as different individuals, media accounts or primary documents, enhances both your credibility and the confirmability of your findings. Thus, because there are no statistical tests to rely on, qualitative studies put a greater premium on showing the data itself and the aggregation and analytical processes employed.

Elsbach and Kramer started their Data and Methods section with a detailed description of how Hollywood pitch meetings work. It is also here where, in a somewhat unusual but effective move, they provided the rationale for their methodological approach. Without revealing their informants' identities, they provided lots of detail about who their informants were—which helps assess the credibility and confirmability of their findings. They also provided details about the number of interviews they conducted, how they collected their data, the questions they asked, and the waves in which their data were collected. They observed over two dozen pitches, and they described how many were live, how many were taped and how many were recreated by their informants (who had delivered the pitches to studios). Finally, they described how Kim Elsbach sat in on screenwriting classes where pitching was discussed, and described the archival data they collected (e.g., books written by screenwriters and producers). They also devoted considerable space to describing the four-stage process they used to analyze their data and the new insights that they developed at each stage of the analysis. They ended by describing their "member checking," demonstrating the credibility of their insights with their informants.

Results/Findings Differences

The starkest differences between writing qualitative and quantitative articles come in presenting the results of your analysis, typically referred to in qualitative studies as the Findings. This is because the Findings in qualitative studies are completely narrative, and you are revealing the model, typology or process along with the new theory it suggests, rather than using statistics to test a theoretical model you've already described. Bansal and Corley (2012) noted that the Findings section weaves two different narratives together, which they called the data narrative and the theory narrative. The data narrative is the story of what happens in your context. It develops your main and supporting theoretical characters within your context; they explained (p. 511):

> The data are needed to give the theory context, and the theory is needed to give the data meaning. Qualitative articles, thus, use current theory as the backdrop for interpreting the data, the data to provide the context and describe the phenomenon in-depth, and the emergent theory to expose the phenomenon in a new light.

Thus, in writing the Findings section you must pull the reader into your story, which can make the language and storytelling more complex than in quantitative results sections. Editing and focusing both stories can be a challenge as you try to figure out a data story that will capture and hold your reader's attention and a theory story that provides new theoretical insight and adds to the conversation.

Another difference is that in qualitative studies you need to "show" your data to a far greater degree than in quantitative studies. Because you are analyzing textual data, you must demonstrate that the themes you claim exist are actually there by providing multiple quotations illustrating them in both the body of your paper and in tables. The quotes in the body of the paper must also differ from the quotes in the table. No recycling. Otherwise readers may think you've just cherry-picked the one quote that supports the story you want to tell. Further, like the interwoven narratives, which you can structure in a variety of ways, the data tables don't have the standardized formats typical of results tables in quantitative studies. Thus, you have to decide how best to present your data. The figures accompanying the narrative also do not follow standard formats; and you can use a figure at the beginning of the Findings section to summarize your findings, which you then describe in detail, or at the end of the Findings section to pull your story together. This creates greater latitude for creativity, but also puts a greater burden on you to come up with something that will be meaningful and illuminating to others.

Using a baseball metaphor, Elsbach and Kramer (2003) began their Findings section by summarizing the two processes that "catchers" (those to whom the project is being "pitched") use to categorize the screenwriters pitching their ideas as creative or uncreative. The first process uses the pitcher's behavioral and physical cues to classify them into one of several well-known individual prototypes, and in the second process they use cues based on their interactions with the pitchers to employ relational prototypes.

Elsbach and Kramer then walked the reader through each process and the seven individual and two relational prototypes they inducted. They followed the same structure for both processes: summarize the conclusions, then walk readers through them. They didn't try to hide the ending for a "big reveal." In doing so they wove their theory into the narrative about their findings; for example, in several places they noted where the catchers' assumptions about what leads to more creativity contradicted what research has shown actually increases creative output. This broke up the "listy-ness" of going through all the prototypes and really enhanced their motion and pacing. They also summarized their findings again at the end of each process. In presenting their findings they used lots of quotes, and the quotes in the paper were different from the quotes in the tables. Their main results tables were clear and conveyed the essential information about each prototype. Their footnotes explaining each column were also useful to someone just skimming the article and trying to glean the main insights from the tables. They used a figure, which included clip art, at the end of their Findings section to help summarize their dual process model.

Discussion Differences

The Discussion section differences, although less pronounced than the Methods and Findings differences, are still significant. A qualitative article's Discussion section must fulfill all the same purposes described in Chapter 8. However, unlike in quantitative articles, where you develop most of the new theory before presenting the results, in qualitative studies you consolidate and develop the new theory in the Discussion based on your Findings. Thus, the Discussion needs to "move up" a level of abstraction from the Findings, and describe the study's implications in terms of your main and supporting characters' theoretical constructs, rather than in terms of the research context described in the Findings. This is why qualitative article Discussions tend to be longer.

You may provide some evidence of the generalizability of your new theory beyond your specific research context (often at the reviewers' behest), even though generalizability isn't the method's strength or purpose. It's typically a good practice to do this unbidden, as it enhances your trustworthiness, and your study's potential contribution, by demonstrating your theory's transferability to similar contexts. However, make sure you acknowledge any applicable boundary conditions, and avoid overclaiming the generalizability of your new theoretical insights. Finally, some qualitative studies, particularly those that have a somewhat more positivist orientation, may also provide a set of theoretical propositions to help summarize their new theoretical insights. These are not hypotheses (I'll discuss the difference in the next section on theory articles), and although uncommon they can be useful summarizing devices. I don't recommend including them just as a means of "legitimacy seeking," or to make your study seem more familiar to quantitative scholars, however. Only include them if you think it really helps readers understand your insights.

In their Discussion, Elsbach and Kramer (2003) restated their study's purpose and findings, but in more general theoretical rather than context-specific terms. They also described their theoretical contributions in more general terms, rather than in context-specific ways, and some of the theoretical issues they highlighted in their Findings (e.g., the catchers' inaccurate assumptions about enhancing creative output) were developed further here. They also related their Findings to some literatures they hadn't discussed previously—social judgment and impression management—suggesting the broader applicability of their insights. These additional theories also helped set up some of their practical implications, which they discussed more extensively than many studies do, and they finished by noting their study's limitations and with a nice concluding paragraph (other than their use of the phrase "present study") (p. 300):

> In his 1983 memoir about Hollywood, the legendary screenwriter William Goldman asserted that, when it came to picking hit ideas for movies, "Nobody knows nothing." The results of the present study suggest, to the contrary, that experts have well-developed perceptions about the prototypes of writers they believe are likely to produce creative ideas, as well as the kinds of cues that signal those prototypes. Being savvy to such judgmental processes, therefore, may make the difference between a mere pitch, and a hit.

Thus, qualitative empirical studies differ in significant ways from quantitative studies. I hope this section gives qualitative scholars a better understanding of where your quantitative counterparts are coming from, and also the confidence to avoid succumbing to pressures to make your studies more "familiar" to inflexible quantitative scholars. I also hope it gives quantitative scholars a better understanding of, and openness to, a "different land," so that you understand and accept qualitative articles on their own terms, rather than trying to force them through the prism of quantitative norms and expectations.

WHAT'S DIFFERENT ABOUT THEORY ARTICLES

The biggest difference between theory and empirical articles is, of course, that theory articles have no data. Thus, they include no Methods and Results sections. A key mistake many authors make, however, is assuming that theory articles are then just equivalent to the front end of a quantitative empirical paper. This is far from the case.

Former *Academy of Management Review*[2] editor Martin Kilduff (2006: 252) noted "The route to good theory leads not through gaps in the literature but through an engagement with problems in the world that you find personally interesting." As such, theory articles can serve a wide variety of purposes. At their best they present big ideas that can run ahead of empirical evidence (Kilduff, 2006); that is, they generate insights that are subsequently tested (such as Einstein's general theory of relativity, as described in Chapter 1) rather than based only on what's already been empirically tested, or is easily empirically tested. Their theoretical models explain relationships similar to those that empirical studies explore, but they also consider broader sets of relationships that are more complex than a single empirical study could handle. Theory articles are also often used to understand processes that are more difficult to study empirically, such as processes that operate at higher levels of analysis (e.g., the interorganizational field) or that are unobservable (e.g., psychological processes). Others use theory articles to develop typologies of a phenomena (e.g., Creary, Caza & Roberts, 2015), review and integrate a literature (e.g., Magee & Galinsky, 2008), clarify a construct that scholars have defined in different ways (Adler & Kwon, 2002), or introduce a new construct (Rindova et al., 2006). Finally, theory articles sometimes take an essay format, where the authors discuss some specific issue or set of issues. These essays stake out a position on a controversial issue or recognize some ill effect, such as the self-fulfilling nature of theory (Ferraro, Pfeffer & Sutton, 2005) or the negative effects of bad management theory (Ghoshal, 2005), or address some topic that is missing in the literature or is under-considered, such as the role of context in theorizing (Johns, 2006).

To illustrate the differences in theory and empirical articles I will use my article, "The shackles of CEO celebrity: Socio-cognitive and behavioral role constraints on 'star' leaders," that I co-authored with Jeff Lovelace, Jon Bundy and Don Hambrick (Lovelace et al., 2018). I chose this article because it's a hybrid that serves two different purposes; thus, it has a complex structure, which made it an interesting and challenging storytelling task.

This study was originally motivated by a phenomenon: Why does CEO celebrity create value for the CEO but not always for the firm, and why does the firm only benefit some of the time? To answer this question we developed a typology of celebrity CEO roles (creator, transformer, rebel and savior) into which the media casts celebrity CEOs, and then integrated the typology into a theoretical model explaining how a CEO's celebrity archetype "shackles" them into engaging only in the proscribed set of behaviors consistent with their celebrity archetype, and how this in turn affects firm performance. The

---

[2]   *AMR* is the premier theory article-only outlet in management.

shackling process is moderated by factors that increase the likelihood the CEO will perform true to type, and the relationship between the CEO's celebrity archetype and firm performance is mediated by both sociocognitive and behavioral factors, and is also moderated by whether or not the firms' internal and external environments are stable, or change. Thus, it's a very complex model that would be impossible to test in a single study. There are lots of difficult-to-observe pieces to the model, and the relationships are contextualized by moderators at multiple junctures, making it tough to test empirically, too. There is also currently a limited amount of empirical research on CEO celebrity, so the theory in this model definitely runs ahead of the empirical findings to date.

Storytelling Structure Differences

Because they serve a wider variety of purposes, theory articles also employ a wider variety of structures. They all have Introduction and Discussion sections, but whereas the Introduction is generally about the same length as for quantitative and qualitative empirical studies, the Discussion is shorter because you aren't recapping findings or linking your study back to the broader theoretical conversation in the same way—that's what the guts of your article has been about. Further, although they are similar to empirical article Introductions, one difference about theory article Introductions is that you have to very clearly define what is and isn't within the bounds of your theorizing, and then defend those boundaries during the review process, because you don't have data to create natural boundaries. Thus, you must specifically state what you are and aren't going to consider, and have reasons why and why not. The sections between the Introduction and Discussion employ a variety of structures, depending on the paper's objective. The section headings and their organization typically follow the structure and organization of the model you're developing. However, the main character constructs are generally defined early, and often get their own definition section or sections up front.

Applying Freytag's Pyramid (see Figure 9.2), the exposition is about the same length as in empirical papers, but like qualitative studies the rising action will usually be short and steep, and the theoretical deliverable—the model or argument developed in the article that unties the knot—is the long falling action. The dénouement is shorter than in both quantitative and qualitative articles because it doesn't require the same summarizing and linking functions as in empirical studies.

Because our "Shackles of CEO celebrity" article (hereafter I'll just call it the "shackles" article for brevity) developed both a typology and a theoretical model, I'll note the length of each separately. All in, the body of the paper, including tables and figures, is about 20 pages. The Introduction provided

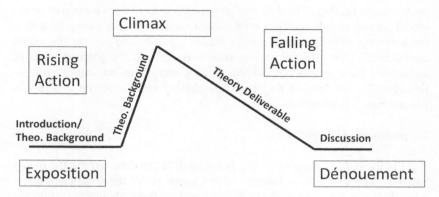

Figure 9.2   Proportional Freytag's Pyramid for theory articles

the exposition and comprises 11 percent of the article. The theoretical background—which comprises the rising action—is 8 percent. The typology comprises the next 15 percent of the article. As I'll discuss shortly, in our study I consider the typology part of the rising action. The falling action, where we develop our theoretical model, is 51 percent of the article. The Discussion is the final 15 percent. These percentages map pretty closely onto the rules of thumb suggested in Chapter 3.

A couple of things to note about our story's structure. We followed our Introduction with a major section that defined the celebrity construct. In addition to defining celebrity, we had to differentiate it from related constructs (i.e., reputation, status, fame and infamy), and we discussed some of its antecedents. Discussing the antecedents was useful because it helped us foreshadow some of our eventual moderators, and it provided a transition to the typology. This section helped us to quickly tie the knot as part of the rising action.

Developing the typology was part of the rising action in our study because it didn't start answering the question; rather, it provided more exposition and set up how we went about answering our research question and untying the knot with our theoretical model. We structured this section by first defining key terms and laying out the criteria for a heroic drama, and then describing the criteria we used to create the typology in general terms (arena/firm life cycle stage; attributions of valiance and prescience; and adversary). We then applied the criteria to describe each of the four celebrity CEO archetypes.

The typology also effectively represented the initial part of our theoretical model, which we developed next. We presented our model in a figure, and then walked through it in the rest of this section. We used the main components of the model (Sociocognitive Outcomes; Moderators, Behavioral Consequences of Celebrity and Celebrity's Influence on Organizational Performance) as the main section headers. The different sub-components of each main part of the model served as sub-headings within each section. So, for example, within the Sociocognitive Outcomes section the main sub-headings were "increased confidence," "felt pressure to stay true to type," and "heightened sense of authority." Each sub-section within a major section ended with a proposition. Finally, we labeled the major concluding section of our article—its dénouement—Implications.

Propositions vs. Hypotheses

Writing the bulk of a theory article is not so different than writing the theory and hypotheses section, as I described in Chapter 6. All the discussions about what theory is not, construct clarity, and how to think about organizing the different pieces of your theory applies equally here. One significant difference, however, is that theory articles don't have hypotheses, although they may have propositions.

Propositions are different from hypotheses because they are not intended to serve as testable statements; rather, they are summarizing statements of the arguments as you develop your theory or theoretical model. They help readers digest sometimes complex arguments, signal transitions to the next part of your argument, and provide easily skimmable summaries of your main ideas. Some propositions do resemble hypothesis statements—specifying the nature, direction, shape, strength and temporal aspects of the constructs and relationships in ways that could be empirically tested. However, propositions are often longer than hypothesis statements. They may identify clear relationships, but may be double- or triple-barreled (i.e., discuss multiple relationships in a single proposition). They may also include some of the constructs' antecedents or consequences, or may describe the mechanisms at work. All of these characteristics are considered "bad" if included in hypotheses, because they make them hard to test. Propositions can also simply describe or summarize a theoretical mechanism or claim. Finally, theory articles can include significantly more propositions than could be feasibly tested as hypotheses in a quantitative empirical study.

Depending on the nature of the article, propositions may also be unnecessary. Kilduff (2006: 254) noted that the notion you have to "sprinkle propositions throughout the paper" to establish empirical research implications is "superstitious learning." If your theoretical approach is based on something other than logical positivism, or you aren't developing a box and arrow model, propositions are unlikely to be useful. Typologies, reviews and essays, for example, don't need propositions, and including them would muddle rather than clarify the arguments.

In our "shackles" article (Lovelace et al., 2018), we didn't provide any propositions when developing our typology because they weren't necessary and didn't help us tell our story. We used a lot of propositions (12 in all) to help explain and summarize our theoretical model because it was long and complicated, and they provided useful summaries and cognitive breaks. Our propositions took different forms, however. Some main effect propositions looked like typical hypotheses, although they'd be tough to test empirically (e.g., The greater a CEO's degree of celebrity of a given type, the greater the CEO's confidence in actions and behaviors associated with that particular celebrity archetype). Other propositions were summarizing statements (e.g., Role intensity will be greatest for creator celebrity roles, intermediate for savior and rebel roles, and least for transformer roles) and some were triple-barreled (e.g., The greater the role intensity of a CEO celebrity archetype, the stronger the associations between degree of celebrity of a given type and the sociocognitive outcomes [increased confidence to remain true to type, increased felt pressure to stay true to type, and increased sense of authority to act in type-specific ways]). Finally, some reflected moderating relationships, but were wordier (e.g., The relationship between the behavioral outcomes associated with a celebrity CEO archetype and performance is moderated by the continuity of environmental conditions. Specifically, the greater the change in environmental conditions, the more likely a celebrity-led firm's performance will decline). A hypothesis would exclude everything through "Specifically."

Figures and Tables

While figures and tables are de rigueur for empirical articles, they are both optional in theory articles. Most include them, though, and they can play important roles in your storytelling, showing readers what you are telling them and enhancing your motion and pacing. However, there are some differences between the tables and figures found in theory and empirical articles. First, rather than summarizing results or data, tables in theory articles are more often used to summarize aspects of the theory, make comparisons or provide examples. As in empirical articles, figures often are boxes and arrows (if there are propositions, mapping them on the figure helps); but they can also take a wider variety of forms to illustrate processes or capture relationships that would be hard to test empirically (e.g., 3-D models).

We included one table and three figures in our "shackles" article (Lovelace et al., 2018). We used the table to summarize our typology of the four celebrity CEO archetypes. Its columns listed the celebrity CEO archetype, a short description of the archetype, the four dimensions we used to distinguish each archetype, and the types of behaviors the archetype engaged in. This table summarized what we described narratively, making it a useful tool for others who employ our typology. We also included three figures. Figure 1 summarized our overall theoretical model, which we then walked through. Figure 2 was a 2x2 that illustrated the role intensity of each archetype (i.e., the degree to which role expectations are salient to role holders, and they immerse themselves in the role) based on two dimensions: perceived likelihood of a firm's imminent failure, and the archetypes' normativity (i.e., did they reflect the in-group or out-group). We used this figure to summarize and illustrate our arguments about why creator celebrity CEOs would experience their celebrity CEO roles the most intensely, transformer CEOs would experience their role the least intensely, and rebels and saviors would be in-between.

Figure 3 was a graphical representation of the Arc of Celebrity, a concept we introduced as a moderator in our model to describe how quickly a CEO became a celebrity, and how long they maintained their celebrity. We used this figure to show readers what we were talking about in our description, which provided a nice visual for our argument that the quicker the rise and the longer the duration of the arc of celebrity, the stronger the relationship between the CEO's degree of celebrity of a particular type and the sociocognitive outcomes described earlier.

Discussion Differences

Theory article Discussion sections are shorter than in empirical articles; because you've just spent the bulk of the article describing your new theoretical insights, you don't need to do it again. Like empirical articles, they do explore the article's contributions to the theoretical conversation, its practical implications, its implications for future research, and its limitations. However, unlike empirical articles they also often include a sub-section describing how to empirically test the theory.

As noted earlier, we labeled our Discussion section in the "shackles" article "Implications," because that was our primary focus. We first briefly summarized our objectives, and then described the theoretical implications of our study. Within this sub-section, however, what we really talked about were directions for future research, such as other factors to consider or use to extend our model. We also assessed the relationships among CEO celebrity and other related constructs, both as antecedents and as consequences. These discussions were interwoven with some of our model's limitations, which resulted from the choices we had to make about what we were and were not going to theorize about. Thus, it was somewhat of an omnibus section that identified the different conversations we were contributing to, limitations and future research directions, and how others could empirically test our theory. The remainder of the Implications section focused on our model's practical implications for boards of directors and CEOs themselves.

I hope you now have a better understanding of the differences in writing quantitative, qualitative and theory papers. Each is a unique discipline. In the remainder of this chapter I discuss what's different about writing book chapters, another common way we present our research to the world.

BOOK CHAPTERS

Book chapters are the most versatile outlet we have for publishing. They can be structured like conventional quantitative, qualitative or theory chapters. The book editor may also stipulate a specific form; for example, handbooks on particular topics and encyclopedia entries often follow the same format. Some book chapters are shorter than typical journal articles, while others are much longer. Book chapters can also take some really non-traditional forms, like ethnopoetics (self-reflective qualitative studies written in the form of a poem), memoirs, or chapters written in the form of a letter. If the book's editor goes for it, it's fair game. If you want to stretch your wings and play with the structure of storytelling, book chapters are where you can more likely do it, not journal articles.

I've published theory, quantitative, review and qualitative book chapters— one of which was based primarily on the book *Moneyball* by Michael Lewis. I have also edited a handbook (*The Oxford Handbook of Corporate Reputation*) where we required the authors to adopt one of two chapter formats (a straight review format or one that provided a case example) so that each chapter would have a similar feel and organizational structure. Writing book chapters can be really freeing and a lot of fun; a couple of my book chapters are among my favorite writing experiences. But that's also the risk. Book chapters can become addictive, too, given they are relatively quick to write and rarely go through the same sort of peer review process as journal articles. Given that most academic departments don't give you much credit for them when it comes to promotion and tenure, writing lots of book chapters can be risky, particularly early in your career. However, if there's something you want to say, or say in a different way, writing a book chapter may be the right way to go.

This chapter concludes part II of this book, focusing on the different sections of an academic article. In the final part of this book I turn my attention from structure and content to process; specifically, the writing process, the co-authoring process, and the review process. I will also discuss other types of writing that academics do (grant proposals, research statements, etc.) and offer some final concluding thoughts.

10. The writing process

As you've probably figured out by now, I see a lot of analogies between what we do in creating academic articles and what my wife Sarah does in creating paintings. This includes the processes used to create the work. Going from a blank canvas, or a blank page, to a finished product can be daunting; getting started and generating enough momentum to carry yourself through the process is challenging, particularly if you try to look at the whole process in aggregate. Novelist Anne Lamott (1994) told a great little story about this. When she was a kid, her brother had a report on birds due for school. He was sitting there in tears, with a big pile of bird books and no idea where to begin. Her Dad told him, "Bird by bird, buddy. Just take it bird by bird" (Lamott, 1994: 19). In addition to being excellent advice, *Bird by Bird* became the name of her memoir/writing guide. I like this story because it's a good reminder that writing—like creating a painting—occurs in stages, and thinking about what each stage entails makes the process more understandable. Far too many works on the writing process either start in what's really the middle of the process, or compress time and conflate different parts of the process that occur across time. In this chapter I lay out the four stages of the writing process, as I see them, using the process of creating a painting as an analogy. I then discuss some of the practicalities of enhancing your writing productivity.

THE FOUR STAGES OF THE WRITING PROCESS

The Core Activities of Writing

Several years ago I served on a panel about writing with Charlotte Cloutier, who at the time was an assistant professor at HEC Montreal (she has since earned tenure). Charlotte was on the panel with more senior scholars—most of us current or former journal editors—because she started a fantastic blog called ProjectScrib (projectscrib.org) where she posted the edited transcripts of interviews she did with senior scholars about how they write. Although she has tapered off posting these interviews now, the 25 interviews she has posted are still available, and I recommend them to everyone. Because Charlotte does qualitative research, most of the folks interviewed (22 of the 25) were also qualitative scholars; however, their insights about the writing process apply regardless of your methodological orientation.

Charlotte did an inductive analysis of her interview transcripts and wrote an article, "How I write: An inquiry into the writing processes of academics" (Cloutier, 2016), in which she synthesized the different activities that comprise the "writing" process. Recall that in Chapter 1 I discussed the differences between writing and typing, arguing that writing occurs in places other than just in front of your computer. I put writing in quotes here because Charlotte's article pushes this notion further. In addition to writing itself, she identified reading, talking, thinking and drawing as activities that are also part of the writing process. To this list I add working with data, because it's in collecting, coding and analyzing your data—whether quantitative or qualitative—that additional insights arise, ideas coalesce and your story starts to come together. I use these six writing activities to structure the four painting-inspired stages of the writing process: (1) Preparing the ground; (2) Blocking in the scene; (3) Adding detail, refining and focusing; and (4) Finishing and framing. While these six activities generally occur during all four stages, what they look like changes as you progress through the writing process. I highlight these differences across each stage.

Stage 1: Preparing the Ground

Before you can start painting you have to prepare to do so; this involves preparing the surface you are working on (i.e., the ground), gathering your other materials (e.g., paint; thinning agents; texture enhancers) and tools (brushes, palette knives, etc.) and perhaps doing preparatory sketches or color studies. Figure 10.1 shows Sarah priming boards for painting. Before you can begin writing you similarly have to prepare *your* "ground" by getting your mind ready to accept the raw materials you've accumulated to tell your story. It's also when you do your own "preparatory studies," experimenting with what to include and exclude.

   Writing. Before you start writing your manuscript you'll write lots of other things, such as notes, memos, meeting summaries and working hypotheses. You may also write research materials like survey questions, experimental protocols, scripts, scales, case histories and historical timelines and grant applications. What you write depends on the linearity of your thinking and research process, and the type of research you do. These are your preparatory studies that help you start identifying your main and supporting characters, your story's theme, the storylines the characters will follow, and how you will go about tying the knot. You may not be thinking of them in these terms yet, but you are preparing your "ground"—thinking about your story and getting your mind ready so that it's receptive when you put the pieces together.

   Reading. Preparing the ground also involves immersing yourself in the literature, so that that the main theories, findings and studies are at your mental

Figure 10.1   Preparing the ground

fingertips when you begin to craft your story, construct your conversation and identify your contributions. Thus, you are likely to read the literatures you think you'll be building on and contributing to as you figure out whether your idea has been done or not, and how you will join the conversation. This includes what's been recently published or is available on journals' in-press sites, as well as key articles or other work in the area. Your reading may be wide-ranging and eclectic, depending on how well versed you are in the literature and how clear your study is in your mind.

Drawing. For many scholars, a big part of preparing the ground is trying to capture your idea or model in a figure—boxes and arrows, or otherwise. This can take place on an office white board, in PowerPoint, in an idea notebook, or on napkins, paper from your recycling can, department meeting agendas or whatever you like to draw and doodle on. Drawing can help you work through ideas by visualizing how your different characters relate to each other, and it can help you work out problems or inconsistencies. At this stage of the process it's like storyboarding in animated films, where the storylines and the story's characters and relationships start to form.

Talking. A great deal of time is also spent talking—to your co-authors; to others, such as your students or practitioners; and to colleagues, perhaps in brown bag sessions or hallway conversations. Talking helps you process the different information and ideas you're encountering; it's how you start to figure out what your story is and what's interesting and to test out parts of your narrative with audiences. To that end, remember that a big part of talking is therefore *listening* to what others have to say and using it to improve your story.

Thinking. Thinking occurs both in front of and away from your computer. You'll be thinking about your study while you are doing other things like exercising, cooking, cleaning, sleeping, doing yard work, and working on other projects or writing reviews. During this stage you are putting your ideas together and trying to convince yourself, as well as thinking about how you can convince others.

Working with data. This stage occurs while you are collecting and analyzing your data. Writing neither completely precedes nor completely follows data collection and analysis. They most often co-occur and overlap. Working with the data at this stage stimulates your thinking and helps you figure out what your story is and which characters you need and don't need to tell it. Writing provides insights into the data analyses needed, other variables you need to collect and the types of analyses you want to conduct.

Stage 2: Blocking in the Scene

Once you've prepared the ground, you can start blocking in the scene. For a painting this involves laying down the underpainting, sketching out the big shapes or sections of the scene and putting in the color notes (see Figure 10.2). Thus, at this point you are laying out the broad contours; you'll fill in the details later. Likewise, as you start writing your article you'll be roughing in your Introduction, developing your storylines and the general arguments supporting your hypotheses, and drafting your Methods and Results. This isn't the time to worry about getting all the detail in and making the prose pretty, because you are writing the *shitty first draft*.

Writing. Anne Lamott (1994: 21) offered this important observation: "Shitty first drafts. All good writers write them. This is how they end up with good second drafts and terrific third drafts." I call writing during this stage "new" writing because you are working from scratch. It's the hardest kind of writing to do. One of the biggest challenges less experienced writers, and many experienced writers, have is that they think their articles must be polished, logically coherent, near-finished works right out of the chute. Nothing could be further from the truth. The first draft is the shitty draft meant for an audience of one—you. It's where you put together all the ideas, parts and pieces that you accumulated while preparing the ground in an order that has some resemblance to a story. The ideas can be half-developed; you can insert notes like "[Add

Figure 10.2   Blocking in the scene

more here]" and "[Example]," and your reference parentheticals will mostly say "(Cites)."

Once you get your first draft written, then you can start to reorganize, edit and fill in the details in the next stage. You'll likely end up revising your paper dozens of times before you even send it to a journal, so your writing during this stage is just the first step. Thus, don't censor yourself during this process, nor try to create the "perfect" first draft; that can lead to paralysis. And don't try to write it all at once, either. Follow the bird by bird approach, and give yourself short assignments that you can complete in one sitting, such as drafting the Introduction, writing the argument for hypothesis 2, or writing the Theoretical Background section for one theory you're using. You also don't have to start at the beginning. The part you write first may be the part that's clearest in your mind's eye, or that you think is the easiest to write. If you still have problems getting started you can try freewriting, where you just type whatever comes to mind, recognizing up front that you'll end up throwing most of it away. If you freeze when you sit in front of your keyboard, get dictation software and a headset, and just start talking.

One question many people have at this stage is whether to outline before writing. I find no particular virtue in outlining, nor is there a problem with it. If it works for you, do it. If it doesn't, don't. If you don't normally outline but you're having trouble getting going, try it. And if you compulsively work on your outline without ever actually turning it into a paper, or feel caged in and trapped by it, then maybe you should chuck it and just start writing.

I have personally never outlined an article. That's not the way I think, and it isn't the way I like to write. However, I do typically use an outline format when I write my class notes for teaching. I taught the material in this book as a doctoral seminar, and I wrote the first four chapters before the semester started, two more chapters during the semester, and the rest after the class concluded. Thus, I effectively wrote outlines for over half the chapters before I wrote the chapters themselves. This was an interesting experiment for me. To be honest, I didn't find much difference between writing my class note outlines from drafts of my chapters and writing chapter drafts from my outlines. Collectively it took me the same amount of time to do both no matter which I started with. So, do whatever works for you, but make sure you distinguish between what's comfortable and familiar and what works. Even if it's comfortable and familiar, if it isn't working it's time to try something different.

I tend to write my first drafts in chunks. I usually write the hypotheses with a couple of sentences of justification when preparing the ground, so I know what my basic story is going to be. During this stage I write the Introduction first, because it helps me organize my thoughts, identify my main and supporting characters, and provides a thumbnail sketch of the rest of the paper. I then go back and expand the logic supporting the Hypotheses and develop the Theoretical Background. I write the Methods and Results sections after I draft the front end. By that point I know what the measures and results generally are. I write the Discussion last—often during the next stage—because the theory, contribution and results can change as the paper evolves. Thus, it usually makes sense to wait until I have developed and polished the rest of the paper more.

Reading. Your reading during this stage becomes a bit more focused, as you start to lay down the broad contours of your paper. You'll be doing a bit more reading to fill in gaps in your logic or story, get definitions for your key constructs, and make sure you aren't missing any major studies on your topic. If you're doing a qualitative study, you'll also likely be iterating between the literature and your data as you develop your findings.

Drawing. You'll likely continue drawing during this stage—refining your figure, and perhaps adding or deleting components and relationships as you develop your Theory and Hypotheses or Findings sections further. You'll also graph interactions, if you have them, think about what kinds of tables to include, and start to develop them.

Talking. As when you're preparing the ground, most of your conversations will be with co-authors and colleagues. Your co-author conversations will likely become more focused, as you encounter particular problems and start working through the issues. There may also be some negotiations over definitions, ordering and how to best frame your contributions. Talking with colleagues will look much the same as during preparing the ground—informal hallway conversations and idea development brown bag sessions.

Thinking. When and where your thinking occurs won't change much during this stage, but you'll now be thinking more about how to develop the fuller arguments for each hypothesis and put them together, rather than about the rudiments of your story. Thus, your thinking becomes more focused as you put the parts and pieces together and start playing with structures and storylines.

Working with data. At this point you'll have established your main results, but you are likely conducting robustness tests and other analyses—such as exploring potential mediating and moderating relationships—to flesh out your story and rule out alternative explanations. If your study is qualitative, you're likely still working with your data to develop your Findings section. Some of these analyses may result in changes to other parts of the paper if a new and interesting storyline emerges, or an early, promising result goes away after making some analytical or measurement change. This may prompt more thinking about what's really going on. If you are doing experiments, you may even decide another experiment is necessary to explore some new wrinkle or nuance to your story.

Stage 3: Adding Detail, Refining and Focusing

Once the artist blocks in the piece, they proceed to add detail, color, light and nuance to the work (see Figure 10.3). They'll focus on different parts of the scene, but also move back and forth across the different sections as the scene develops to keep the whole painting balanced. You'll do the same during this stage of the writing process; adding detail, connections and examples that turn your shitty first draft into a fully developed piece.

Writing. My favorite quote from William Zinnser's book *On Writing Well* is "Rewriting is the essence of writing well: it's where the game is won or lost" (Zinnser, 2006: 83). I love this quote because it emphasizes that most of what we think of as "writing" is actually "rewriting." I find rewriting considerably easier, and more fun, than the "new" writing required for blocking in the scene. This is where you get to craft the language and employ all the tools and techniques discussed in Chapters 3 and 4, like the human face, showing and telling, motion and pacing, and rhythm and cadence. You also begin to address the pathologies you ignored during the block in—the cluttered sentences and unnecessary words; the passive constructions, buried leads, overstuffed sentences and pompous prose; the missing definitions, assumptions and connections between ideas that require mind reading. You root them out over successive rounds of rewriting.

This stage is also where you work out your theme and storylines and turn the two-dimensional "cardboard cutout" (King, 2000) characters of your block-in into fully formed constructs. That's why it's "where the game is won or lost," because it's what you do during this stage that makes or breaks the storytelling. You attend to your story's structure, answering questions such as: Where do I need more, or less, exposition to set the scene? Are all the pieces there to effectively tie the knot? Where and how do I introduce the context? In what

Figure 10.3   Adding detail, refining and focusing

order should I present the hypotheses? How, and whether, do I include all the cool stuff and needed detail in the Methods and Results? During this stage you'll also write the Discussion. Does it link back to your claimed contributions in the Introduction, and are you creating an effective dénouement that brings catharsis and advances theory, or do you just summarize your findings again? Have you landed on a strong concluding paragraph yet? By the end of this stage you'll have a manuscript that's nearly ready to go.

Reading. You tend to do less reading at this stage. What reading you do typically involves tracking down specific information to address questions and issues that have come up as you craft and polish your manuscript and respond to friendly reviews.

Drawing. You may still be tinkering with your model, particularly if you're doing a qualitative study or coming up with additional figures and tables, but you are wrapping up the drawing, at this point.

Talking. This is where the biggest change from prior stages is likely to occur. During this stage you'll submit your paper to conferences, and perhaps present it at invited talks. You'll also get friendly reviews, which is another form of talking, and use them to make further refinements. Thus, most of your "talking" during this stage will really involve "listening" to feedback.

Friendly reviews are a critical part of the writing process. After working on a paper for so long, you start to lose perspective on what's interesting and what's not, what requires mind reading, and what's overexplained. My favorite line from Stephen King's book *On Writing*, about one of his childhood babysitters, says it all with respect to friendly reviews: "In many ways, Eulah-Beulah prepared me for literary criticism. After having a two-hundred-pound babysitter fart on your face and yell Pow!, the Village Voice holds few terrors" (King, 2000: 20–21). This is the point in the writing process where you need to open yourself up to some much-needed criticism and ask your friends to let it rip (in a helpful, constructive way, of course). Journal reviewers will not hold back, so you need to do some sparring first, toughen your manuscript up, and make sure it's in as good a shape as possible for the big event. That way, when you get to the review process, the reviews you get back will be less intimidating. You'll be ready, having already responded to some of the most obvious problems, and you'll be more equipped to haggle with the reviewers over other issues you expect will come up.

In our "From the Editors" column discussed in Chapter 3, Joyce Bono and I (Pollock & Bono, 2013) talked about the team of helpers you'll want to ask for friendly reviews. Each plays a distinct role. One helper is the supportive reviewer. This person delivers critical feedback, but is also unfailingly positive and supportive, encouraging you to keep going and assuring you that you can do it. You'll also want to recruit some topical experts on your theory, context and/or method. You may ask them to read the whole paper, or just specific parts where you have questions on which they can be most helpful. Asking for comments just on specific parts also reduces the magnitude of the request, increasing the likelihood they will help. Try to develop a cadre of close colleagues and co-authors you can turn to, and who can also turn to you for friendly reviews.

A third type of helper is someone with little expertise in your area, and perhaps even in academia, such as first year doctoral students, spouses, or friends and neighbors. They can tell you whether your narrative is clear, interesting and easy to read. Finally, you'll also want a Eulah-Beulah, that crusty reviewer with deep expertise and little tact, who will tell it to you straight. You'll have to resist the tendency to argue with them (I often fail); but listening to what they have to say will help you avoid the mines that can sink your paper when you send it out for review. In all instances, it's important you seek *specific* feedback, rather than unhelpful generalities. You can ask specific questions up front or press your friendly reviewers to elaborate on how to address the issues they raise. Even if you don't take their suggestions, they may spark some additional ideas.

Thinking. At the beginning of this stage you are thinking deeply about all the issues I discussed above in writing. As you progress through this stage you'll think more about resolving lingering problems and how to phrase things most effectively.

Working with data. You may be doing a few supplemental analyses based on friendly reviews—or finding the right quotes and finalizing tables if your study is qualitative—but the data work should be largely done by now. Your main analyses are all in place.

Stage 4: Finishing and Framing

This is the final stage where artists put the finishing touches on the work. They dry, varnish and frame the painting, and put on the backing paper, hanging hardware and wire. It's now ready to sell (see Figure 10.4). In writing, this is where the final polishing and scrubbing of the manuscript occurs. Once that's done, your manuscript is ready to submit to a journal.

Figure 10.4   Finishing and framing

Writing. This is where the final, careful copy-editing occurs. It's also where you check your references to make sure you include all the articles and books you cite, and you delete any references that have disappeared through the rounds of revision. It's also when you make sure your references are formatted consistently. Every journal has its own formatting style, but I personally don't worry about following the journal's particular reference format until I've at least received an R&R. It's a ton of work, and the editor and reviewers generally don't pay any attention. Instead, I make sure that all the references consistently employ my preferred format.

Reading. Your reading is done.

Drawing. Other than minor editing and proofing of labels and titles for consistency and formatting, the drawing is done.

Talking. You may want to engage one last helper at this stage: a good copy-editor. They will help you make sure your prose, grammar and punctuation are all clear and tight. I've used copy-editors, and I always learn things. The better your article reads, and the freer it is from typos, the more successful you're likely to be. Other than that, talking at this stage is mostly back among your co-authors and focuses on any unresolved details, where to send it, what editors and reviewers to suggest, and rounds of congratulations on a job well done.

Thinking. The thinking here turns mostly to review process issues, which I cover in Chapter 12. There isn't much left to figure out with respect to the paper.

Working with data. This is done.

Once you've completed this stage, your manuscript is ready to submit. I hope that the analogy of the four stages of creating a painting helps illustrate that writing is indeed a process, and I hope that you better understand what occurs at each stage, both on the page and off. Thinking about the writing process in this way makes it more tractable, and helps you understand where you are and what needs to be done without worrying so much about things that don't require your attention at the moment. In the remainder of this chapter I will discuss some tactics and approaches to help you enhance your writing productivity.

ENHANCING YOUR PRODUCTIVITY

Writing requires focus; the greater your ability to tune out distractions and home in on what you're writing, the more you'll be able to produce in a given amount of time. That's why I think focus is more important than time; you can get a lot out of a little time if you manage it right, and you can get little out of a lot of time if you don't manage it well. However, in this digital age we face all manner of distractions—phones, texts, emails, the lure of the Internet and its sirens Facebook, Twitter and 24-hour news. Add to this the demands of modern family life, teaching, and various service requirements and bureaucratic demands and it seems there's never enough time to get any writing done. It becomes, "once the semester's over," "once summer comes," or "once I get my sabbatical" then I'll crank the writing out, but something always seems to get in those "once's" way. So, what's a willing but distracted scholar to do?

Deep Work

Self-improvement author and theoretical computer scientist Cal Newport argued that what we need more than ever, and what's increasingly hard to achieve, is "deep work." In his book of the same name (Newport, 2016), Newport defined deep work as "Professional activities performed in a state of distraction-free concentration that push your cognitive capabilities to their limit. These efforts create new value, improve your skill, and are hard to replicate" (Newport, 2016: 3). Sounds awesome, right? So how do you do it? Newport argued there are four ways to engage in deep work: (1) The monastic approach; (2) The bimodal approach; (3) The rhythmic approach; or (4) The journalistic approach.

The *monastic* approach is where you cut yourself off from all possible distractions for prolonged periods (or forever) so that you can focus solely on your single goal. This approach is unrealistic for all but a few, and I think it requires some significant misanthropic tendencies.

The *bimodal* approach is where you establish regular periods of time when you become monastic and shut yourself off from all distractions, but otherwise engage with your distracting world. This approach can fit the academic lifestyle; for example, we can stack our teaching in single semesters, leaving the other semester open for research. You can employ the bimodal approach even if your teaching isn't stacked, because you can use it for periods of days (e.g., 2–4 days once or twice a month), not just for weeks or months at a time. If you can manage your schedule to allot extended blocks of time, and have the willpower to stay away from all your communications and technology distractions for that long, this may work for you. It may also work if you can isolate yourself physically by going somewhere that takes you out of your usual milieu—a cabin in the woods or at the beach, for example. Newport (2016) provided some extreme examples, such as J.K. Rowling checking into the expensive Balmoral Hotel to finish the last Harry Potter book, *Harry Potter and the Deathly Hallows*, or another writer who, with only two weeks to meet a book contract deadline, booked a flight to Tokyo and back, using the plane trip each way to write most of the book.

The *rhythmic* approach is what many aspire to. This is where you write daily for a fixed amount of time. It is also the approach that Paul Silvia (2018) advocated in his book *How to Write a Lot*. He argued that writing a lot requires writing regularly, and to do so you have to figure out when's the best time for you to write, allot that time to writing, protect it (you wouldn't schedule a meeting while you are supposed to be in class, for example, so accord your writing time the same importance), figure out a good place to do it, and give yourself writing goals to accomplish during each session. Stephen King (2000) offered novelist Anthony Trollope as an exemplar of this approach. He wrote for exactly two and half hours every day before going to his job with the British postal service. He would stop mid-sentence if his time were up, and if he finished a book before his writing session was over he'd put a fresh sheet of paper in his typewriter and start the next novel.

During the Covid-19 pandemic shutdown, many folks inside and outside academia who were forced to work from home adopted some form of this approach as they balanced their work demands, their kids' schooling and demands for attention, and their significant others' own work time require-ments. They worked for certain hours each day while their spouse wrangled the kids, for example, and then traded to give each other their own undivided work time. Or they scheduled their work around when their kids were sleeping. One of my neighbors, a CFO and single parent, told me he got up at 4:30 each morning to get his focused work done before his son woke up at 7:00, and then he handled phone calls in between home schooling. You may have adopted similar practices yourself.

The *journalistic* approach is where, like a journalist working on deadlines, you switch into deep work mode whenever the opportunity arises. You can plan ahead for these periods, but they change from day to day and week to week. This approach is a tough one for new writers to employ, because it requires training yourself to drop into deep work quickly and having the confidence that you'll be successful. Rather than a fixed schedule, as with the rhythmic approach, you figure out—perhaps on a weekly basis—when you will have blocks of time to write, and you take advantage of them. You may update these assessments daily; for example, an unexpected meeting cancel-lation frees up your afternoon, or your dog gets sick and your planned writing time gets blown up taking her to the vet. Thus, it's not random, but it's not as rigid and regular as the rhythmic approach either.

Whichever approach you choose, during your deep work periods you don't answer email, texts or the phone, and you don't use the Internet, except to look up articles or other information to inform your writing, and you work somewhere that you won't be interrupted by children, colleagues or students. No one said it's easy, and you need to figure out which approach is best for you. Personally, while I aspire to the rhythmic approach, in reality I practice the journalistic approach. Every week is different, even when I'm not teaching, and it's hard for me to block out whole days or weeks. I've always been able to focus and concentrate narrowly, and I've become pretty adept at dropping into this state quickly when I write. For example, the day I first wrote this section on the four approaches to deep work, I had to do our weekly grocery shopping, followed by a meeting about a student's dissertation, then I took my dog to physical therapy, followed by a research team meeting about an R&R. I drafted this section after that meeting and before taking my dog for a walk and making dinner. Two days prior I had nothing on my schedule and I accomplished more, drafting the introduction to this chapter and the sections on the first two stages of the writing process. It just depends on the day.

Organization

Staying organized will also enhance your productivity, if for no other reason than that you aren't spending hours looking for misplaced files or replicating what you've already done. It makes it easier to get going when you start writing, and reorganizing your files may be part of your stopping ritual (discussed shortly). It doesn't have to be pretty, or work for others; it just needs to work for you. In my pre-academic days, I had a "pile" organizing system where I had a pile on my desk for each project, and I knew where in each pile things were. While my system horrified some of my "clear desktop" co-workers, it worked for me. In the more paperless world of today, I have folders on my computer. Some are for broad areas where I do multiple studies, like IPOs (each study has its own folder), others are labeled by co-author, and include folders for each project we have, and others are for stand-alone projects. I use sub-folders within them to keep data separate from documents, articles, etc. I also date my files and save new versions frequently. I put the dates at the end so that I can sort by title and then see the dates in order. Do whatever works for you, but do develop and stick to a system.

Routines and Rituals

Many prolific writers, and highly productive people of any profession, have a set of routines and practices, or rituals, that help them get into and stay in the flow of their writing. These involve when and where to work, getting started, how long to work, and how to stop.

When to work. When to work depends on your life situation, deep work approach, and biorhythms. If you employ the bimodal approach, your calendar and other factors will influence when you can block out large chunks of time. If you employ the rhythmic or journalistic approaches, whether you're a morning person or a night owl, have young kids and other factors will influence when during the day is best for you. Paul Silvia (2018) noted that about two-thirds of people are morning people and a third are night owls. I personally am better in the morning, so I try to keep my mornings as open for writing as possible. Stephen King (2000) is also a morning person. He said for him, mornings were for writing, the afternoons were for other non-writing work activities (and naps), and evenings were for family pursuits and watching Red Sox games. I've had colleagues who start working very early (between 4:30–5:00 am), ending their workdays by 2:00–3:00 pm so they can do other things. In contrast, my co-author Jung-Hoon Han will work all night. If I get a paper from him at 6:30 am, I know it's because he hasn't been to bed yet. It's whatever works for you.

Where to work. Wherever you can best engage in deep work is where you should work. That may be at home, in your school office, at the library, in a coffee shop, or in an isolated environment like a hotel room or a cabin in the woods. Where you work depends on the deep work approach you employ and your ability to stay away from the Internet, social media and other distractors. It doesn't have to be fancy. Stephen King wrote *Carrie* and *Salem's Lot* in the laundry room of a double-wide trailer, balancing a kid's school desk on his thighs (he's well over six feet tall) while typing on a typewriter. I'm sure his current writing digs are posher. King argued that the most important characteristics are that your writing space is free from distractions, and that you can close the door, at least metaphorically. Cal Newport and Paul Silvia echo these sentiments. An actual door is great, but if you end up in a public space like a coffee shop or library, headphones and music that helps you shut out the world will also do. I have current and former students that work in coffee shops who use this approach.

I write primarily at home. Figure 10.5 shows my current home office. It's the coolest office I've ever had. My house was built in 1927 and my office was originally an outdoor porch. It's like a treehouse for me, overlooking my driveway and the street. At the start of my career I wrote in my school office, but after I married and we moved to Maryland in 2002, Washington DC traffic plus getting our first dog, Annie, made that harder. The concurrent advent of residential broadband access made working from home more feasible. I've written at home ever since. While I also write on planes and in airports, hotels and sitting in the street at outdoor art shows, home is primarily where I get deep work done. I prefer silence while I write, so I don't listen to music. It's hard for me to hear words while writing words. My wife's studio occupies the second floor of our house, so she has her own distinct space, and we can't hear each other.

Getting started. Once you've figured out when and where to work, you'll want to consider developing routines for starting a writing session. As they become habituated, they can help you get to deep work more quickly. If you've ever wondered about the elaborate rituals that musicians, athletes and other performers engage in, this is part of the reason. They help them prepare and achieve the necessary focus. There may be particular things that help you focus, like clearing your desk or organizing your support materials (notes, books, etc.), turning off Internet access or closing your email client. Or, they may involve some food or drink-related ritual, like getting a cup of coffee or making your favorite snack. It could also be something more physical, like exercising, or meditating for ten minutes to clear your mind. Even just shutting the door or putting on certain music can signal to yourself it's time to

Figure 10.5   Where I write

write. Once these pre-game rituals are concluded, how will you start the actual writing process? For example, will you pick up right where you left off, or reread what you wrote the day before, or start at the beginning of the article every day to get into the flow?

My getting started ritual typically involves getting a cup of coffee before heading to my office in the morning and a mug of green tea after lunch. I usually at least read what I've written in the previous session or day to see if I still like it, I make edits, and then I keep going. To the extent you can ritualize these activities, it can help you achieve the focus you need to get into deep work more quickly.

How long to work. I recommend at least a 90-minute session, if you can, because it allows you to get into the flow, and for most people concentration starts to flag after about 90 minutes to two hours. You may want to build in breaks, and perhaps plan a couple of sessions. Many people revel in the fantasy of marathon writing sessions but they really don't yield a good product. Quality declines precipitously after a point. Just think of all the crappy papers you've gotten from students who pulled all-nighters before the assignment was due. Cal Newport (2016) cited research showing that it's hard to be really creative and focused for more than about four hours a day. If you have the time, particularly if you're using the bimodal approach, I'd suggest identifying a couple of writing sessions with a break in between. For example, ideally I prefer to write for a couple of hours in the morning, from about 9–11, take a break to walk the dog and have lunch with Sarah, then write for another couple of hours before turning my attention to other things. Remember, this is just the "writing" part of writing; all the other associated activities (reading, thinking, talking, drawing and working with data) can occupy the other hours of your workday.

You may also want to consider working towards a specific goal, rather than for a specified period. Pretty much everyone who has opined on writing productivity advocates setting writing goals. Shooting for a particular number of words or pages per day is one option. In his book King (2000) said he targeted writing about 2,000 words a day, although I've also heard him say in interviews that he writes for four hours a day. Silvia also suggested creating a to-do list, focusing on finishing a particular section, or setting goals for how many words you write in a specified amount of time, like 25 minutes.[1] Setting goals creates a sense of progress and accomplishment, and helps you figure out when to stop for the day. Don't get too obsessed with a particular goal, though. If you need to spend some time drawing, reading or thinking, do it and don't worry about missing your word count for the day.

Stopping. It's also important to figure out how to stop working, both for a given session and on a project. It may be simply that you hit your time limit, word or page goal, or complete the desired section, or finish your to-do list. You may also want to develop some stopping rituals to signal to yourself that you're done with the session, such as saving and closing the file, closing your laptop, putting away all the stuff you've been working with, opening the door, or some other physical act that signals completion. When to stop working on the article and send it to a co-author, or a journal, can be more challenging. It's important to figure out how to get yourself to stop tinkering and get something out the door. Perfectionism can be the enemy. One option is to manufacture deadlines. If you blow through your self-imposed deadlines, ask others to set them for you. In his interview with Charlotte Cloutier on projectscrib. org, Mike Pratt said that when he gets to the point where he's just "moving commas" then it's time to send the paper out (Pratt interview, posted April 24th, 2016). You might also establish a practice such as when you think the

---

[1]   These are sometimes referred to as "Pomodoros," named after old-fashioned kitchen timers that look like tomatoes, used to time these sessions (Silvia, 2018).

paper is ready you let it sit for three days or a week, read it one more time with fresh eyes, then submit it, no exceptions.

I don't have a particular closing ritual. Once I run out of time, or finish what I wanted to accomplish for the day, I usually just stop writing. I don't even shut off my computer; I just let it go into sleep mode eventually. At the project level, I'll set targets for what I want to accomplish and dates for sending something to a co-author, usually in conjunction with my co-author so that the commitment's public and they're looking for it. When I read through my papers and I'm not doing much copy-editing, then I'm ready to send it off to a journal. I don't have trouble letting go; my tendency is to send things out too early. That's where co-authors can help, as we'll discuss in Chapter 11.

In this chapter I've described breaking up the writing process into discrete stages. I've also discussed how to enhance your productivity during whatever time you have—or make—for writing. As I've said several times, there's no one best way to go about this; if it works for you, do it. And what works best may change over time as your life and work circumstances change. The key is to recognize when certain things are and aren't working, and to make changes when necessary. In writing this chapter I've also talked about the writing process as a largely solitary act. While parts of it are, other parts involve working with co-authors, which I discuss next.

11. The co-authoring process

Academic writing is paradoxical in that it's both solitary and highly social. With a few exceptions, when you are actually writing you do it alone; at the same time, odds are you also have co-authors with whom you develop your ideas, share the writing duties, and who edit your work, just as you edit theirs. The frequency and number of co-authors varies widely across fields. Some fields, like history, still hew mostly to sole-authored works, whereas natural science articles can have dozens of authors.

Chengwei Liu, Christopher Olivola and Balázs Kovács (2017) explored co-authoring trends, both across different social sciences disciplines and within different subfields of management, and they conducted a survey to identify authors' co-authoring preferences. They found that over the last 30 years the number of authors has gone up across all the social sciences they studied (economics, psychology, political science, sociology and management). Although psychology had the highest average number of authors per article (2.3) when their study ended in 2012, they predicted management (2.2) would overtake psychology by 2020. Political science had the lowest average number of authors (1.4). They also observed increases within all subfields of management (entrepreneurship, human resources, organizational behavior, organization theory and management science). Entrepreneurship (2.6) and organizational behavior (2.5) had the highest author averages and steepest trajectories, and human resources (1.8) had the lowest average. Thus, although there are some variations across domains, co-authoring is increasingly prevalent.

I looked at my own personal statistics; of my current published articles and book chapters, 2 percent are sole-authored, 33 percent have two authors, 43 percent have three authors and 22 percent have four authors. I also have one working paper with five authors, and one with six authors. All told, including working papers, I've co-authored with 57 different individuals between one and eight times each. This book is only the second thing I've ever sole-authored. Co-authors can make you more productive, and I'm fortunate that the vast majority of my experiences are positive. However I also know of many co-author horror stories entailing free riding, permanently damaged relationships, authors leaving papers and then attacking their former co-authors, and even retractions due to falsified data.[1] In this chapter I discuss the pros and cons of co-authors, different types of co-authoring collaborations, the mechanics of writing with co-authors, and the processes involved in inviting, working with and dropping co-authors.

THE PROS AND CONS OF CO-AUTHORS

Pros of co-authors. There are many benefits to working with co-authors. The biggest benefit, to me, is I get to have fun working with friends. Another benefit is that you learn new things. Your co-authors need to share some common interests and understandings, but they ideally also have complementary skills you don't possess. They can expose you to new literatures, methodological techniques and ways of thinking that enhance your repertoire. At the same time, you can leverage each other's skills by focusing on the things you do best. Good co-authors play off each other to generate superior insights. Together, they produce better products than any one of them could have produced alone. A related benefit is enhanced productivity; since you share the workload with others, co-authors allow you to work on more, and more varied, articles.

Co-authoring can also increase your motivation to get things done, because you know other people are waiting and counting on you to do your part. This is especially true for more senior scholars working with doctoral students and junior scholars who face career-determining deadlines. You don't want to let them down or hold them back. A related benefit is that co-authoring provides senior scholars opportunities to mentor and share their knowledge with more junior scholars, which can be intrinsically motivating (at least for some of us). It also provides junior scholars with the opportunity to learn from senior scholars about how to develop and present research effectively, and how to navigate the review process. Co-authors can also keep you from sending out a paper too soon or yank it out of your hands when you're hanging onto it too long, depending on your proclivities.

Co-authoring offers some instrumental benefits as well. It can provide access to data without having to go through the effort of developing the dataset yourself. And if you don't have doctoral students or research assistants, but your co-author does, it can provide access to the labor necessary to collect and code data. Having a high-profile co-author can enhance your research visibility, because anything your co-author publishes is more likely to be read and cited (Merton, 1968). Finally, it can enhance your odds of publication. In most cases an experienced co-author knows how to avoid many of the mistakes

---

[1]   See http://retractionwatch.com for up-to-date listings of all retracted articles.

less experienced authors make (I address some of these issues in Chapter 12 on the review process). Their track record of success may also reduce editors' perceived uncertainties about their ability. As a result, they may be more likely to invest scarce journal resources in their submissions—such as assigning them better reviewers—or give them an opportunity to revise and resubmit their papers on close calls because the editor has more confidence they have the skills and experience to successfully pull it off. There are no guarantees that either of these things will happen, but the probabilities are higher.

Cons of co-authoring. Although there are many benefits to co-authoring, there are also costs. Even in a well-functioning relationship, co-authoring increases coordination costs, and the more co-authors you have the higher these are likely to be. Getting a paper done requires that the whole author team focuses on the project at the same time, and schedules may vary for a variety of reasons, such as teaching in opposite semesters, service obligations, other co-authoring commitments and differing levels of interest in and commitment to the project. If the project isn't on the front burner for any of the co-authors, it's unlikely to go anywhere. I've had projects take over a decade to complete because the study wasn't anyone's top priority. Someone needs to pick up the ball and run with it to focus the team. If you are facing the job market or are on the tenure clock, having a co-author with other priorities who slows down your progress can damage your career. You'll have to make some tough decisions about how much effort to devote to those projects, and whether it's better to keep pushing them with little result or focus your attention elsewhere until your co-authors are ready to work on the project and move it forward.

Most of the benefits I discussed occur when everything goes well; however, it isn't always that smooth. Rather than leveraging each other's skills, you may have a co-author who is a free rider, benefitting from your hard work without making equivalent contributions. Power dynamics within teams can also become problematic, and some authors may be afraid to speak up to more senior colleagues, particularly if they're in the same department. If you failed to have clear discussions early on there may also be disputes about authorship order or who owns the data. It can also damage your reputation if you have a co-author who behaves unethically, for example by falsifying data or results. All these outcomes can end relationships and friendships, and at worst could cost people their jobs.

On a more instrumental level, while having a high-profile co-author can bring many benefits, it can also affect internal and external attributions of credit. Internally, senior co-authors can fail to recognize their junior co-authors' contributions, forget who suggested what, or how the project evolved, and (intentionally or unintentionally) take more credit than they deserve. At the same time, junior co-authors can mistakenly equate time with contribution—even if the most time-intensive activities aren't the highest value-added activities—and become resentful or demand more credit than they deserve. Externally, because of the Matthew effect (Merton, 1968)—named after the verse in the book of Matthew suggesting that the rich get richer, which Robert Merton used to describe the benefits that accrue to high status—the most prominent author will most likely be attributed the greatest credit for the study, regardless of their actual contribution or the authorship order. Finally, if you are not the first author on a paper with three or more authors, the convention of using "et al." after the first use of the reference, rather than listing all authors' names, reduces all but the first author's visibility when the paper is cited. Despite all these limitations, if the process is managed well the benefits generally outweigh the costs. In the next section I will discuss different types of collaborative relationships, and how they affect the writing process.

TYPES OF COLLABORATIVE RELATIONSHIPS

Liu and colleagues (2017) found that 48 percent of the scholars they surveyed prefer to co-author with their peers; of the other 52 percent, most preferred working with senior rather than junior colleagues. However, their analysis also showed that senior scholars preferred working with junior scholars. Of my 57 co-authors, at the times the collaborations occurred 32 percent were doctoral students, 25 percent were junior colleagues, 30 percent were peers and 14 percent were more senior than me.

Preferences for co-authoring with more junior, peer or senior colleagues can lead to different types of collaborations. In their study "'Only if I'm first author': Conflict over credit in management scholarship," Steve Floyd, Dean Schroeder and Dale Finn (1994) inducted a co-authoring typology from the qualitative portion of their survey data. It focused on two dimensions—(1) Whether the collaboration's motivation was to build a social relationship or enhance productivity; and (2) Whether the power balance among the co-authors was equal or unequal—yielding four types of collaborations: Collegial (social, equal power), Meritorious (productivity, equal power), Mentoring (social, unequal power), and Directive (productivity, unequal power). Although their focus was on how the collaboration types affected authorship order (which I'll get to in a bit), they also affect how the writing collaboration transpires.

Collegial. Collegial collaborations are trusting, egalitarian relationships where no one seeks to dominate. Consequently, these relationships are also the most likely to result in what Adam Grant and I dubbed "ruthless rewriting" (Grant & Pollock, 2011), based on a quote from one of the award-winning authors we surveyed. Ruthless rewriting means that you don't show undue deference to your co-authors nor hesitate to rewrite what they've written. Rather, you show "little pity and great trust" (Grant & Pollock, 2011: 875) as you try to make each other's work better. Each author may be responsible for drafting different parts of the manuscript, but all authors rewrite the whole paper, passing around the manuscript frequently and rewriting whatever they think doesn't work or requires clarifying. Of course, it's always better to discuss these changes before or right after they're made.

Even though it can be personally painful to see something you've spent a bunch of time on deleted or substantially rewritten, if you trust your co-authors' intent it makes you more open to the changes they make, and to assessing whether, or what parts of, their changes have improved the manuscript. My long-time co-author Violina Rindova and I have always been peers and have always ruthlessly rewritten each other. We are both blunt and direct, so our discussions get interesting, but we trust and respect each other, we always work things out (even if it takes reinserting something the other deleted a few times), and the final product is better than what we could have produced alone.

Meritorious. Meritorious collaborations are also egalitarian but are productivity based; thus, although they can result in ruthless rewriting, it's somewhat less likely. There are two reasons. First, the focus in these collaborations is on relative contribution; if you delete or rewrite everything your co-author has done their contribution will appear smaller, and they'll resist your changes. Conflict can arise more quickly in these relationships because the collaboration isn't built on deep social bonds. To avoid conflict, rewriting each other often amounts to little more than copy-editing grammatical and punctuation issues. Second, given that the collaboration exists to enhance productivity and leverage each co-author's strengths by assigning them specific roles, each co-author will focus on their agreed upon sections, and may be less likely to rewrite others' sections unless one of their roles is to be "the writer" who brings the whole paper together. Ideally papers should have one voice and sound like they were written by one person. Since co-authors have equal power in a meritorious collaboration, assigning a co-author the "writer" role, even if they aren't the first author, can help create a unified voice and avoid timid rewriting.

Mentoring. Mentoring collaborations are trusting, but they're more benevolent than egalitarian because the power balance is unequal. The senior co-author seeks to assist the junior co-author's career development and understanding of how to conduct and publish research. In return they have someone who does most of the work involved in collecting, and perhaps analyzing, the data. Even though they trust each other, because their power is unequal the senior co-author will have no compunction about ruthlessly rewriting their junior co-author, but the junior co-author may be reluctant to rewrite their senior co-author. Thus, although the manuscript is passed back and forth regularly, and all authors are likely to rewrite all parts of the paper, the senior author will emerge as the writer whose voice dominates the final product. My collaborations with doctoral students tend to take this form. My goal is to teach and help them, so I encourage them to learn by initially writing all parts of the paper, but I rewrite all of it.

Directive. Finally, because directive collaborations are driven by relative contribution and have unequal power, the first author runs the show. Thus, they are the least likely to involve mutual ruthless rewriting. Authors are tied by respect but not necessarily the trust that comes with social motivations, and the unequal power makes it more difficult for co-authors to rewrite the first author, although the "director" won't hesitate to rewrite others. Indeed, the first author may do most of the writing, particularly the front end and discussion. Please keep in mind that, as Floyd and colleagues recognized, these are "pure types." Co-authoring relationships are often hybrids reflecting aspects of more than one collaboration type.

THE MECHANICS OF CO-AUTHORING

Passing the paper. The most common way in which rewriting occurs is that authors pass around a version of the manuscript, each making their edits and/ or adding comments for their co-authors to address. These editing rounds are often punctuated by periodic meetings, either face to face, on the phone or via video-conferencing. My strong preference is that everyone uses the track changes function so that we can easily see what each other has done. I also use the comment function liberally. I have one colleague who prefers putting comments in brackets in the main text and has a system for color coding the text and using different colored highlighting to indicate different things. I find this a little harder to read because it clutters up the text; but you need to be flexible with your co-authors and try to adapt to their quirks, just as they adapt to yours. The more flexible you are, the easier it is to co-author with a wide variety of people. The onus to be more flexible also tends to fall on the less powerful co-author in an unequal relationship.

Not everyone likes to track their changes, though. In her interview with Charlotte Cloutier on projectscrib.org, organizational scholar Martha Feldman (Feldman interview, posted November 10th, 2014) said she doesn't like to use track changes because she feels it makes people too invested in what they've written, rather than truly creating a collaborative work. For the same reason, she also prefers that everyone writes every part of the paper rather than parceling specific pieces out to different co-authors. I appreciate her sentiment, but not using track changes is one behavior that drives me crazy. If I don't like a change or want to put some old text back somewhere else, I don't want to stop and hunt for it in an old version. You can adopt her perspective while still tracking changes, as I try to do, but it means suppressing your ego. This is easier to do in collaborations motivated by social bonds because of the higher degree of trust among co-authors.

   Contemporaneous co-authoring. Some scholars also prefer to sit down and write with their co-authors side by side, or screen to screen. Organizational theorist Nelson Phillips discussed this approach in his interview with Charlotte Cloutier. Phillips said,

> I'm incapable of working alone. Both figuring out ideas and writing is a very social activity. Much of the time I write with my co-authors, so in the same room. So I'll go to visit a colleague somewhere, and we'll spend five days sitting in his study writing. Or another colleague will come down to London and we'll spend twelve hours sitting in my apartment.

He went on to note that,

> The actual technical way we probably would start doing it is to have quite long and detailed discussions over the phone or on Skype. We often use something like Google Docs, so we can both see the document at the same time, and then begin to sort of sketch out some sections and pieces. Ideally we do a bit of writing, merge stuff back together, then have another long call and again, work through and talk through each part. If I can go to where he is, we would get together for a couple of days and try to really structure the argument and get down the main points and generate a bunch of text. Then we'd go back to the Skyping. (Phillips interview, posted March 8th, 2013)

In his own interview, Nelson's co-author Tom Lawrence elaborated that

> If you were typing, that means another person was dictating … but you wouldn't be writing what I'm dictating. You would be adapting it as you went. (Lawrence interview, posted July 31st, 2013)

I've written with co-authors both ways Phillips described. My early collaborations with Violina Rindova involved one of us traveling to visit the other and sitting together to work through issues, often in front of the computer talking and typing. We always accomplished a great deal in a short time. If you have trouble finishing a paper, this approach may help move it forward. You can also block out time at conferences to sneak away and work together.

   My earliest experience with contemporaneous co-authoring was as a doctoral student. My advisor Joe Porac lived in Chicago because his wife worked in advertising there, and he commuted down to Champaign to teach. As a result, he was often in Chicago and I was in Champaign. This was in the mid-1990s, so many of today's online conferencing technologies didn't exist. However, Joe had a program called Laplink that allowed him to dial into his computer in Champaign from Chicago using a dial-up modem, and then we could share a screen. We talked on the phone (he had to install a second phone line in his office) while he typed, and I could take control of the mouse and type and he could take control back. This is how I learned to write academic papers, by literally watching Joe write and think through the argument in real time. While this was by far the least efficient way I've collaborated, it was also the richest learning experience.

However you choose to work with your co-authors, make sure you openly discuss the process and what your preferences are, but be flexible in accommodating your co-authors' preferences and quirks. You'll find you are very simpatico with some people; others you'll only work with once. The key is to be aware of your preferences and talk about them as you begin your collaboration.

CO-AUTHOR TEAM MANAGEMENT

Inviting co-authors. You can add co-authors at any stage of the process, not just at the beginning. I've added co-authors to papers after they've received revise and resubmits, and I've been added to papers at this stage. As an editor for *AMJ*, I handled one paper that had two authors at its initial submission, three authors when the first R&R was resubmitted and four when the second R&R was resubmitted. Whenever you add a co-author, make sure your existing co-authors agree before you make the invitation. Also be sure to clarify the role the co-author will play, so they know what you expect them to contribute.

There are two primary reasons to invite someone to co-author a paper with you: (1) They have something to offer, whether it's analytical or theoretical skills and expertise, or access to data; and (2) It's someone you like and want to do a project with. Sometimes it's a relationship in search of a project, and other times it's a project in search of collaborators. The best collaborations, though, meet both criteria. A bad reason to invite someone is simply because they are prominent. If they only bring their name to the project and contribute little else, it's unlikely to go well. Another bad reason is to help someone pad their CV, or to attempt to mutually pad CVs by adding each other to all your papers. In addition to being unethical, it won't yield a very robust or defensible record. If it's just the two of you, it will yield no productivity gains, and if there are other co-authors, they won't react well to including a co-author who adds nothing but dead weight.

If someone invites you to join their paper and you don't know them, or aren't sure about them, you can also run a "background check." Look at their publication record; if they never co-author with the same person twice, or only co-author with people junior to them, there may be reasons. When running my own background checks I've also talked to others who co-authored with the individual to find out what their experience was like before accepting their invitation.

When making the invitation, I usually ask the potential co-author if they'd be interested in joining the project, making it clear it's perfectly fine if they don't have the time or interest. I don't want them to feel pressured. Depending on the project's stage, this may follow getting a friendly review from them, or a good conversation. If it's a project that's further along, I might send them the current version to read, but I always talk to them first. Avoid sending a surprise email saying, "Hey, you want to be on this paper?"

It's also important to distinguish between an assistant and a co-author. While a graduate student co-author can also be paid for their labor on the project as part of an assistantship, if they engage in paid work only, and are not going to continue their involvement once they stop getting paid, then I don't think they merit authorship (although you should be clear about this early on and thank them for their help in the acknowledgments). If they're paid but will continue to be involved even if they are no longer paid for it, then they deserve authorship. If they do any writing, though, then they deserve authorship. Although I prefer to see authors remain involved throughout the entire process, if the person is promised authorship for doing specific things and they do them, then they should get authorship. A final, awkward situation is where the individual isn't an academic, or is dropping out of academia. If they don't want to continue being involved, and they haven't been promised authorship for a specific deliverable, then it's probably reasonable not to give authorship. Be sure to discuss this with the person, though.

Dissertation-based papers are an important special case. On the one hand, this is where emerging scholars can establish independent identities and demonstrate their capabilities by sole-authoring a manuscript, which can be important when going up for tenure. At the same time, although this varies by person and field, dissertation chairs may expect to participate as a co-author on a paper from the dissertation in recognition of the substantial time and effort they contributed (assuming they did their job well). Ideally, you'll have designed your dissertation so that it yields more than one paper. You and your chair should discuss early on which paper they will be a co-author on, if any. The best and easiest course of action is usually to offer them authorship on a paper; they can always decline. I generally try to leave the "main" empirical paper to my student, unless they want me to join that paper. If your chair joins the paper as a co-author, they should be an active co-author all the way through the process.

Authorship order. The first important decision your co-authoring team needs to make is what the authorship order will be. It's important to discuss this up front so everyone has the same expectations. As I'll discuss, it can always be renegotiated later. Co-authoring teams can use a variety of means to assign authorship order. In some fields, such as finance and accounting, the norm is to list authors alphabetically. In others, such as management, sociology and psychology, author order presumably reflects relative contribution and is used to assess authors' likely thought leadership in promotion and tenure decisions.

However, what activities count as "bigger" contributions are often a whole separate negotiation, and can vary from project to project. Is it the part that takes the most effort, the most time, requires the most expertise or was the most critical to moving the project forward? This can vary from project to project, and different individuals may have different algorithms. The American Psychological Association, for example, publishes an "authorship determination scorecard"[2] where they provide weights for 17 different activities that author teams can use to determine authorship order. While I personally wouldn't let someone else determine how much different activities should count, it can be a starting point for a discussion, and it highlights that you can employ a rational system to determine authorship. This is particularly useful for meritorious and directive collaborations.

There are times, however, when you may want to consider other factors or approaches. For example, if the paper is student driven (i.e., a second-year working paper or a dissertation-based paper) then the student should be the first author, regardless of how much rewriting their advisor does. The senior scholar often takes a lower authorship position in other types of mentoring collaborations, as well, to help build their junior co-author's career. More egalitarian co-authoring teams may want to consider equal authorship, perhaps listing authors alphabetically and adding a footnote that both authors contributed equally. Overall, half of my co-authorships were co-equal. If you are co-authoring with the same individual across papers, you may rotate authorship order. This was the approach Violina and I took for most of our papers. Given the way we worked, it didn't make much sense to parse out relative contributions. I know of other co-authoring duos that employ the same approach. If you are working on multiple papers with the same co-authors, you should also consider discussing authorship order across the different papers, switching up the order so the same people aren't always first or last.

Finally, just as you can add co-authors at any stage of the process, you can also renegotiate and change the authorship order. Co-authors' contributions may change over time as the project evolves, other things come up that lead different co-authors to take greater or lesser roles, or you may discover new skills are needed that necessitate adding another author and you'll have to negotiate their position in the author order. I had one project where a co-author and I brought on a new third author to help with data issues, the new co-author brought on his doctoral student, and the student ended up first author because

---

[2]   See: https://www.apa.org/science/leadership/students/authorship-determina tion-scorecard.pdf

of his contributions. I've demoted myself in the author order several times to recognize others' contributions. I've also been added to projects late where I came in high in the author order because I fundamentally changed the paper. It all depends. Be open to changing the author order, and re-evaluate it periodically.

Working with co-authors. In addition to negotiating authorship order, if you are conducting an empirical study it's important to discuss who owns, or has rights to publish with, the data you collect. If one or more co-authors paid for the data, or paid research assistants to collect it, they may be the owners. If it's a student-led project, the student typically has ownership rights, but if their advisor was involved in the data collection, or paid for it, they may have some claims as well. If a co-author was paid to collect the data—for example, as part of their assistantship—they may or may not have ownership rights, even if they did all the work. It depends on what you negotiate. You also need to determine whether all those with some ownership interest in the data are automatically included on all projects using the data, have a right of first refusal to participate but don't get automatic authorship, or if each author can use the data for their own purposes. It's whatever you agree to, but have the discussion early on and don't make unspoken assumptions because your co-authors might not share them.

Open communication is key to working effectively with co-authors. It is also helpful if everyone knows who's responsible for what, and if one of the co-authors (it doesn't have to be the first author) takes on the role of project manager. The project manager keeps things moving forward, schedules meetings and keeps track of timelines. This can be the same person throughout the process, or it can rotate. But having someone crack the whip generally makes projects move faster than if everyone is waiting for someone else to do something. My co-authoring teams always discuss timelines, and we make sure we all know when different folks will and won't be available to work on the project. It's also helpful to meet regularly—virtually or face to face—particularly as milestones approach. And if you break up into sub-teams to work on specific tasks, make sure you keep everyone in the loop on what's happening. If you see that a major change is required, discuss it with the team before making it.

Finally, if there are problems, don't let them fester. If you're having issues, talk about it, but do it live, not via email. Email is the best way to create hard feelings and make a problem worse. Try to avoid "ganging up" on a co-author and making them feel like the odd person out. If one of your co-authors isn't keeping their commitments, rather than making assumptions about why and lobbing accusations, find out the actual reasons. There may be something going on in their life you aren't aware of. It may also be the case that one team member will have to act as the go-between with feuding co-authors to get the project done.

Dropping a co-author. Despite your best efforts, sometimes things just don't work out and a co-author needs to go. This is tricky. It's best and easiest if they no longer want to be part of the project and leave voluntarily. If they don't want to leave voluntarily, one option is to just let them be the last author but ask them to no longer participate in the project. They can still list the publication on their CV and get credit for it in annual evaluations, which may be what they are most concerned about. It goes against what I discussed earlier, but it's a relatively costless solution that can end the stress and rancor. You may also consider agreeing to let them have access to the data for their own purposes as a condition of leaving the project. If they aren't contributing anyway, or you think what they want to do is wrong-headed, this again can be relatively costless, as the likelihood they will publish anything using the data may be low. Finally, be prepared to defend your decisions with editors or others, especially if this happens during the review process. If you are having problems with a co-author, create a paper trail. Save all email correspondence, and document face-to-face meetings with a follow-up email about what was said. It can get ugly, and it's best to have the facts on your side. I've seen these kinds of situations play out, and it never ceases to amaze me how badly some people behave.

Even if you complete the project together, you need to decide whether you're willing to work with a co-author again on future projects. I've only had a few co-authors I didn't want to co-author with again. If I enjoy working with the person, they do their part and they communicate, then I'm willing to work with them again. If they created a negative dynamic, didn't come through on their promises, or I felt like I was doing all the heavy lifting, then I'm unlikely to work with them again.

On that happy note, I'll bring this chapter to a close. Understanding the norms and dynamics of working with co-authors can be confusing to the uninitiated, and most folks I know have co-authoring war stories. If you're clear-eyed about who you're dealing with, and follow the steps I suggest, your positive experiences should far outweigh the negative.

12. Navigating the review process

I did a rough tally, and to date I've received approximately 440 reviews of my journal submissions and written about 120 response letters. If you add in friendly reviews, editors' letters, feedback on book chapters and conference submission reviews, the number of reviews probably increases by 50 percent. I've written approximately 300 journal reviews (a number that again goes up by about half when you add in friendly reviews, conference paper reviews and dissertation competition reviews) and over 280 editor's decision letters. As an editor and reviewer I've also read over 2,000 reviews of others' work and over 300 response letters. I can say unequivocally that my articles have all improved for having gone through the peer review process, as have all the accepted articles I've been involved with as a reviewer or editor. The system is inherently subjective and far from perfect, but it's better than any alternative available for ferreting out problems, ensuring quality and improving manuscripts. It also requires a thick skin, perseverance, the ability to read between the lines, confidence and a great deal of emotional control.

The reviewers' job is to vet your work and make sure it meets the journal's standards of rigor, importance and interestingness. Your job is to convince them of these things. That's why it's so important that you are clear, complete and transparent in your writing and explanations. You want the reviewers to like and trust you, even though they don't know who you are. However, that isn't enough. I've seen many promising papers get rejected because the authors made mistakes managing the review process.

In this chapter I explain how to navigate the journal review process. I start with a word about emotional control, and then discuss two issues pertaining to your initial submission—choosing the journal to submit your manuscript to and learning from rejections. In the remainder of the chapter I discuss how to navigate the revision process in the happy event you receive an invitation to revise and resubmit your work.

EMOTIONAL CONTROL

The biggest challenge in the review process is managing your emotions, especially negative emotions like anger and annoyance. These emotions are natural when receiving negative feedback, which comprises about 95 percent of the content in decision letters and reviews. It's okay to experience these emotions and to vent them within your close circle. I sometimes get pissed off by the reviews I receive and rant to my co-authors about them, even when we get an R&R. However, you then need to get over it, put the negative emotions aside, and get to work. You can't let emotions tinge your responses to reviewers; you also can't let them keep you from working on rejected papers and sending them back out for review.

It's easy to forget as you read page after page of negative comments, but editors and reviewers are by and large trying to help you improve your manuscript. Cooling-off periods are thus an extremely important part of the process. Whether the news is good or bad, set the decision letter aside for at least a week and then come back to it calmer, and with a more dispassionate eye towards the issues raised (except after conditional acceptances—get on those right away). Don't let the letter and paper sit too long, though. You're more likely to lose your ambition, particularly if it's a rejection or a difficult R&R, and the editor's and reviewers' interest may wane. You might also get scooped by another study. As you revise the paper, either to resubmit or send to another journal, take it in small bites so that the emotions don't build back up and overwhelm you.

INITIAL SUBMISSION

Choosing a Journal

As you prepare your article for journal submission, you need to decide where you want to send it. As you consider your options, it's important to understand the differences across journals, and which may be the best fit for your article. The following are some important considerations:

General (big tent) vs. domain specific. Some journals are "big tent" journals that consider any method or topic area within an academic field. Others are more focused, and only accept articles about certain phenomena or topics, or focus on specific levels of analysis. Big tent journals (in my field of management this includes journals such as *Academy of Management Journal, Academy of Management Review* and *Journal of Management*) are always safe bets in the sense that everything falls under their umbrella, but there aren't that many of them. Other journals may still be relatively broad, but will only consider articles at particular levels of analysis. Examples in my field include *Administrative Science Quarterly* and *Organization Science*, which both require some organization-level or higher implications, as opposed to a strictly individual-level focus. If you send a paper to a domain-specific journal (in my field these would include journals such as *Journal of Business Venturing* [entrepreneurship], *Personnel Psychology* [human resources] and *Strategic Management Journal* [strategy], among many others), you need to make sure your article actually fits within the journal's domain and contributes to the conversations happening there, or starts a new conversation its readers will find interesting.

Empirical only, theory only or mixed. Make sure the journal accepts the type of article you've written. This is basic, but you'd be amazed how often people screw this up. Some journals accept both empirical and theory papers, but many only accept empirical research, and a few, like *Academy of Management Review*, are theory only. Read the domain statements and look at recent issues if you aren't sure. Along these lines, try to assess whether the journal publishes articles employing the same methodology you've used, or is at least likely to be open to it if it's a new methodology. Although it's rare for journals to say explicitly "we don't publish articles using 'X' methodology," reading a few issues and talking to others sometimes makes it clear whether the journal has the expertise or willingness to handle certain methodologies.

Emphasis on theoretical or empirical contributions. Some journals put a premium on theoretical contributions, while others focus more on empirical contributions. For example, in my field *Administrative Science Quarterly* probably puts the highest premium on making a significant theoretical contribution (although the empirics have to be really strong, as well), whereas journals like *Psychological Science* and *Academy of Management Discoveries* expressly focus on interesting empirical contributions and don't emphasize theory. Most other journals fall between these two extremes. Make sure the journal you submit to fits your study's contribution.

Publishing outside your academic domain. You may also have a study that crosses disciplinary boundaries, or really lies outside your home academic discipline. For example, management scholars sometimes publish in adjacent disciplines such as psychology, sociology, economics, marketing and communications. Some marketing scholars publish in management journals, and, although rarer, I've seen accounting scholars publish in management journals, and management scholars publish in finance journals. Please recognize, however, that even though the different disciplines share some common theoretical underpinnings, publishing norms and expectations vary significantly across fields. For example, since I do research on initial public offerings (IPOs), I've occasionally reviewed articles that were clearly written for finance journals but apparently didn't get accepted there, so the authors thought they'd take a shot at a management journal, but without ever having read or cited a management article on IPOs. If you try to publish outside your discipline, I strongly encourage you to find a co-author who is "native" to the discipline and can help guide your study so that it fits the discipline's norms. And read some articles from that field and cite them!

General Rules of Thumb for Initial Submissions

Before sending an article to a journal:

- Make sure your paper's structure conforms to the journal's length require-
  ments. Some journals won't even send the paper out for review if it's too
  long.
- Match the journal's emphasis on theory versus empirics. If the journal is
  empirically focused, keep the theory section short. If it's theory heavy,
  make sure you have more than a theory paragraph.
- Look at how the papers in the journal are written (structure, use of hypotheses, etc.) and ensure your structure fits within the journal's norms.
- Consider whether your paper fits the conversation going on in the journal.
  If you don't cite any studies published in the journal, or the journal's field,
  it's the wrong outlet.
- Assess whether your style fits the journal's style. The way you think and
  write may naturally fit certain journals' styles and emphases better than
  others. I've certainly had more success at some journals than others, at
  least partly for this reason. If your articles don't look much like the articles
  published in the journal, and it's too much of a stretch to make them look
  that way, then it's probably not the right outlet.

Learning from Rejections

Rejections suck. There are no two ways about it. However, rejections also offer
the opportunity to learn and improve your manuscript for the next journal. For
example, early in my career the reviewers advised my co-author and I to split
a paper they had rejected into two papers. We did, and one of them is now my
highest-cited paper and the other won an award. Never send out the exact same
version of a rejected paper to another journal. There are always things you can
improve on for the next outlet. There's also the risk you may draw the same
reviewer at the next journal, who would be displeased if you ignored their
comments entirely. As discussed above, give yourself a little break to calm
your emotions, but then get back to it and turn it around for the next journal.

As you work your way through the reviews, the issues the editor focuses
on in his/her letter are likely to be the biggest problems you face, and typically reflect common themes and major flaws. The amount of feedback
you get depends on the journal, its editorial norms and the particular editor.
Developmental decision letters and reviews can provide excellent guidance
about how to revise your paper. Others, unfortunately, provide limited insights.
In either case, you want to read the reviews carefully. As you do, don't assume

that what they talk about first is the biggest issue. Some reviewers order their reviews by importance, while others are more chronological as they go through the paper and don't necessarily say "this is my major concern."

You'll also want to separate the common themes and major flaws you need to address from idiosyncratic comments you can probably ignore. If only one reviewer brings up an issue and the editor didn't mention it, the issue is likely idiosyncratic to that particular reviewer. Think carefully about whether you want to address this issue, and how much attention to give it. Making a big deal out of something that otherwise wouldn't be a big deal to the next set of reviewers can draw unnecessary attention and create problems. I've made this mistake more than once. In making your decisions, take the risk–reward ratio into account. Fix the things you can reasonably fix; all theory issues are fixable, but data issues may not be. If you have an unfixable data issue, you'll have to figure out how to minimize the flaw's effects. This may require changing your story, conducting some additional robustness tests to assess if it's really an issue in your context, or identifying it as a limitation and area for future research in the Discussion. What you don't want to do is ignore it and hope nobody notices. They will.

Finally, don't let the reviewers push you towards a story you don't believe in. After all, the rejected paper isn't going back to them. At the same time, if the reviewers suggest a different story, or a lot of different stories, they're telling you that you didn't do a good job persuading them that your story was the best story. Otherwise, they'd focus on the details of and holes in your story rather than suggesting something wholly different. Give yourself enough time that you can read the reviews somewhat dispassionately, and just ignore any snide or ill-considered comments. At the same time, keep in mind that if the reviewers didn't get something, that's ultimately your fault. You need to explain issues so clearly and so well that there's no mistaking them, even if the reviewer is reading quickly or is distracted. And don't sit on the paper too long. If the paper's in your hands and not at a journal, the odds of it not getting accepted are 100 percent.

YOU GOT AN R&R! CONGRATULATIONS! NOW WHAT?

First, celebrate! This is a big deal. Your acceptance odds just went from less than 10 percent to 50 percent, because about half of the papers editors give revise and resubmits to ultimately make it through. I've often seen new scholars get depressed when they get an R&R because the revision is labeled high risk, and because of the amount of work they'll have to do. They don't realize what a big accomplishment this is. So, savor it, but then get to work. In this section I discuss how to manage the revision, and then address dealing with second revisions, conditional acceptances and the journal production process.

Keep your Goal in Mind

As you begin work on your revision, what's your goal? To get all the reviewers to recommend acceptance? That almost never happens. Getting the editor and most reviewers on your side, and wearing down the most negative reviewers so they run out of concrete objections, is more feasible. This means you need to assess who seems the most positively predisposed to your paper, and who's probably never going to like it. You want to make sure that you don't lose the positive reviewer in the process of trying to convince the intransigent reviewer. At the end of the day, the editor has to like your paper, along with hopefully the majority of the reviewers. If the editor is positively predisposed, then one positive (plus maybe one neutral) reviewer may be enough.

Does this surprise you? If so, it's probably because you've heard the popular myth that editors are looking to reject as many papers as they can, or that there's a limited amount of white space available. Editors put out new issues of their journals on a monthly, bimonthly or quarterly basis—to do that they need inventory. Indeed, an editor's biggest challenge isn't running out of white space, it's having enough accepted papers in inventory. You can't build inventory and publish a journal if your default position is to reject everything unless convinced otherwise. Reviewers don't always get this, but they aren't the decision makers. The editor is. As both an editor and a reviewer, my default position is to give a revision unless convinced otherwise. Unfortunately, many authors are good at convincing editors and reviewers to reject their papers. If you've received an R&R, you're over the first big hurdle. You don't want to blow it now.

Evaluating the Comments

Former *AMJ* Editor Jason Shaw wrote a useful "From the Editors" column (Shaw, 2012) on responding to reviewers. In it, he recommended going through all your comments and classifying them into one of three categories: (1) Those that improve the paper; (2) Those that are neutral (they won't improve, but they also won't hurt the paper); and (3) Those that, if you followed them, would hurt the paper. You should follow every comment and suggestion that improves the paper. These are the critical changes and will likely make up the bulk of the changes you discuss in your response letter. They're also most likely to be the comments the editor singles out in the decision letter.

If the comment is neutral, do it if you can. It's not going to hurt the paper but will likely make the reviewer feel better—it shows you're being responsive to their concerns, and it will help you earn the reviewer's trust. I'm often surprised, and disappointed, at how unwilling many authors are to make even basic changes that cost them nothing but a little time and effort. By failing to make these changes you appear defensive, which generally leads reviewers to respond negatively. If the suggestion will hurt the paper, or fundamentally tries to move the paper in a direction you don't want to go, then don't do it. This can be tricky, and I'll discuss how to defend your choice in the next section. But you don't have to do everything reviewers suggest. You're still the author, and reviewers aren't always right. They also may not care that much about the issue, or it may have been an offhand suggestion.

The trick, of course, is identifying which category the comments fall into. You are making the judgments, and your judgment may not be exactly unbiased. For example, it's likely that most comments will fall into the "helps" and "neutral" categories. So, if you have identified a lot of "hurts the paper" comments and few helps and neutral comments, then you're likely being too defensive. By the same token, if you categorize most comments as helping, then you may need to be a little more discerning or your study could turn into a muddled mess. Although the distribution varies as a function of the reviewers you draw, on average I find "neutral" comments make up the largest category and "hurts" comments the smallest, with "helps" in between. If you deviate from this rough ordering, give the comments a second look, or ask an experienced colleague to look at the letter and offer their opinion.

Figuring Out your Responses

Once I've categorized the comments, I then start sketching out responses to each of them. You won't draft the whole letter, but you'll want to develop a game plan for how to respond before diving into the paper. Usually, I like to go through all the comments by myself first, while my co-authors are doing the same thing, and then get together with them to discuss what we think we need to do and assign tasks. Assign responsibility for responding to each comment to the author best equipped to handle it. Don't leave everything for the first author to do. You're all invested in getting the paper through the revision process.

Drafting the Letter and Responding to Reviewers

The first step is to convert the decision letter into a response letter. First, I delete all the parts of the editor's letter other than their specific comments, as these are what you are responding to. We'll talk about that in a bit. I also convert the editor's and reviewers' comments to italics so they are easier to distinguish from my responses. I prefer italics to bolding because bolding just makes the words blockier and the letter longer. Number the reviewer's points if the reviewer was inconsiderate enough not to have already done so, because it makes them easier to reference. I also sometimes break up compound points that address multiple issues into sub-points. I don't renumber them, but I put my responses in after each part of the comment, rather than waiting until the end of the point.

As you think about how you'll respond to each comment, keep in mind that revisions are both a conversation with the editor and reviewers, and a nego-tiation. Once you send a paper to a journal it's no longer just "yours"; you are asking others for something (acceptance), and they'll want some input in return. I therefore recommend you treat revisions as integrative negotiations, which look for win–win outcomes that satisfy both parties' needs, rather than as distributive negotiations which adopt a zero sum, I win–you lose stance (Fisher, Ury & Patton, 2011). In a distributive negotiation with someone who has all the decision-making authority, you will lose. So be as open-minded and responsive as possible to their comments and suggestions. Because this is an integrative negotiation, look for ways to acknowledge their concern even when you disagree with the point. This may mean addressing the spirit of the issue, even if you don't do what they suggest. Most editors and reviewers are okay with that. They're (usually) more concerned that you address the problem than that you do exactly what they recommend. If they aren't okay with that on some specific point, they'll let you know.

Although you aren't interacting face to face, you still want to try and create a connection with the reviewers, and making your letter conversational helps do this. So, use conversational speech that employs contractions and other more informal communication modes, and address the editor and reviewers directly using personal pronouns. It's also okay to be frank—if you made a mistake, take responsibility for it (e.g., "We now see that we omitted some important details about how we constructed our measure"), and if you can't do something, say so (e.g., "We'd love to do what you suggest, but the data are unavailable"). Don't be afraid to apologize. It isn't a sign of weakness. Most often you are apologizing for being unclear. Even if you think you were clear, or you did say something and the reviewer missed it, apologize anyway for not being clear enough, but then go on to say that you've revised the paper to make this point clearer (and make sure you do something to the manuscript. They'll notice if it's unchanged.).

When you make changes in response to a reviewer's comment, give them credit whenever possible (e.g., "In response to your suggestion," "As you suggested," "Following your suggestion"). When reviewers see things in your paper based on their ideas and suggestions it increases their psychological ownership of the paper and their desire to see it succeed, even if they aren't getting direct credit for their ideas. As you make these changes, explain how the change addresses the concern they raised, particularly if you aren't doing what they suggested but something that was "inspired" by their comment. You should also thank them for their suggestions, but don't be a kiss-ass. If they raise a really good point (these are at least some of the "improves the paper" comments), thank them for raising the topic or for pushing you on the issue. Don't do it for every point, though, or it loses its effectiveness. If it's a "neutral" comment, you can simply say thanks for pointing it out, or note that you made the change they suggested.

When you disagree with a comment or suggestion, to the extent possible use facts and data and not just argumentation to support your position in your response. For example, do supplemental analyses, if you can, to rule out alternative explanations, or provide data or other studies that refute their assertions. If they ask you to use an analytical technique you think is inappropriate, explain why the method is inappropriate, but then do the analyses they ask for anyway and show them that the results came out as you predicted because of the reasons you identified. You can include these analyses in the letter only. Try to do something that at least addresses the spirit of their concern, though. And if it's a gray area issue, or a matter of preference as opposed to a clear right or wrong, say that you'll report the alternative analysis, or include a more detailed discussion in the paper, or whatever the issue is, if the reviewer *and editor* really want you to. This shows your flexibility, and it also puts both the reviewer and editor on notice that the editor has to give his/her express blessing.

Another challenging circumstance is when reviewers make opposing suggestions. Ideally the editor will point you towards their preferred option; then you can just say, "Following the editor's recommendation ... ." But if the editor doesn't provide guidance, or you don't like their preferred option, then you'll have to address the conflict directly. The easiest way to do this is to thank them for their suggestion, point out the conflicting recommendations, and then say you followed the other reviewer's recommendation and explain why.

If the editor or reviewers suggest references, try to incorporate them to the extent they are relevant and make sense. This is one of those neutral issues. If there are lots of references to the same author's work, there's a good chance that this person is the reviewer. Citing some of their *relevant* work is costless, and can also increase their desire to see your paper published.

As you draft your responses keep in mind that your response letter will be long no matter what, so do things to keep it as short as possible. For example, when you've made changes in the paper in response to some comment, don't repeat chunks of text in the letter. Instead, provide the page number for the spot in the paper where you made the change. They are going to read your change when they read the paper; they don't need to read it twice. While drafting the letter and editing the paper I put markers for page number references in the letter (e.g., p. XX) and highlight them in yellow to make them easier to find later. You can then search on "XX" at the end of the process when you're sure the page numbers in the paper aren't going to change and replace them with the actual numbers.

Finally, if two reviewers make the same point, or if the editor summarized a point that the reviewers made, don't repeat your response verbatim multiple times. Do it once, and for the others refer them to the full response, identifying the reviewer or editor and point number. I usually say something like "The Editor, Point Y, and Reviewer X, Points Z and ZZ, raised similar issues ..." to highlight the commonality and direct them to the specific response. So they don't feel neglected I then say, "However, to summarize ... ," and provide a short summary to give them a little personal attention, or address a nuance in their comment that might not be part of the other answer. Finally, provide the full references used in your responses to the editor and each reviewer at the end of each response. Although this may add length because you repeat some references, it's a courtesy to the reviewers.

Revising the Manuscript

Although I've focused most of my attention on the letter to this point, that doesn't mean it's all about the letter. Indeed, one major reason revisions fail is that the authors spend too much time on the letter and don't sufficiently change the manuscript. If you don't fundamentally change your manuscript to address the reviewers' concerns, it doesn't matter how artfully crafted your letter is—your paper will get rejected. Thus, you want to make sure you adequately address the editor's and reviewers' comments in the paper, too.

Just as assigning a project manager can help get a paper out the door (see Chapter 11), making one of the authors the revision's project manager helps ensure everything gets done (Agarwal, Echambadi, Franco & Sarkar, 2006). It can be the lead author, or it can be the co-author who is the most organized. As I noted earlier, each author should be given responsibility for addressing specific questions and rewriting that part of the paper consistent with their expertise, and one person should pull it all together and make sure it sounds unified.

Once you have your game plan, start by doing all the necessary data stuff; depending on what's required, you may also need to simultaneously work on the Introduction and Theory and Hypotheses sections. If you are developing and testing new hypotheses, you'll need to know what your revised story is to do the analyses. Be prepared to conduct major surgery. Your theory, the story, the hypotheses, the measures and the types of analyses done are all on the table. This is your best chance to convince the reviewers and the editor, so you need to do all that you can. At the same time, don't overdo it and scrap the whole paper, unless that's really required. If you aren't sure, ask someone you trust to read the reviews and offer their opinion. Be open to improving your story, but don't lose your story in trying to be responsive. I've made that mistake before. One of my articles was rejected the first place we sent it, and although we received R&Rs at the next two journals, it was rejected after the revisions. We went through two rounds of revision before getting rejected at a fourth journal. My co-authors and I finally stepped back, re-established the story *we* wanted to tell, and successfully moved the paper to publication at the fifth journal where we submitted it.

So how do you avoid our fate? Part of it is gut feel. If the reviewers are pushing you towards a story you simply don't believe yourself, or that you don't find interesting, don't do it. Also, keep the primary aspects of your story in mind. Are your main and supporting characters clear? Are you spinning out too many storylines based on too many theories? Do you know what your theme is? This is where we lost our way; we lost track of our storyline and brought in too many different theories. If you tell a plausible and coherent story, reviewers are more likely to look for ways to refine your story than for different stories to tell.

This is also the point where you want to put a lot of effort into your Discussion section. Reviewers may not have read it carefully on the first round, but they will now. The Discussion section always gets longer on this round, if for no other reason than you add limitations and directions for future research in response to the reviewers' comments. Now that you've entered into a negotiation with the editor and reviewers your story is likely to focus and deepen, and you can make the specific edits to your Discussion that highlight your contributions more clearly, and position it more effectively within the theoretical conversation you are participating in. I'm not going to say more about revising the paper here, because everything I discussed in the first nine chapters applies equally to revisions. Do that.

Communicating with the Editor

Another area shrouded in myth and misunderstanding is how to communicate with the editor handling your manuscript. If you've received an R&R, then the editor wants to see you succeed. To that end, many, but not all, prefer that you ask for clarifications about questions you have, rather than guessing at the answer and guessing wrong. If you have questions, or you aren't sure what a reviewer is asking, or you need guidance on dealing with conflicting requests, ask the editor if you can talk with him or her. I've encountered a few editors who don't want to communicate with authors outside of decision letters, but most are happy to talk. Some prefer email, while others will do a phone or video call. It never hurts to ask, politely, and then accommodate their preference.

A few pieces of etiquette: please don't call the editor out of the blue. Email your request first, remind them of your manuscript number, and detail your issues and questions so they can think about them ahead of time. While your paper is your paramount focus, the reality is the editor probably doesn't remember that much about it once they've hit send on the decision letter. They have lots of manuscripts to deal with, so they've sent the information on yours to their mental off-site storage. You need to give them a little time to retrieve the particulars so that your conversation is focused and productive. When you get on the call be respectful of their time and be clear about what you're looking for. Also understand, and reassure them you understand, that just because you do what they say it doesn't guarantee your revision will be successful. Editors will provide guidance, but they aren't going to make promises. Finally, don't forget to thank them for their time. It also doesn't hurt to send them a thank-you email when they give you an R&R. Editors are people too; they've put a lot of effort into their decision and appreciate their efforts being recognized. Again, don't be a kiss-ass, but acknowledge the opportunity they're giving you, and say thanks.

Finally, most revisions come with a deadline. Some are longer than others, but they typically range from three months to a year. Do your best to meet the deadline, but I've yet to encounter an editor who won't give you more time if you need it. They want you to do the best job you can. Just communicate with them and give them a reasonable time when you think you'll be done. It's annoying if you ask for two weeks, and then in two weeks ask for another two weeks, and on and on. Although I've had to ask for multiple extensions for different reasons, give your best estimate of how long it will really take, add a couple of weeks, and then ask for that. No one complains if you set a longer deadline than you need and then submit the revision earlier.

Polishing it Up and Sending it Off

Once you think the paper is done, return to the response letter and edit it as necessary to reflect how the paper actually evolved as you rewrote it. You may also find points you forgot to respond to, and that you need to incorporate into the paper. If you haven't already done so, provide a general comment at the beginning of each reviewer response thanking them for their suggestions, personalizing the responses as appropriate, and letting them know that you'll be referring them to your responses to the Editor's and other reviewers' comments if you've already answered a similar question elsewhere.

The last thing I do after the responses are done is write a one-page (approximately) cover letter to the editor. Many editors ask for one, but even if they don't it's useful to provide a summary of all your major changes so they know what's coming. It helps the editor if you include the manuscript number and title in the opening paragraph. My opening paragraphs are some variant of this example:

> Dear [Editor's Name]
> Thanks for giving us an opportunity to revise and resubmit our manuscript AMJ-2017-0144, "Too many peas in a pod? How overlaps in directors' local and global status characteristics influence board turnover in newly public firms," for further publication consideration at the *Academy of Management Journal*. We have worked hard to address all of your and the reviewers' comments, and we think our manuscript has taken a significant leap forward. To summarize the major changes that we've made:

I then follow this with a numbered point-by-point summary of the major changes. Don't list everything you did; hit the highlights, and condense the smaller stuff into a single line, such as "and we addressed all of the reviewers' other methodological concerns." I close the letter with some variant of

> Overall, we think our theory is now more refined, our contributions clearer, and our findings are robust. We hope these changes address your and the reviewers' concerns. In the rest of this letter we address each of your and the reviewers' specific comments and suggestions. We look forward to hearing from you regarding the disposition of our manuscript.

Once this is done, replace all the XXs in your letter with page numbers and give the paper and letter another careful copy-edit. That's it. You're ready to resubmit.

Subsequent Revisions and Acceptance

Second (or more) revision. The same general steps apply for subsequent revisions. If the first revision was really major, the second round may be almost like the first round, but hopefully not. As the negotiation progresses there should be fewer issues to work out in later rounds, and they will typically be more focused. Don't get defensive at this point because you are tired of the process, and of changing stuff. Suck it up and keep putting lots of effort into the revisions. It depends on the journal, but many editors look to make a decision after the second R&R. Unfortunately, some also take you through more revisions. Be super responsive to their points, because they reflect what they're looking for to say yes.

Conditional acceptance. Now you can really celebrate! You're almost home. At this point you won't be working with the reviewers anymore, just the editor. Unless the editor notes otherwise, direct your responses to him/her, address all the editor's points, and simply tell them what you did in response to any remaining reviewers' points that the editor didn't specifically mention. Be responsive, and turn it around quickly. Everyone wants to be done at this point. This is also where the editor may ask you to shorten the paper to meet particular page limits. If you've added stuff to placate a reviewer's idiosyncratic demands that takes up space, and it's not a big issue for the editor, it may be a candidate for deletion. As an editor I took two papers through two rounds of revision at the conditional acceptance stage, and I've been taken through two rounds of revision at this stage myself, but in general this is your last round. After this should come the final acceptance.

Preparing the article for publication. Once you've submitted the final, accepted version of your manuscript for publication, the only thing left will be the copy-editing and reading the page proofs. Some journals do this right after acceptance, so the only thing that changes between the in-press version and the published version is the volume, issue and page numbers. Others handle copy-editing right before your article goes to press. Either way, the paper will go through a final copy-editing process. Journals vary in how they handle this process, but more and more are outsourcing the copy-editing and layout to third-party services. This sucks, because you don't get to communicate directly with the copy-editor like you do at journals who do their own in-house copy editing. I've learned a great deal from in-house copy-editors. Third-party services also don't typically send you a copy-edited version of your manuscript, which makes it easier to see the changes. They make their changes, put the text and images into the publication format, and then send you a pdf of the page proofs with a list of queries, which are requests for clarifications on different items. Thus, you have to pick through the page proofs and try to spot their changes.

Read the page proofs carefully, including the tables. Numbers are sometimes screwed up, or they forget to put in significance identifiers. Respond to all the copy-editor's queries. Don't go overboard on making changes at this point, though. And you don't have to just accept what the copy-editor does. Most changes fix errors you made or pertain to the journal's house style and formatting; however, some changes are a matter of taste or preference, and sometimes they change things that alter the sentence's meaning. Push back on these changes if you need to. Copy-editors also often give you very short turnaround times with no notice. If you can't meet the deadline they give you, say so, and let them know when you'll have it back. Try not to take more than a week.

This chapter concludes the processes involved in conducting and publishing your research. In the next chapter I will focus on some other common types of writing that academics do that are also persuasive tools.

13. Other kinds of writing

One reason we have so little time for academic writing is because we spend so much of our time, well, writing. We write syllabi and lesson plans, annual reviews describing our year's accomplishments, and reviews of others' work. Much of this writing helps others accomplish their tasks. In this chapter I'm going to focus on three documents we write for our own benefit that are related to research, and where we use storytelling to persuade others: grant proposals, research statements, and cover letters. In describing how to write each document effectively I will focus on their audiences, purposes, tone, content and structure.

GRANT PROPOSALS

Most scholars need money to carry out their research. The amount required can range from a few hundred to hundreds of thousands of dollars, or more. Further, at many schools summer research support is awarded on a competitive basis. While some schools provide faculty with budgets that cover research expenses, many do not. Thus, whether it's applying internally for research grants and summer support, or chasing research grants from external granting organizations, at some point most scholars write grant proposals. Unlike STEM fields, funding opportunities and institutional norms are less well-developed in the social sciences. Grant money is often available, however, and there are steps you can take to improve your grant proposals' odds of getting funded.

Science writer Vid Mohan-Ram wrote a great set of blog posts for *Science Magazine* titled "How not to kill a grant application" (2000)[1] that I highly recommend to anyone new to grant writing, or who has been unsuccessful thus far. Although geared towards natural scientists, his recommendations apply equally to social scientists and echo many of my storytelling recommendations. I also recommend reading others' successful grant proposals, particularly if you are applying to the same granting agency.

Audiences and purposes. Grant proposals fulfill a variety of purposes. On a personal level, grant proposal writing is a sensemaking process where you figure out what study or stream of studies you want to conduct, what's involved

---

[1] See: http://www.sciencemag.org/careers/where-search-funding

in conducting them, and why they are worth doing. Writing grant proposals helps you work through a lot of issues, details and logistics associated with conducting your research before you actually begin. It also helps you develop the story for your academic article and puts some momentum behind the study.

Beyond that, a grant proposal's most obvious purposes are to convey information about studies you want to conduct to funding organizations who may be interested in giving you the money needed to conduct them, and to convince them that doing so is a worthwhile investment that helps them meet their needs and interests. If you don't know who will be reading your proposal and what their interests are, it will be difficult to persuade them to give *you* the money so many desire. Thus, critical to successful grant writing is understanding who will read the grant proposal, and what their levels of expertise and interests are.

One of the biggest mistakes grant writers make is that they assume their proposals are read by technical experts in their area. If you get such reviewers, you're lucky. But there are a variety of audiences to consider. The first is the granting organization's decision makers. Depending on the organization, these folks may or may not be academics; thus, you need to make sure that non-academics can understand your proposal and why your study is interesting and important. That means avoiding lots of technical jargon. The granting agencies are also likely to have a variety of interests they are trying to address. First and foremost is the granting organization's mission. For example, I received a grant from the Oxford Centre for Corporate Reputation which, as the name implies, is interested in promoting research on corporate reputation. They fund reputation research across academic disciplines, but do not fund research in unrelated areas.

The granting organization may also have political interests that they need to meet; thus, there may be certain topics they are particularly eager, or disinclined, to fund. They may also look to promote certain kinds of individuals or initiatives, and/or have concerns about equity. For example, I was one of the last people who was neither Oxford faculty nor working on a project with one of their postdoctoral research fellows to get a grant. Shortly after I received my grant, the Centre's leadership decided that they wanted to prioritize funding folks within the Centre or Oxford University more generally—a perfectly reasonable choice. Thus, in selecting whom to submit your proposal to, and how to frame your study and contribution, you'll need to take this audience and their interests into account.

A second audience is the reviewers who read your grant and make specific recommendations to decision makers. These may be the members of the research grant committee in your school, outside reviewers in your domain, such as those enlisted by the National Science Foundation, or others. Again, they are likely to vary in their level of technical expertise and knowledge of your specific research domain. Understand who is likely to review your proposal, and make sure it's written so that even non-experts can follow it.

A final audience is other constituencies within your college or university, including the institutional review board (IRB), research deans and even internal grant committees. IRBs have to approve studies that involve human subjects, so they will be interested in and have to approve the details of your proposal. Research deans will be interested in any research that brings money to the school, particularly if the granting organization also pays overhead.[2] And although this is not yet common in the social sciences, demonstrating you can successfully raise grant money may be part of your tenure and promotion assessment. Finally, internal grant committees will be interested if you are applying for external funding as well. Some committees like to provide "seed" funding only if you are actively seeking funds from other sources, whereas others may decide that if you are pursuing outside funding you are less likely to need their funding, and will commit the resources to others with fewer options. I've seen both happen when serving on research grant committees.

Tone. The tone of grant proposals is formal but not jargony; in other words, similar to the tone of an academic article. You will want to keep it succinct and to the point, focusing on what your study will provide and how you'll go about doing it. Reviewers and decision makers plow through a lot of proposals, and you don't want to make the process any harder on them than it already is.

Content and structure. Much of a grant proposal's content and structure mirrors the opening sections of an article. Whether or not the granting organization has a particular format they want you to follow, they all ask for the same information.

As with an article, the first three components are the title, abstract and introduction. Mohan-Ram's (2000) recommendations for these largely mirror mine in Chapter 5. He suggested that your *title* be clever and contain all the information necessary to know what your study is about. Next, the *abstract* needs to capture the essentials of your study in a few hundred words, explaining what's been done before, why your study is important and how you'll do it, all in a non-technical way. Titles and abstracts are particularly important for grant proposals because they are frequently used to route the proposal to the relevant agency or reviewer. They may also be the only part of your proposal some folks read. Thus, it also behooves you to include key words from their requests for proposal (RFPs) in your abstract. The *introduction* does all the good stuff

---

[2]   Overhead is money paid to the university to help defray general costs the school covers on behalf of the research, such as utilities, office or lab space, administrative support and costs, etc. It is typically a major source of revenue for research universities.

that introductions do, answering the questions: "Who cares?," "What do we know, what don't we know, and so what?" and "What will we learn?"

Following the introduction are the *problems you'll address*. This is where you'll review the literature and discuss the problems you hope to solve and why they're important, present your research questions and, if you're doing a quantitative study, the hypotheses they suggest. Thus, you'll identify your main and supporting characters and lay out their storylines.

Since you haven't done the study yet, rather than presenting a methods section explaining what you have done you will instead describe *how you intend to conduct your study*. You'll describe your context, sampling, measures and analytical approach, but it will be in the future rather than past tense (i.e., "we will ...," "we intend to ...," "we plan to ..."). Depending on the magnitude of your grant and the funding organization, Mohan-Ram (2000) also recommended describing a plan B and a plan C in case your first study doesn't work out. You don't want to propose a set of studies that are contingent on the first one working, because if the first study fails then the money has gone to waste. This may be less of an issue for smaller grants, and particularly for internal grants.

Two important additional topics you'll need to cover are a *realistic timeline and budget* that lays out the cost and *project team biographies and roles*. I'm always surprised when a proposal doesn't say how long the study is likely to take, doesn't include a clear financial request, or just states the maximum grant available but doesn't explain how it will be spent. You need to show the decision makers that you will spend their money wisely, and that you understand what it will take to conduct the study you're proposing. Thus, you need to provide some details about what you'll spend the money on. Make sure you look carefully at what the granting organization is and isn't willing to cover. For example, some will help cover summer support for the principal investigators or the costs of conference travel to present the study, while others won't.

It's also important for the granting agencies to know who is on the team and what their prior experience is. Scholars who have a successful record generally find it easier to get grants because the granting organizations always worry about their money going to waste. That's why new faculty and doctoral students really need to polish their proposals; they don't have their reputations and prior experience to fall back on. This is also why it's a good idea to have an experienced co-principal investigator.

Finally, you'll end your proposal with a *conclusion*. Mohan-Ram suggested that your conclusion focus heavily on the "so what?" issue, and what you intend to accomplish. It's also nice if you can say how many articles the project is likely to generate, where they will be presented and what journals you'll target. The more information reviewers and decision makers have that increases their confidence in you, the more receptive they're likely to be to your proposal. You'll also include a complete *reference section* of the articles you cited.

RESEARCH STATEMENTS

A research statement is a narrative where you tell the story of who you are as a researcher and what you've accomplished. It's where you connect all the different studies you've been involved in, along with your research in progress, to help others understand who you are. Thus, it's a statement of your scholarly identity.

Audiences and purposes. Your research statement plays important roles throughout your career. It helps you get a job, it helps you get tenure, and it helps you get promoted and reviewed positively when post-tenure reviews roll around. It does so by serving as a sensegiving device that helps you shape how others perceive you and what you do. It also serves as a sensemaking device, because it allows you to find coherent themes across what might otherwise seem like disparate projects and articles, and to figure out who you are as a scholar. As you progress through your career it helps you figure out whether your identity has changed. Reviewing my old research statements, although my interests and research topics have evolved some, my scholarly identity has changed remarkably little over the years. Other scholars' research identities may change more substantially.

Your research statement is read by a wide variety of audiences who vary in their level of technical expertise and familiarity with your field. If you're a doctoral student, your first audience is likely your advisor and dissertation committee members. Once you've figured out who you are as a researcher, you need to help those advocating for you to understand what your scholarly identity is. They will then reinforce and amplify it in their recommendation letters, and/or in conversations they have with others at schools where you're applying for jobs. It plays the same role for whoever is writing your recommendation letters for subsequent jobs as well. When I write a recommendation letter for someone, the two documents I always ask for are their vita and their research statement.

If you are looking for a job, the next audience is the recruiting committee selecting the candidates to interview. They also want to know who you are as a scholar, what's novel about your research and how it overlaps with or complements others in their department. If you get an interview, deans may also read your research statement for the same reasons.

If you are up for tenure and promotion, committees and deans within your schools will read your research statement to assess whether you've developed a clear scholarly identity and coherent record of achievement that merits the promotion. Although tenure processes vary by institution, these committees will typically exist at the department, college and university levels, and at each level committee members will be less and less familiar with the specifics of your field and research domain. Thus, you need to write your statement in a way that even those with no experience in your field can get a basic understanding of who you are and how all your work fits together. Deans at the college level, and provosts, chancellors and/or presidents at higher administrative levels, will also read your research statement and use it to make their decisions and draft their letters supporting your case.

Finally, as you move through the tenure and promotion process, the individuals reading your research statement will also rely heavily on outside letters written by prominent scholars in your field evaluating your research program. These outside letter writers are your final audience; your research statement will help them understand who you are and give them the language they can use to describe you in their letters. You want to make their jobs describing your research and what's unique and important about it as easy as possible.

Tone. I describe the tone of research statements as "semi-formal." You want it to be conversational, but not too chatty and informal. Your research statement conveys key information about your research and its unique contributions, but in an accessible way. It's also where you make the case for yourself and your capabilities, so you should freely and liberally use the pronoun "I," even when you're discussing research you've co-authored. Everyone reading the documents recognizes that you didn't do the work alone, but you are making a statement about your abilities and contributions that cuts across all your studies with all your different co-authors. This is where you're supposed to take credit for what you've done.

Content and structure. Research statements vary in length depending on what you have to talk about. For new graduates, they will typically be 2–3 pages; if you are going up for tenure or promotion, they could be 3–6 pages or more. Although a research statement's structure isn't set in stone, there are several important issues you need to discuss, and they tend to flow naturally into a particular structure that looks like a pyramid, going from the most abstract characterizations of your research to more detailed descriptions of your specific studies.

The first thing your research statement needs to do is succinctly introduce your scholarly identity with an elevator pitch.[3] This is the most abstract description of your research program at the pyramid's top. A good elevator

---

[3]   The term "elevator pitch" comes from entrepreneurship, and it is based on the idea that you need to develop a description of your business idea and why it's valuable that it is clear and succinct enough that you could present, or "pitch," it to someone in the amount of time it takes to ride an elevator together.

pitch uses an economy of words to capture the essential aspects of what you study using key words and phrases that readers will understand. Thus, research statements typically open with a paragraph that succinctly summarizes what your research is all about. For example, the opening paragraph in my research statement reads,

> My goal as a scholar is to create a greater understanding of the complex mix of forces that socially construct the way rationalized organizational outcomes—whether it is the value placed upon a company or the compensation paid to a CEO—are determined, presented and justified to the public. In all of my research I have tried to focus on how the social and political contexts that individual and organizational actors face influence the way they make sense of the world, and in so doing shape the value placed on the organizational outcomes that are the focus of the actor's attention.

Some of the key ideas here are that (1) I'm interested in how outcomes typically treated as rational are in fact socially constructed; (2) I'm interested in how these social construction processes affect not just how the outcome is determined, but also how it's publicly presented and justified; and (3) that I focus on social and political constructs and mechanisms at both the individual and organizational levels, and explore how they shape cognitive processes of sensemaking. Although there's more detail to come in the next paragraph, that already tells you a lot about what I do and where I'm coming from as a scholar.

The next paragraph or two elaborate on your research program by highlighting what you've contributed to the field theoretically and methodologically (if relevant), and what's unique about your research program. You are still summarizing your overall body of work here, but you now begin to elaborate on what you do and add key details, creating the next, wider level of the pyramid. As part of this, you'll need to identify the major research streams your work fits into. One question that always comes up is how many streams you should discuss. Although individuals vary in their recommendation, two to three is generally fine. You may have only one stream, but that can seem a bit narrow. Too many streams suggest you're an intellectual dilettante who lacks focus. I used to present three research streams—corporate governance, strategic choice, and the social construction of markets—but I now collapse the first two streams into a single stream. I elaborate on my elevator pitch in my second paragraph by saying

> My research follows two broad but interrelated topical streams: (1) corporate governance and the strategic choices of top management, and (2) the social construction of value in markets, particularly the initial public offerings (IPO) market. A common theme that cuts across both research streams is my focus on the role of social evaluations, such as reputation, status, celebrity and stigma. Within these streams, I pursue common theoretical themes that draw on literatures in a variety of

disciplines and use them to understand how individuals and organizations acquire, interpret and act on information in uncertain and ambiguous circumstances to assign value.

Thus, I highlight more specifically what types of phenomena I study, the social contextual features I'm interested in, that I focus on uncertain and ambiguous environments, and that I draw on a variety of theories and literatures. My major stream labels are both phenomenological, but that's because of the nature of my research. If you work primarily within a specific theoretical domain you may choose to use the theory as your label instead. Whatever labels you choose, make sure they are broad enough to encompass the breadth of your research.

Next, you'll want to highlight what's unique about your research program. This is again a summary statement, but it adds additional detail that broadens the pyramid, so you need to be more specific than in your elevator pitch. It doesn't have to be earth shattering, but you'll want to identify some theme or approach that sets your research apart. In my case, one of my potential challenges is that some may find the fact that I draw on a lot of different theories problematic. However, I present this as a feature, rather than a flaw,

> One hallmark of my research is that I integrate micro-level theories of power and social cognition with macro-level theories of strategy, networks, social approval and markets to develop more nuanced and comprehensive theoretical models … I believe this theoretical pluralism is a strength of my research because it allows me to explore the substantive issues I am interested in from a wide variety of perspectives, and to develop more integrated theoretical explanations of the processes and phenomena that I observe.

Some version of these two sentences, including the term "theoretical pluralism," has always been in my research statement. This section highlights that I incorporate individual-level theories of cognition and social psychology into the more macro-level organizational and industry-level theories typically used to explain the phenomena I study. I follow this paragraph with one highlighting some of the unique methodological aspects of my research—that I use the content analysis of text data in most of my studies—and the breadth of methodologies I've employed. You might also highlight unique datasets you've built or have access to, or specific programming or data mining skills you possess.

It's also useful to provide evidence of your research impact. This could be a separate section or could be integrated into descriptions of your research streams. This is more difficult to do if you are a doctoral student, but if you've won any research awards or received press coverage, for example, you can mention that here. Demonstrating impact becomes more important when going up for tenure. If you have articles more than a few years old when you go up, you can talk about citation counts in Web of Science and Google Scholar. Reference both sources because different people and institutions put more weight on one than the other. Many assistant professors don't have a lot of citations yet, so if you do, that's a plus. Awards and other recognition are also still useful to mention. When you go up for full professor, however, demonstrating impact is a must.

The remainder of your research statement describes your specific research studies by research stream. This is the broad base of the pyramid. The research stream labels serve as your section headers. One option for opening this section—which I employ—is to explain why you're motivated to study what you study. I think it personalizes and adds richness to your story. You could instead introduce this information early in your research statement when you describe your general interests, or as an opening hook before giving your elevator pitch. When discussing my research stream on corporate governance I talked about my prior work experience as a compensation consultant and in designing non-qualified benefit plans for senior executives, and how my observation that it was often social and political considerations that had the greatest influence on our engagement outcomes led to my research interests.

Within each stream, create a narrative about the limitations in the conversation you're responding to, and how your studies fit together. For each study provide a short summary of what the study was about, and make sure you identify what's important about it (i.e., have a sentence starting with "This study is important because" or "These findings are important because" for every study). This helps the reader understand what you're contributing to the field.

For example, when describing my corporate governance research, I opened this section by stating, "Given that an extensive set of political factors unrelated to performance appear to influence CEO compensation, one question I have raised is how boards of directors justify their politically motivated compensation practices to shareholders." This set up descriptions of several different studies. Here's how I described one of them:

> In a more recent study (Pollock, Fisher & Wade, 2002), I took advantage of a unique fluctuation in the stock market to conduct a "naturally occurring experiment" and explored how CEO power and impression management concerns affected whether the CEO's stock options were repriced. I found that factors which increase the CEO's structural power also increased the probability that the CEO's options would be repriced. However, I also found that direct CEO stock ownership decreases the likelihood of option repricing, even though it increases the CEO's power. Further, I found that factors which increase the decision's visibility, and that increase CEO power by decreasing the board's power (thereby making it appear weak), decrease the likelihood of repricing. These findings are important because they highlight the influence of impression management concerns in executive compensation decisions. They also demonstrate the limitations of using stock options as the primary

mechanism for aligning management and shareholder interests—the purpose for which they are expressly intended.

Developing a clear and concise research statement is thus not only a valuable marketing document for yourself, it helps you figure out who you are as a scholar and makes it easier to convey your identity to others.

COVER LETTERS

Everyone goes on the job market at least once in their careers, and most do it multiple times. Besides your CV, the one document you can be sure almost everyone reads is your cover letter. It is your key sensegiving tool and plays a major role in determining whether you make it past the first round of the hiring process. Readers will use it to assess who you are, what you do, why they would want you as a colleague, and your interest in the school and position.

Audiences and purposes. Your cover letter has two primary audiences: (1) The recruiting committees at the schools where you apply for jobs; and (2) The folks writing recommendation letters for you. Hiring committees use your cover letter to glean information about you that isn't readily discernable in your CV. This includes whether you're a fit for the position, the research interests and skills you'd bring to the department, whether you share the department's values and focus with respect to research and teaching, whether you're likely to make an interesting colleague, and what kind of shot they have at getting you if they ended up making you an offer. Thus, your cover letter needs to capture their attention and get them to look at you seriously, convey the information they're looking for, and persuade them to move you to the next step in the process. For your letter writers, it provides them with additional information and details they can build on and reinforce in their recommendations.

Tone. Cover letters should be conversational, what I'd call "business casual," so it's okay to use contractions. They should be engaging and easy to read and can include personal biographical information. The committees are reading a lot of these letters, so the easier and more interesting you can make it to read, the more they'll like you.

Content and structure. I try to keep a cover letter to no more than two pages. If it drags on too long, people stop reading it. I'll use my cover letter from when I went on the job market as a minty-fresh PhD to illustrate the basic structure and content. Some of the details will obviously change as you progress in your career, but the essentials don't change all that much. After the salutation, the first paragraph should identify your title and current institution ("I am currently a doctoral candidate in organizational theory at the University of Illinois at Urbana-Champaign") and include essential information about the position you're applying for, since some schools recruit for more than one at a time. If you're a doctoral student, state when you defended your proposal and intend to defend your dissertation (so they know you'll be done when the job starts), and summarize the information included in your application packet (so they know what else you sent). In my case I said,

> I have included a current copy of my vitae and writing samples consisting of a summary of my dissertation proposal, a paper entitled "Worth, words, and the justification of executive pay" which was recently published in a special issue of the *Journal of Organizational Behavior* dedicated to computer-aided text analysis, and a paper entitled "The politics of the comparable firm and CEO compensation" which has been provisionally accepted for publication in *Administrative Science Quarterly*.

Thus, by the end of the first paragraph readers knew what school I'm from, when I'll graduate, that I have publications and where, and a little something about the kind of research I do.

In the next few paragraphs you'll need to include the following: (1) Your elevator pitch; (2) Information on your research interests; (3) A summary of your dissertation; (4) Additional personal information that makes you more interesting and attractive, or signals experiences they'll find valuable; and (5) Any awards, grants or other recognition you've received. How you structure this information depends on what you have to sell and what creates the best narrative structure. For example, you could start with your elevator pitch, perhaps mixing in some personal details along the way, followed by your dissertation summary which leads into your research stream discussion and accomplishments. Or you could invert this order, or discuss your dissertation last and use it to illustrate how your research streams come together.

In my letter I started by using the personal background information mentioned earlier to introduce my research interests and elevator pitch, noting how this influenced the research I worked on with my advisors Joe Porac and Jim Wade (this is how I worked my significant relationships into the letter). In writing this section I repurposed a fair bit of material directly from my research statement, which creates consistency across documents.

In the next paragraph I talked about a different set of experiences that shaped my interest in entrepreneurship (I was applying for entrepreneurship, strategy and organization theory jobs)—helping my parents with their independent pharmacy as it faced a changing competitive environment, and my work with the Ewing Marion Kauffman Foundation. I then said,

> Over the past two years I have leveraged these experiences into scholarly research by assisting the Kauffman Foundation in its efforts to develop what has become

one of the most extensive databases of high-growth firms currently in existence. Working with management narratives solicited from well-known entrepreneurs, I have been conducting research exploring managerial sensemaking and how management's interpretations of a firm's competencies shape expansion plans and determine financial outcomes for a sample of high-growth enterprises.

This served two purposes: (1) It let me talk about another of my research streams, and (2) It signaled I was affiliated with a prominent foundation funding a lot of entrepreneurship research. I followed this paragraph with a summary of my dissertation, also noting that I had won a well-known dissertation proposal competition. Collectively this section made up a little over half of my letter and presented key details about me and my experience.

The final topic you want to cover is teaching—both your experience and future interests. If you've already taught one or more different courses you'll want to list what they are; and if you did well, mention your ratings. You'll also want to list the courses you'll be interested in and capable of teaching at the new institution. It also helps to provide a couple of sentences on your teaching philosophy.

You can employ the tools and techniques of storytelling in a wide variety of writing. Grant proposals can not only help you garner financial resources, they are a useful way to kick-start writing articles. Research statements and cover letters not only help you achieve career milestones, they are also introspective documents you can use to figure out your research identity and how that meshes with your other life experiences. Recognizing the multiple roles other kinds of writing play not only makes what you write more effective, it can make the process of writing them more invigorating.

14. Conclusion

There's something about generating a well-turned phrase that's deeply gratifying. Reading over something you've written and thinking. "Wow, that's pretty good. I can't believe I wrote that" can be something of an out of body experience. However, I also recognize that for many, writing is one of the more difficult and unpleasant aspects of what we do. If you want to be a successful academic, expressing yourself clearly and convincingly using the written word is an essential skill. I wrote this book to help demystify the process and show how the sausage gets made. It contains as much of what I've learned in my lifetime as I could fit into about 75,000 words. I hope you'll find, as I have, that the better you become at writing, the more fun and less frustrating or onerous it is. I want to conclude by talking about how to become a better writer by practicing what I've described in this book.

THE PRACTICE OF SCHOLARLY WRITING

Anyone who has ever seriously studied music, art, martial arts, cooking, yoga or a sport understands what I mean when I say that writing is a practice. With a practice, there is no end point; the journey as you continually improve and refine your skills is the goal. And in the beginning, no one's very good at whatever they're pursuing. I was no different when I started my doctoral studies. While I like to think I was at least a slightly better than average writer, generally I knew nothing about the discipline of academic writing. Although I have read constantly my whole life, I didn't have an extensive background in academia (and by that, I mean I had zero background), so journal articles and academic books were pretty much virgin territory. Thus, like many newbies I struggled to make sense of them. During the first few weeks of my doctoral program I remember calling more senior doctoral students for advice on how to get through it all, and my fellow student Lenny Holbrook telling me, "You just have to put on your reading pants and do it."

I eventually got better at comprehending academic writing, particularly once we got to material written in the latter half of the twentieth century. As I read more and more, my mental map of the literature started to form. Later, as I took more statistics classes, the methods and results sections started to make sense. Then I had to take my first stabs at writing an academic article for my seminars. The research I was immersed in with my advisors also gave me opportunities to write parts of papers. Of course, what I wrote wasn't very good, but I learned from the changes they made and kept working at it. And as I mentioned in Chapter 11, watching Joe Porac write was hugely influential.

As we try to become academics we all struggle with some parts of the job more than others. For me, it was learning how to *think* like an academic. Going into my final year as a doctoral student, I had a conversation with Joe and asked him for a frank assessment of my strengths and weaknesses; he said my biggest weakness was that I wasn't theoretical enough. And he was right. Because I've always been drawn to phenomena first, I wrote and made arguments in a very phenomenological rather than theoretical way. I determined that I was going to learn how to be more theoretical, but it took my first five years as an assistant professor, and lots of journal rejections, before I started seeing consistent evidence that I was getting the hang of it. To this day I continue to try and improve on this skill.

It is a very rare person who is immediately good at what we do. If you encounter someone who seems good at it from the get-go, a little more digging will likely reveal that they had experience prior to officially beginning their academic careers that gave them a head start. We all have to learn the practice of academic writing, and the more focus and effort you put into it, the better you're going to get at it. Stephen King (2000) said the only way to become at least a competent writer is to read a lot and write a lot. He's correct. But it takes more than just doing something a lot, it takes *deliberate practice*. Psychologist Anders Ericsson (Ericsson, Krampe & Tesch-Römer, 1993) has been one of the foremost researchers on the subject of why some people are so much better at certain things than others, and his conclusion was that they spent more time engaging in deliberate practice and focusing on specific skills they needed to improve. *Fortune Magazine* editor Geoff Colvin (2008) provides a very interesting exposé on deliberate practice in his book *Talent is Overrated*. He defines deliberate practice, why it works and how to apply it in our lives in an interesting and accessible way. He notes that,

> Deliberate practice is characterized by several elements … It is activity designed specifically to improve performance, often with a teacher's help; it can be repeated a lot; feedback on results is continuously available; it's highly demanding mentally, whether the activity is intellectual … or heavily physical … and it isn't much fun. (Colvin, 2008: 66)

Although I didn't realize it when I started, deliberate practice (which goes hand in hand with deep work) is how I have improved as a writer. Doctoral seminar papers, working on research projects with my advisors, and writing and rewriting papers that were rejected repeatedly by journals were a big part of how I learned. I also engaged in the activities I've recommended in this book; for example, selecting a couple of articles I thought were really good and really well written, and then dissecting them line by line and paragraph by paragraph to assess how they build their arguments, and how one idea led to the next. I've also spent countless hours reading about writing. I just counted, and I have 42 writing books on my office shelf. Some of these books are as much memoir as how to write books, making them a pleasure to read; others, such as several I have on grammar and punctuation, aren't exactly potboilers, although they are extremely useful.

Further, all the time I've spent reviewing others' work has also been hugely beneficial to my writing, particularly since I've tried to be a developmental reviewer and suggest solutions to the problems and issues I identify. This requires the same kind of creativity and problem-solving you need to refine your own work. I know for certain that serving as an editor has made me a better writer, and I guarantee that reading and commenting so much on others' work was highly demanding mentally. I've also sought and received tons of feedback on my writing from friends, co-authors and reviewers. While delivering and receiving a lot of negative feedback isn't that much fun, it has helped me become a better writer. I dispute that deliberate practice is never much fun, though. A lot of what I did was deeply gratifying, even if stressful in the moment, like when you have 20-plus manuscripts waiting for decision letters. I've also enjoyed most of the writing books I've read, and dissecting others' work. To this day I continue to try and improve my writing skills. Indeed, I've learned new things while writing this book that have improved my recent research.

I'm not saying this is what you have to do if you want to become a good writer. It's the path I took, and I think I still have much to learn. What I'm suggesting is that if you want to become a better writer you can, but it takes work. You need to identify both your strengths and where you need the most improvement, and then you have to develop practices and routines that both allow you to improve on your weaknesses and further develop and refine your strengths. The more effort you put in, the better you'll get. You can see substantial improvements quickly, but your efforts must be deliberate rather than haphazard—otherwise, to paraphrase innovation scholar Andy Hargadon, you won't end up with 20 years of experience, rather you'll have one year of experience repeated 20 times. To become really proficient you will need to engage in deliberate practice for a substantial amount of time. As I noted above, it took me about ten years before I felt like I was getting the hang of it. Even if your goal isn't to become a great writer, given its importance to our career success I encourage you at least to try and become a better writer; writing is something we all need to come to terms with, so you may as well learn to enjoy it.

To that end, on my website I've posted some exercises associated with the different chapters that you can use for deliberate practice (www.timothypollock

.com/writing). If you come up with exercises you'd like to share, send them to me; if I like them, I'll post them. I also encourage you to get as much reviewing experience as you can. If you're a doctoral student and have never reviewed before, volunteer to review papers for your professional association's annual meeting. The various divisions are always looking for reviewers. You and your fellow doctoral students can also practice by writing reviews for each other. If you are a senior doctoral student or new assistant professor, sign up as a reviewer at journals where you publish, or want to publish, your work. Once you've done so, contact the editor in chief and/or the associate editors who handle the papers in your topic areas, and let them know of your interest. Editors rate every review they receive, and reviewers are picked in part based on their reviewer scores; thus, if you haven't reviewed for the journal before it's hard to get selected as a reviewer unless the editor knows you. Do a good job and turn your reviews around quickly, and you will get more and better manuscripts to review. Also volunteer to give friendly reviews to your friends and colleagues. Finally, if your department has a working paper group, become an active participant. And if it doesn't, think about organizing one. The more experience you get giving and getting feedback, the better writer you'll become.

WHEN WRITING GOES WELL

When things are going well and you're really in the flow, writing sings. The more you read, engage in deliberate practice, and then get in the game and actually write, the more frequently your writing will sing beautifully, rather than sing out of key.

Storytellers have been venerated in all societies for eons. Before written languages—not to mention TV, video games, the Internet and streaming video—the oral storytelling tradition was essential for passing down knowledge, history, culture and values. When writing, and later printing, were developed, the written word became pre-eminent. Despite all the other communication modes we have today, the written word continues to hold a special place and offers a more permanent record of our thoughts, ideas and stories than any other medium. You are a storyteller, and writing is your medium. The students in my doctoral seminar—who read and gave me feedback on every chapter as I've developed them—told me the class made them more interested in and excited about writing than they ever thought they'd be. It was a joy to watch them try new things, take chances and really push their writing. It was also gratifying to hear that what I told them had demystified so much of the research enterprise. I hope this book has done the same for you, in at least some small way. And as we come to the end of our journey together, and our paths again diverge, I hope you'll continue on your journey more excited about and confident in your ability to use the techniques of storytelling in your academic writing.

References

Adler, P.S. and S. Kwon (2002), 'Social capital: Prospects for a new concept', *Academy of Management Review*, **27**, 17–40.

Agarwal, R., R. Echambadi, A.M. Franco, and M.B. Sarkar (2006), 'Reap rewards: Maximizing benefits from reviewer comments', *Academy of Management Journal*, **49**(2), 191–196.

Ashford, S.J. (2013), 'Having scholarly impact: The art of hitting academic home runs', *Academy of Management Learning and Education*, **12**(4), 623–633.

Atinc, G., M.J. Simmering, and M.J. Kroll (2012), 'Control variable use and reporting in macro and micro management research', *Organizational Research Methods*, **15**, 57–74.

Baker, T. (2007), 'Resources at play: Bricolage in the toy store(y)', *Journal of Business Venturing*, **22**, 694–711.

Baker, T. and R.E. Nelson (2005), 'Creating something from nothing: Resource construction through entrepreneurial bricolage', *Administrative Science Quarterly*, **50**, 329–366.

Bansal, P. and K. Corley (2012), 'Part 7: What's different about qualitative research?', *Academy of Management Journal*, **55**(3), 509–513.

Baum, J.A.C., T.J. Rowley, A.V. Shipilov, and Y.-T. Chuang (2005), 'Dancing with strangers: Aspiration performance and the search for syndicate partners', *Administrative Science Quarterly*, **50**, 536–575.

Boivie, S., S.D. Graffin, and T.G. Pollock (2012), 'Time for me to fly: Predicting director exit at large firms', *Academy of Management Journal*, **55**(6), 1334–1359.

Briscoe, F. and S. Safford (2008), 'The Nixon-in-China effect: Activism, imitation and the institutionalization of contentious practices', *Administrative Science Quarterly*, **53**(3), 460–491.

Campbell, R., S. Jeong, and S.D. Graffin (2019), 'Born to take risk? The effects of CEO birth order on strategic risk taking', *Academy of Management Journal*, **62**, 1278–1306.

Casagrande, June (2014), *The Best Punctuation Book, Period*, Berkeley, CA: Ten Speed Press.

Chatterjee, A. and D.C. Hambrick (2007), 'It's all about me: Narcissistic CEOs and their effects on company strategy and performance', *Administrative Science Quarterly*, **52**, 351–386.

Chatterjee, A. and T.G. Pollock (2017), 'Master of Puppets: How narcissistic CEOs construct their professional worlds', *Academy of Management Review*, **42**(4), 703–725.

Cloutier, C. (2016), 'How I write: An inquiry into the writing practices of academics', *Journal of Management Inquiry*, **25**(1), 69–84.

Colvin, Geoff (2008), *Talent is Overrated: What Really Separates World-Class Performers from Everyone Else*, New York: Penguin Books.

Cortina, J.M. and R.S. Landis (2009), 'When small effect sizes tell a big story, and when large effect sizes don't', in Charles E. Lance and Robert J. Vandenberg (eds.),

Statistical and Methodological Myths and Urban Legends, New York: Routledge, pp. 287–308.

Creary, S.J., B.B. Caza and L.M. Roberts (2015), 'Out of the box? How managing a subordinate's multiple identities affects the quality of the manager–subordinate relationship', *Academy of Management Review*, **40**(4), 538–562.

Daft, R.L. (1985), 'Why I recommended that your manuscript be rejected and what you can do about it', in L.L. Cummings and Peter J. Frost (eds.), *Publishing in the Organizational Sciences*, Homewood, IL: Richard D. Irwin, pp. 193–209.

Dane, E. (2011), 'Changing the tune of academic writing: Muting cognitive entrenchment', *Journal of Management Inquiry*, **20**, 332–336.

Davis, G.F. and C. Marquis (2005), 'Prospects for organization theory in the early twenty-first century: Institutional fields and mechanisms', *Organization Science*, **16**, 332–343.

Davis, J.P. and K.M. Eisenhardt (2011), 'Rotating leadership and collaborative innovation: Recombination processes in symbiotic relationships', *Administrative Science Quarterly*, **56**(2), 159–201.

Davis, M.S. (1971), 'That's interesting! Toward a phenomenology of sociology and a sociology of phenomenology', *Philosophy of the Social Sciences*, **1**, 309–344.

Derfus, P.J., P.G. Maggitti, C.M. Grimm, and K.G. Smith (2008), 'The red queen effect: Competitive actions and firm performance', *Academy of Management Journal*, **51**(1), 61–80.

Douglas, Yellowlees (2015), *The Reader's Brain: How Neuroscience Can Make You a Better Writer*, Cambridge, UK: Cambridge University Press.

Elsbach, K.D. and R.M. Kramer (2003), 'Assessing creativity in Hollywood pitch meetings: Evidence for a dual-process model of creativity judgements', *Academy of Management Journal*, **46**(3), 283–301.

Ericsson, K.A., R.T. Krampe, and C. Tesch-Römer (1993), 'The role of deliberate practice in acquisition of expert performance', *Psychological Review*, **100**(3), 363–406.

Evans, Harold (2017), *Do I Make Myself Clear? Why Writing Well Matters*, New York: Little Brown.

Feldman, M.P., S. Ozcan, and T. Reichstein (2019), 'Falling not far from the tree: Entrepreneurs and organizational heritage', *Organization Science*, **30**(2), 337–360.

Ferraro, F., J. Pfeffer, and R.I. Sutton (2005), 'Economics language and assumptions: How theories can become self-fulfilling', *Academy of Management Review*, **30**(1), 8–24.

Fisher, Roger, William Ury, and Bruce Patton (2011), *Getting to Yes: Negotiating Agreement Without Giving In*, New York: Penguin.

Fiss, P.C., M.T. Kennedy, and G.F. Davis (2012), 'How golden parachutes unfolded: Diffusion and variation of a controversial practice', *Organization Science*, **23**, 1077–1099.

Flaherty, Francis (2009), *The Elements of Story: Field Notes on Nonfiction Writing*, New York: HarperCollins.

Floyd, S.W., D.M. Schroeder, and D.M. Finn (1994), '"Only if I'm first author": Conflict over credit in management scholarship', *Academy of Management Journal*, **37**(3), 734–747.

Freytag, Gustav (1865), *The Techniques of the Drama 3rd Edition*, trans. E.L. McEwan (1900), Chicago, IL: Scott, Foresman.

Geletkanycz, M. and B.J. Tepper (2012), 'From the Editors, Publishing in AMJ–Part 6: Discussing the implications', *Academy of Management Journal*, **55**(2), 256–260.

Ghoshal, S. (2005), 'Bad management theories are destroying good management practice', *Academy of Management Learning and Education*, **4**, 75–91.

Gioia, D.A. and K. Chittipeddi (1991), 'Sensemaking and sensegiving in strategic change initiation', *Strategic Management Journal*, **12**, 433–448.

Gomulya, D., K. Jin, P.M. Lee, and T.G. Pollock (2019), 'Crossed wires: Endorsement signals and the effects of IPO firm delistings on venture capitalists' reputations', *Academy of Management Journal*, **62**(3), 641–666.

Grant, A.M. and D.A. Hofmann (2011), 'It's not all about me: Motivating hand hygiene among healthcare professionals by focusing on patients', *Psychological Science*, **22**(12), 1494–1499.

Grant, A.M. and T.G. Pollock (2011), 'From the Editors, Publishing in AMJ–Part 3: Setting the hook', *Academy of Management Journal*, **54**(5), 873–879.

Grant, A.M., E.M. Campbell, G. Chen, K. Cottone, D. Lapedis, and K. Lee (2007), 'Impact and the art of motivation maintenance: The effects of contact with beneficiaries on persistence behavior', *Organizational Behavior and Human Decision Processes*, **103**, 53–67.

Greenwood, R. and R. Suddaby (2006), 'Institutional entrepreneurship in mature fields: The Big Five accounting firms', *Academy of Management Journal*, **49**, 27–48.

Guldiken, O., M.R. Mallon, S. Fainshmidt, W.Q. Judge, and C.E. Clark (2019), 'Beyond tokenism: How strategic leaders influence more meaningful gender diversity on boards of directors', *Strategic Management Journal*, **40**(12), 2024–2046.

Guler, I. (2007), 'Throwing good money after bad? Political and institutional influences on sequential decision making in the venture capital industry', *Administrative Science Quarterly*, **51**(2), 248–285.

Hale, Constance (2013), *Sin and Syntax: How to Craft Wicked Good Prose*, New York: Three Rivers Press.

Hambrick, D.C. (2007), 'The field of management's devotion to theory: Too much of a good thing?', *Academy of Management Journal*, **50**(6), 1346–1352.

Han, J.-H. and T.G. Pollock (2021), 'The two towers (or somewhere in between): The behavioral consequences of positional inconsistency across status hierarchies', *Academy of Management Journal*, forthcoming.

Hirsch, P.M. and M. Lounsbury (1997), 'Ending the family quarrel: Toward a reconciliation of the "old" and "new" institutionalisms', *American Behavioral Scientist*, **40**(4), 406–418.

Hollenbeck, J.R. (2008), 'The role of editing in knowledge development: Consensus shifting and consensus creation', in Yehuda Baruch, Alison M. Konrad, Herman Aguinus, and William H. Starbuck (eds.), *Journal Editing: Opening the Black Box*, San Francisco, CA: Jossey-Bass, pp. 16–26.

Hollenbeck, J.R. and P.M. Wright (2017), 'Harking, sharking and tharking: Making the case for post hoc analysis of scientific data', *Journal of Management*, **43**(1), 5–18.

Huff, Anne S. (1999), *Writing for Scholarly Publication*, Thousand Oaks, CA: Sage.

Johanson, L. (1994), 'Writing as a storyteller's art'. Presented at the Academy of Management Annual Meeting, Dallas, TX, August, 1994.

Johanson, L.M. (2007), 'Sitting in your reader's chair: Attending to your academic sensemakers', *Journal of Management Inquiry*, **16**, 290–294.

Johns, G. (2006), 'The essential impact of context on organizational behavior', *Academy of Management Review*, **31**(2), 386–408.

Johnson, M.D., J.R. Hollenbeck, S.E. Humphrey, D.R. Ilgen, D. Jundt, and C.J. Meyer (2006), 'Cutthroat cooperation: Asymmetrical adaptation to changes in team reward structures', *Academy of Management Journal*, **49**(1), 103–119.

Judge, T.A., D.M. Cable, A.E. Colbert, and S.L. Rynes (2007), 'What causes a management article to be cited: Article, author, or journal?', *Academy of Management Journal*, **50**(3), 491–506.

Kilduff, M. (2006), 'Editors comments: Publishing theory', *Academy of Management Review*, **31**(2), 252–255.

King, Stephen (2000), *On Writing: A Memoir of the Craft*, New York: Simon & Shuster.

Lamott, Anne (1994), *Bird by Bird: Some Instructions on Writing and Life*, New York: Anchor Books.

Lashley, K. and T.G. Pollock (2020), 'Waiting to inhale: Removing stigma in the medical cannabis industry', *Administrative Science Quarterly*, **65**(2), 434–482.

Leblebici, H., G.R. Salancik, A. Copay, and T. King (1991), 'Institutional change and the transformation of inter-organizational fields: An organizational history of the U.S. radio broadcasting industry', *Administrative Science Quarterly*, **36**, 333–363.

Lee, P. and E. James (2007), '"She"-E-Os: Gender effects and investor reactions to the announcements of top executive appointments', *Strategic Management Journal*, **28**(3), 227–241.

Levitt, B. and J.G. March (1988), 'Organizational learning', *Annual Review of Sociology*, **14**, 319–340.

Lincoln, Y.S. and E.G. Guba (1985), 'Establishing trustworthiness', in *Naturalistic Inquiry*, Newbury Park, CA: Sage, pp. 289–331.

Liu, C.W., C.Y. Olivola, and B. Kovács (2017), 'Coauthorship trends in the field of management: Facts and perceptions', *Academy of Management Learning and Education*, **16**(4), 509–530.

Locke, K. and K. Golden-Biddle (1997), 'Constructing opportunities for contribution: Structuring intertextual coherence and "problematizing" in organizational studies', *Academy of Management Journal*, **40**, 1023–1062.

Lovelace, J., J. Bundy, D.C. Hambrick, and T.G. Pollock (2018), 'The shackles of CEO celebrity: Socio-cognitive and behavioral role constraints on "star" leaders', *Academy of Management Review*, **43**(3), 419–444.

Magee, J.C. and A.D. Galinsky (2008), 'Social hierarchy: The self-reinforcing nature of power and status', in Arthur P. Brief and James P. Walsh (eds.), *Academy of Management Annals*, **2**, Essex, UK: Routledge, pp. 351–398.

McGrath, J.E. (1982), 'Dilemmatics: The study of research choices and dilemmas', in Joseph E. McGrath, Joann Martin, and Richard A. Kulka (eds.), *Judgement Calls in Research*, Beverly Hills, CA: Sage, pp. 69–103.

Merton, R.K. (1968), 'The Matthew effect in science', *Science*, **159**, 56–63.

Mishina, Y., B.J. Dykes, E.S. Block, and T.G. Pollock (2010), 'Why "good" firms do bad things: The effects of high aspirations, high performance and prominence on the incidence of corporate illegality', *Academy of Management Journal*, **53**(4), 701–722.

Mohan-Ram, Vid (2000), 'How not to kill a grant application', accessed July 15th, 2020 at http://www.sciencemag.org/careers/where-search-funding

Molinsky, A., A.M. Grant, and J. Margolis (2012), 'The bedside manner of homo economicus: How and why priming an economic schema reduces compassion', *Organizational Behavior and Human Decision Processes*, **119**, 27–37.

Newport, Cal (2016), *Deep Work: Rules for Focused Success in a Distracted World*, New York: Grand Central Publishing.

Oppenheimer, D.M. (2006), 'Consequences of erudite vernacular utilized irrespective of necessity: Problems with using long words needlessly', *Applied Cognitive Psychology*, **20**(2), 139–156.

Pfarrer, M.D., T.G. Pollock, and V.P. Rindova (2010), 'A tale of two assets: The effects of firm reputation and celebrity on earnings surprises and investors' reactions', *Academy of Management Journal*, **53**(5), 1131–1152.

Pfeffer, Jeffrey and Gerald R. Salancik (1978), *The External Control of Organizations*, New York: Harper & Row.

Plowman, D.A., L.T. Baker, T.E. Beck, M. Kulkarni, S.T. Solansky, and D.V. Travis (2007), 'Radical change accidentally: The emergence and amplification of small change', *Academy of Management Journal*, **50**, 515–543.

Podsakoff, P.M., N.P. Podsakoff, P. Mishra, and C. Escue (2018), 'Can early-career scholars conduct impactful research? Playing "small ball" versus "swinging for the fences"', *Academy of Management Learning and Education*, **17**(4), 496–531.

Pollock, T.G. and J.E. Bono (2013), 'From the Editors, Being Scheherazade: The importance of storytelling in academic writing', *Academy of Management Journal*, **56**(3), 629–634.

Pollock, T.G., H.M. Fischer, and J.B. Wade (2002), 'The role of power and politics in the repricing of executive options', *Academy of Management Journal*, **45**(6), 1172–1182.

Pollock, T.G., G. Chen, E.M. Jackson, and D.C. Hambrick (2010), 'How much prestige is enough? Assessing the value of multiple types of high-status affiliates for young firms', *Journal of Business Venturing*, **25**(1), 6–23.

Pollock, T.G., P.M. Lee, K. Jin, and K. Lashley (2015), '(Un)Tangled: Exploring the asymmetric co-evolution of VC firm reputation and status', *Administrative Science Quarterly*, **60**(3), 482–517.

Pratt, M.G. (2000), 'The good, the bad and the ambivalent: Managing identification among Amway distributors', *Administrative Science Quarterly*, **45**, 456–493.

Pratt, M.G., S. Kaplan, and R. Whittington (2020), 'Editorial essay: The tumult over transparency: Decoupling transparency from replication in establishing trustworthy qualitative research', *Administrative Science Quarterly*, **65**(1), 1–19.

Ragins, B.R. (2012), 'Editor's comments: Reflections on the craft of clear writing', *Academy of Management Review*, **37**(4), 493–501.

Rindova, V.P., T.G. Pollock, and M.L.A. Hayward (2006), 'Celebrity firms: The social construction of market popularity', *Academy of Management Review*, **31**(1), 50–71.

Rindova, V.P., I.O. Williamson, A.P. Petkova, and J.M. Sever (2005), 'Being good or being known: An empirical examination of the dimensions, antecedents, and consequences of organizational reputation', *Academy of Management Journal*, **48**, 1033–1049.

Schwab, Donald P. (2005), *Research Methods for Organizational Studies 2nd Edition*, New York: Routledge.

Shadish, William R., Thomas D. Cook, and Donald T. Campbell (2002), *Experimental and Quasi-Experimental Designs for Generalized Causal Inference*, Belmont, CA: Wadsworth Cengage Learning.

Shaw, J.D. (2012), 'Responding to reviewers', *Academy of Management Journal*, **55**(6), 1261–1263.

Silvia, Paul J. (2018), *How to Write a Lot 2nd Edition*, Washington, DC: American Psychological Association.

Smiley, Sam and Norman A. Bert (2005), *Playwriting: The Structure of Action*, New Haven, CT: Yale University Press.

Sparrowe, R.T. and K.J. Mayer (2011), 'From the Editors, Publishing in AMJ–Part 4: Grounding hypotheses', *Academy of Management Journal*, **54**(6), 1098–1102.

Stanley, Matthew (2019), *Einstein's War*, New York: Dutton.

Stokes, Donald E. (1997), *Pasteur's Quadrant: Basic Science and Technological Innovation*, Washington, DC: Brookings Institution Press.

Strunk, William and E.B. White (2000), *The Elements of Style 4th Edition*, Needham Heights, MA: Allyn & Bacon.

Suddaby, R. (2010), 'Editor's comments: Construct clarity in theories of management and organization', *Academy of Management Review*, **35**(3), 346–357.

Sutton, R.I. and B.M. Staw (1995), 'What theory is not', *Administrative Science Quarterly*, **40**, 371–384.

Sword, Helen (2012), *Stylish Academic Writing*, Cambridge, MA: Harvard University Press.

Taylor, Frederick W. (1916), *The Principles of Scientific Management*, New York: Harper & Brothers Publishers.

Tihanyi, L. (2020) 'From the Editors, From "that's interesting" to "that's important"', *Academy of Management Journal*, **63**(2), 329–331.

Truss, Lynne (2003), *Eats, Shoots & Leaves: The Zero Tolerance Approach to Punctuation*, New York: Gotham Books.

Uzzi, B. (1996), 'The sources and consequences of embeddedness for the economic performance of organizations: The network effect', *American Sociological Review*, **61**, 674–698.

Van Maanen, J. (1995), 'Style as theory', *Organization Science*, **6**, 133–142.

Weick, K.E. (1989), 'Theory construction as disciplined imagination', *Academy of Management Review*, **14**, 516–531.

Weick, Karl E. (1995), *Sensemaking in Organizations*, Thousand Oaks, CA: Sage.

Westphal, J.D., S.H. Park, M.L. McDonald, and M.L.A. Hayward (2012), 'Helping other CEOs avoid bad press: Social exchange and impression management support among CEOs in communications with journalists', *Administrative Science Quarterly*, **57**(20), 217–268.

Whetten, D.A. (1989), 'What constitutes a theoretical contribution?', *Academy of Management Review*, **14**, 490–495.

Zhang, Y. and J.D. Shaw (2012), 'From the Editors, Publishing in AMJ–Part 5: Crafting the methods and results', *Academy of Management Journal*, **55**(1), 8–12.

Zinsser, William (2006), *On Writing Well: The Classic Guide to Writing Nonfiction*, New York: HarperCollins.

Index

abstract lengths 62
abstracts 50, 51, 53, 55, 57, 59, 61–3, 160
academic articles 24
acceptance 29
active verb 25, 39, 40
active writing 39–41
adverbs 31, 32, 34, 46
agency problems 35
"air" words 26
alliteration 41
anecdotes 54
aphorism 33
archetype 111, 112
aspirations 13–16
associated hypotheses 72, 75
assonance 41
author order 141, 142
authorship order 4, 134, 135, 140, 141
awareness 29

Baker, Ted 22, 23
Bansal, Tima 100, 102, 104
Baum, J.A.C. 75
Bert, Norman A. 17
bimodal approach 125, 127, 130
body language 23
Bono, Joyce 23, 24, 61
book chapters 113
bricolage 23
Briscoe, F. 27, 28
broadcasting 42, 96
building blocks, storytelling 31–48
    active writing 39–41
    clear writing 32–3
    pathologies of academic writing 33–9
        burying lead 35–6
        fat suit 33–5
        pompous prose 38–9
        read my mind 37–8

sentence stuffing 36–7
"sound" of writing 41–4
stylistic and grammatical dos and don'ts, idiosyncratic list 44–8

cadence 5, 31, 41–3, 61, 81, 86, 120
Carroll, Lewis 28
celebrity 16, 73, 74, 109, 111, 112, 164
CEO narcissism 27
character driven stories 17–18
characters 5, 7, 8, 12, 15–19, 21–3, 115–17
Chatterjee, Arijit 22, 27, 52, 82
clarity 64, 67, 70, 80, 81, 83, 85, 86, 88, 102, 110
clear writing 32–3
climax 9, 11, 14
co-authoring process 5, 113, 132–43
    collaborative relationships 135–7
    cons of 134–5
    contemporaneous co-authoring 138–9
    issues of 4
    mechanics of 137–9
    passing the paper 137–8
    pros of 133–4
    team management 139–43
        authorship order 140–42
        dropping co-author 143
        inviting co-authors 139–40
        working with co-authors 142–3
co-authoring teams 140, 142
cognitive entrenchment 32
collaborative relationships 135–7
    collegial collaborations 135–6
    directive collaborations 137
    mentoring collaborations 136–7
    meritorious collaborations 136
Colvin, Geoff 171
completeness 80, 85, 102
complex sentences 42–4

compound-complex sentences 42, 43
compound sentence 42, 43
confirmability 102–3
consensus creation 60
construct clarity 67–8
construct validity 77
constructs 66
construct's lineage 68
contemporaneous co-authoring 138
contextual realism 78
control variables 14, 17, 83, 84, 87
conversation
    establishing 55–6
    problematizing 56–8
cooling-off periods 145
Copay, A. 42
copy-editors 124, 157
Corley, Kevin 100, 102, 104
corporate illegality 13
credibility 79–84, 87, 95, 102, 103

data 66
Davis, Jason 53
Davis, Murray 58, 59–60, 94
deductive research 99
deep work 125, 126, 128, 129, 171
dénouement 9, 15
dependability 103
dependent (DV) variables 16, 60, 68–70,
    76, 77, 82, 83, 86, 87
Derfus, P.J. 28
diagrams 66
Discussion section 90–97
    flaws 91–2
    future research 95
    limitations 95
    meandering 92
    methodological contributions 94
    overreaching 92
    practical implications 94
    purposes 91
    rehashing results 91–2
    structure 96–7
    superficial interpretations 92
    theoretical contributions 92–4
Do I Make Myself Clear? 33
Douglas, Yellowlees 41, 42
dramatic structure 7–15
Dunlap, Al 52
Dyson, Frank 1

Eddington, Arthur 1, 2
Einstein, Albert 1
Eisenhardt, Kathy 53
The Elements of Story 21
Elsbach, Kim 99, 101, 103, 104, 106
embedded agency, paradox 57
emotions 23, 47, 144, 145, 147
Ericsson, Anders 171
Evans, Harold 33, 35, 39, 40
exposition 8, 12
expressive punctuation 26
external validity 77
extraneous verbiage 33

falling action 9, 11, 14
Feldman, Martha 137
Finn, Dale 135
firm performance 16, 69, 70, 107, 108
first cadence principle 42
Flaherty, Francis 21–7
Floyd, Steve 135
Freytag, Gustav 8–15
Freytag's Pyramid 8–15, 17, 19, 100
    to academic article 12–15

Geletkanycz, Marta 90, 91
Golden-Biddle, Karen 55
Gomulya, Dave 54
Grant, Adam 51, 54, 73
Greenwood, Royston 57, 60, 62
Grimm, C.M. 28
Guba, E.G. 102

Hale, Constance 34, 41, 42
Hambrick, D.C. 27, 82
Hayward, Mat 68
Hemingway, Ernest 12
hidden actions 24
Hirsch, Paul 57, 60
Hofmann, David 54
Hollenbeck, John 58, 60
How to Write a Lot 125
human face 21–4
hypotheses 66
    continuous statements 69
    difference statements 69
    statements 68–70
    tests 11, 84–6, 88

if-then statements 69
inadequacy problematizations 57, 58
incommensurability 57
incompleteness problematization 56
independent (IV) variables 68–70
"Index of the Interesting" 58, 59–60
institutional theory 57, 65
internal validity 76
intervening variables 69
introduction 51–61

Jin, Kyuho 54
Johanson, Linda 7, 12, 37, 96
Johnson, Michael 53, 72, 75, 94, 95, 97
journalistic approach 125–7
junior co-authors 134, 136

Kilduff, Martin 107, 110
King, Stephen 17, 18, 22, 44, 122, 125,
    127, 128, 130, 171
King, T. 42
Kovács, Balázs 132
Kramer, Rod 99, 101, 103, 104, 106

Lamott, Anne 17, 114, 117
Lashley, Kisha 62
Lawrence, Tom 138
Leblebici, Huseyin 42, 44, 96
Lee, Peggy 54
Lewis, Michael 113
Lincoln, Y.S. 102
Liu, Chengwei 132, 135
Locke, Karen 55
Lounsbury, Mike 57, 60

made-up actions 24
Maggitti, P.G. 28
manuscript length 25
Matthew effect 135
Mayer, Kyle 65
McGrath, Joe 78
mental actions 24
Merton, Robert 135
Methods and Results sections 76–89
    three-horned dilemma 78–9
    types of validity 76–7
Methods section
    analysis method 84
    challenges in writing 80–82

clarity 81
completeness 80
credibility 81–2
context and sample selection 82–3
control variables 83–4
dependent variables 83
independent variables 83
purposes 79–80
Mohan-Ram, Vid 158, 160, 161
monastic approach 125
Moneyball 113
motion 24–7

natural actions 24
Newport, Cal 125, 130
"Nixon in China" effect 27–8
non-coherence 56

obtrusiveness 78
Olivola, Christopher 132
On Writing Well 33, 120
onomatopoeia 41
Oppenheimer, D.M. 39
organizational learning 28

pacing 24–7
page-length guidelines 25
paragraph length 43–4
paragraphs 31–48
passive voice 39
"Pasteur's Quadrant" 51
Pfarrer, Mike 73
Phillips, Nelson 138
plot-driven stories 17–18
Plowman, Donde 54
Pollock, T.G. 24, 51, 52, 61, 62
Pratt, Mike 52, 63
predatory clauses 35
The Principles of Scientific Management
    20, 36
process issues 4–5
progressive coherence 56
punctuation 43

qualitative articles
    Discussion section differences
        105–6
    Discussion sections 112–13
    figures and tables 111–12

front end differences 101–2
inductive *vs.* deductive research
    99–100
methods differences 102–3
propositions *vs.* hypotheses 110–11
results/findings differences 103–5
storytelling structure differences
    100–101, 108–10
theory and empirical articles,
    difference 106–8
qualitative studies 25
quantitative manuscripts 25

Ragins, Belle 37
The Reader's Brain 41
recalcitrant 28
"Red Queen" effect 28
references 65
research program 163–5
research question 13, 18, 19, 62, 63, 89,
    91, 92, 96, 101, 102, 109
research statements 5, 6, 113, 158,
    162–6, 168, 169
research streams 164–6, 168, 169
resource dependence theory 48
Results section
    challenges in writing
        clarity 85–7
        completeness 85
        credibility 87
    descriptive statistics 88
    hypothesis tests 88
    post hoc analyses 88–9
    purposes 84
    robustness tests 88
review process, navigating 144–57
    emotional control 144–5
    initial submission 145–8
        general rules of thumb 147
        journal, choosing 145–6
        learning from rejections 147–8
    R&R 148–57
        comments, evaluating 149–50
        communicating with editor
            154–5
        keep your goal in mind 149
        letter drafting and responding to
            reviewers 150–53
        manuscript, revising 153–4

polishing it and sending it off
    155–6
responses, figuring out 150
subsequent revisions and
    acceptance 156–7
rhetorical questions 52, 54
rhythmic approach 125, 126
right-branching sentences 27
Rindova, Violina 67, 68, 73
rising action 8, 13

Safford, S. 27, 28
Salancik, G.R. 42
scholarly writing 170–73
Schroeder, Dean 135
scope conditions 67
second cadence principle 43
section-length estimates 25
senior co-author 134, 136
sentences 31–48
    structures 42, 45, 81, 88
Shaw, Jason 149
Silvia, Paul 125, 127
Sin and Syntax 41
situation-driven stories 17–18
Smiley, Sam 17
Smith, K.G. 28
sole-authoring 4
Sparrowe, Ray 65
The Stand 19
Stanley, Matthew 1
statistical conclusion validity 77
Staw, Barry 65
Stokes, Donald E. 52
story structures 12, 21
story, structuring 7–19
    characters, identifying 15–17
        ensemble 16–17
        main characters 16
        supporting characters 16
    dramatic structure 7–15
    plot-driven *versus* character or
        situation-driven stories 17–18
    storylines and themes 18–19
storylines 5, 7, 18, 19, 64, 115–17, 120,
    154, 161
story's motion 24, 43
story's theme 18, 21, 55, 115
storyteller 1–7, 173
storytelling structure 7, 100, 113

storytelling tools 2–3, 5, 20–30
    conversational, writing 29–30
    human face 21–4
    motion and pacing 24–7
    showing and telling 27–8
Strunk, William 33, 34
Suddaby, Roy 57, 60, 62, 67
Sutton, Robert 65
Sword, Helen 22, 27, 29, 61
synthesized coherence 55

Talent is Overrated 171
Taylor, Frederick 20, 21, 23, 36
technological innovation 53
Tepper, Ben 90, 91
theoretical arguments 55, 64–6, 68, 74,
    93, 100
theoretical model 11, 100, 104, 107–12
theory 64–7
    articles 9, 11, 91, 97, 98, 105–11
    papers 11, 25, 63, 64, 98, 113, 146
Theory and Hypotheses section 64–75
    construct clarity 67–8
    structuring 70–75
        existing constructs 72–3
        main characters and roles 73
        new constructs 72–3
        research context 74
        supporting characters and roles
            73–4
        theoretical domains 70–72
        theoretical figures 74–5
theory of relativity 1, 2
third cadence principle 44
Thomson, J.J. 2

three-horned dilemma 78–9
Through the Looking Glass 28
Tihanyi, Lazlo 94
titles 61–2
transferability 103
turbo-verbs 25, 26
typing 3–4

variables 66

Westphal, Jim 56
White, E.B. 33, 34
words 31–48
writing process 114–31, 135, 137, 138,
    158, 169, 170, 172–4
    core activities of 114–15
    cover letters 167–9
        audiences and purposes 167
        content and structure 167–9
        tone 167
    grant proposals 158–62
        audiences and purposes 158–60
        content and structure 160–62
        tone 160
    painting-inspired stages 115–24
    productivity, enhancing 124–31
    research statements 162–7
        audiences and purposes 162–3
        content and structure 163–7
        tone 163
    "sound" of 41–4
    versus typing 3–4
writing skills 2

Zinsser, William 32, 33, 120